REGIONAL ECONOMICS: Theory and Practice

$$\boxed{F_P}$$

Edited by David L. McKee, Robert D. Dean, and William H. Leahy

# REGIONAL

# ECONOMICS:

## Theory and Practice

*THE FREE PRESS, NEW YORK* · *Collier–Macmillan Limited, London*

Collier–Macmillan Canada Ltd., Toronto, Ontario

Library of Congress Catalog Card Number: 70–94625

*printing number*
1   2   3   4   5   6   7   8   9   10

# Contents

# *Preface*

In recent years people have been becoming increasingly aware of regional influences within national boundaries. Wide disparities in life styles and value systems, not to mention welfare levels, exist between regions within nations. National economies are often composed of sets of smaller, more localized economics. If the national economy is to prosper, then its constituent, regional economies, must be brought into some sort of harmony. Interregional relationships must be complementary rather than competitive. Unfortunately, wide disparities in the level of economic attainment may exist between regions and these may have an adverse affect upon progress at the national level.

The economically advanced nations have been establishing federal agencies to deal with regional problems and it is hardly surprising that economists have been asked for their opinions from time to time. This has led the economics profession to an increased interest in regions and regional analysis. Attempts are being made to adapt economic theory to regional problems and out of this activity a new practitioner appears to be evolving—the regional economist. The recent proliferation of course offerings in regional economics at American universities is evidence of this.

These new practitioners have sprung from the ranks of existing economists, but their backgrounds are diverse. Some of them identify themselves as economic theorists, others are what might have been termed land economists a generation ago. Still others have approached the new discipline with a background in industrial location theory. Regional economics is also gaining increasing interest among economists concerned with the developing countries. Whatever their backgrounds, many economists now share an interest in economic problems that are subnational in nature.

The present volume is not an attempt to collect the work of regional economists, per se. Rather it should be regarded as a selection of ideas put forward by the economics profession in general concerning regional economics. The present writers view the major problems at the regional level as those of expansion and integration. Thus a major portion of the volume is devoted to these issues. The selections in Part II are designed to show the relations of various types of economic theory to problems of regional expansion. Part III concerns itself with the idea of growth poles—a concept developed independently by Professors Perroux and Hirschman. Much of the literature on this topic is in French and thus not widely distributed in the United States—the article by Professor Perroux in the present volume is a translation from the French.

Part IV contains articles on static and dynamic equilibrium theory. Professor Isard's article deals with static equilibrium. He develops a Walrasian-type model with equilibrium conditions specified for N producers and consumers in M regions. The other three articles consider equilibrium tendencies under conditions of growth.

Parts I and V deal respectively with defining regional economics and its tools, and the making of regional policy.

The volume is the product of the generosity and skill of many. Specifically, the late Professor James Young and the Bureau of Business and Economic Research at Kent State University were very kind in providing funds for translations. The translators, Linda Gates and Anne Marie McDermott, are to be commended for a fine job. Mr. Marc-Hubert Henry, a graduate student at Kent State University, was very helpful in preparation of the manuscript. Professor François Perroux of the Institut de Science Economique Appliquée in Paris made some constructive suggestions. Perhaps it should also be mentioned that Professor Perroux has developed his ideas on pole theory well beyond those contained in his "Note on the Concept of Growth Poles" that appears in this volume. However, the present writers felt that since that particular article is really the classic in the field, it should be included. Professor J. R. Boudeville has also been very helpful in securing French material. The authors would also like to thank Professors Niles Hansen, Ben Higgins, and M. L. Greenhut for their encouragement. Our secretary, Miss Mary Ann McCloskey, deserves a special vote of thanks. Of course any criticisms earned by the volume must be accepted "in toto" by the authors.

D.L.McK.
R.D.D.
W.H.L.
Kent, June 1969

# PART I INTRODUCTION

# 1

# *The Definition of Regional Economics*

Regional economics is a new subject. However, its growth has been phenomenal. It has already established a place for itself in university curricula, in international economic conferences, in learned economic journals, and in the thinking of policy-making institutions and planning commissions.[1] Any science, after a stage of development, needs a definition that provides a unifying link between the diverse problems that are considered and analyzed in it by its practitioners, in order to spotlight the essential difference between it and overlapping disciplines. Regional economics has surely reached this stage. It is the object of this paper to examine several definitions of regional economics germane in the writings of regional economists and to suggest a suitable alternative.

One approach to the question of defining regional economics is to deny the possibility of isolating such a discipline. Stress is laid by some writers on the interdisciplinary links of regional economics. Regional studies, according to them, form one indivisible whole. There exists a unified "regional science" in which economic geography, sociology, demography, and even literature are combined for purposes of regional analysis. Any breakdown of regional science into parts parallel to the disciplines employed is not possible. This attitude finds expression in Perloff's statement:

> No fully satisfactory way of classifying regional studies was found . . . . Regional studies tend to deal with many features and often involve the use of several academic disciplines. Thus no general system of classification can be expected to provide self-contained categories; there is inevitable spill-over.[2]

However correct this approach may be as to the content and nature of existing regional studies, it cannot be accepted as an approach to the definition of regional economics. Robbins long ago expounded the idea that economics is not distinguished by its subject matter, "the ordinary business of life," but by its point of view.[3] There is much overlapping among various academic disciplines with regard to the field of study, but they are fairly clearly distinguished by the point of view adopted. If we accept the Robbinsian argument that economics

1. See, for example, Meyer[8] and Isard and Cumberland[5].
2. Perloff[10; p. v].
3. Robbins[11; Ch. 1].

*Dubey, Vinod, "The Definition of Regional Economics," Journal of Regional Science, V, No. 2 (1964), pp. 25–29.*

studies not a special group of activities but an aspect of all human activities—and most economists do so—then there should be little difficulty in isolating regional economics within the portmanteau of regional science. It follows that regional studies that adopt the economic viewpoint may be considered as studies in regional economics.

A second approach to defining regional economics is the precise opposite of the one just discussed. It is based on the idea that a *group* of problems that form the subject matter of regional economics can be distinguished, and a listing of such problems could serve as a definition of the subject. As an example we have the following passage by Professor Isard:

> An analyst is perplexed with many problems when he looks at a region. One problem may be to identify specific industries which can individually or in groups operate efficiently and with profit in the region. Another related problem may be to improve the welfare of the people or the region, that is, to raise per capita incomes and perhaps achieve a more equitable distribution of income; the auxiliary problem of measurement of income ... is also present. Still another problem . . . is the problem of diversification ....Another pressing problem... is the problem of how to put to best use a limited, if not niggardly, endowment of resources.[4]

Such a listing of problems that are tackled in regional analysis can hardly serve as a definition of the subject. It is true that a list of the problems that are generally considered to lie within the field of investigation of regional economics can be made. But such a list would suffer from a number of defects. First, by its very nature it could never be complete. As new kinds of regional problems become significant the list would grow and become increasingly cumbersome. Secondly, the list method fails to bring out "the distinguishing characteristic" of the problems studied, the unifying link (or links) that make regional economics a distinct academic discipline. Thirdly, a definition consisting of a list of problems tackled in the subject suffers from a logical flaw—it is classificatory instead of analytical in conception. The underlying idea is that a *group* of problems can be isolated, labeled as economic problems, and listed. The implication is that the regional problems not listed are noneconomic problems. The logical weakness of an approach that classifies problems into economic and noneconomic were pointed out by Robbins long ago.[5] Regional economics is not the study of the economic problems of regions, as the "list of

4. Isard et al.[4; p. 413]. The passage is quoted more fully by Meyer[8] as a "definition" of regional analysis.

5. Robbins[11, Ch. 1]. The position of many modern economists is exemplified by Myrdal's statement "The distinction between factors that are 'economic' and those that are 'noneconomic' is, indeed, a useless and nonsensical device from the point of view of logic, and should be replaced by a distinction between 'relevant' and 'irrelevant' factors, or 'more relevant' and 'less relevant.'" See Myrdal[9; p. 10].

problems" definition seems to imply. Rather, it is the study of all the problems of regions from the economic viewpoint.

A third approach to regional economics regards it as the economics of spatial separation. Lefeber[6] emphasizes the necessity for a "spatial general equilibrium theory" and attempts to develop such a theory to study

> optimizing choices of location, agglomeration of products at certain points and not others, occasional mass migrations of labor, patterns of human settlement, intra- and interregional development of resources, development of transport networks, and other problems of social economic adjustment in a spatially differentiated world.

Such a conception of regional economics suffers from two weaknesses. First, it does not describe the whole field of problems covered in regional economics. As Professor Meyer has pointed out, "it would seem to be unduly confining since the policy problems considered in regional economics have been considerably wider in scope from the location problems emphasized by such a definition."[7] Secondly, the characteristic of spatial separation emphasized by this difinition as the source of the problems investigated by regional economics is logically incomplete. The presence of spatial separation is a necessary but not a sufficient condition for the existence of problems studied in regional economics. Spatial separation by itself does not provide both the rationale and the unifying link for regional economics. Consider a situation in which resources and their production and consumption are evenly and uniformly distributed over a continuous plane. Assume that indivisibilities do not exist. In this situation there would be spatial separation, but it would have no modifying influence on economic activities. There would be no regional economics. It appears, therefore, that the definition of regional economics as the economics of spatial separation is to be rejected because the distinguishing characteristic of regional problems highlighted by it is complete, and by itself it fails to explain regional economics.

Another approach to regional economics is to conceive of it as the economics of resource immobility.[8] Professor Meyer considers this to be "a reasonably accurate, though still less than fully comprehensive, description of regional economics."[9] However, the type of resource immobility included in the subject must be specified. There may be resource immobility between two points in space, or between

6. Lefeber[6; p. 1]. A similar point of view toward regional economics is to be found in Beckman[1] and in the writings of Isard.

7. Meyer[8; p. 35].

8. This point of view toward regional economics is exemplified by Borts[2] and Borts and Stein[3].

9. Meyer[8; p. 25].

two industries at the same point, or between two uses in the same
plant. The immobility of resources between two industries in the same
location is clearly not a part of regional economics. The immobility
of a factor between two uses in the same plant is also not necessarily
within the purview of regional economics. Hence regional economics
is the economics of *regional* (spatial) resource immobility.

However, a minor modification does not remove all the weaknesses of the resource immobility definition. By itself regional resource
immobility is not sufficient to give rise to the regional economic
problem. It becomes significant only when considered jointly with the
fact that resources tend to be unevenly distributed over space. This
is clear if we consider again the hypothetical plane in which resources,
products, and markets are all evenly spread over space, and in which
indivisibilities are absent. Suppose that resources are immobile. In
this situation the immobility does not matter; it is inconsequential.
A complete definition of regional economics, therefore, cannot be
couched simply in terms of immobility of resources.

Our discussion of the alternative approaches to defining regional
economics yields us the elements of a new definition of the subject.
The ultimate justification for regional economics derives from three
fundamental and ubiquitous facts about human existence. First,
human activity and its concomitants occupy space. Resources, markets,
and products are not located at mythical points having no length and
breadth. There is spatial separation. Secondly, resources and their
production and consumption are not evenly distributed over space.
Not only do real differentials exist, but they also vary over time. Uneven distribution of resources is not merely a matter of resource immobility. In a plane in which initially resources and activities are spread
evenly, in which resources are completely mobile, but in which indivisibilities (*i.e.*, increasing returns) exist, production would concentrate
at certain points. The initial areal uniformity would be replaced by
areal differentiation.[10] The existence of regional resource immobility
inhibits the erosion of areal differences, but it is conceptually distinct.
Thirdly, though the ends of human activity are many, the resources
to attain them are scarce and capable of alternative uses. In other
words, there exists the economic problem of the allocation and aug-
mentation of scarce resources. All of these fundamental conditions
must exist together for regional economics to develop. Spatial separation or resource immobility by themselves are not enough, as shown
earlier.

Spatial separation, uneven distribution of resources, lack of perfect mobility, and the necessity to economize should all be included in

10. See Lösch [7; Part II, particularly Ch. 9].

a complete definition of regional economics. Regional economics, therefore, is the study from the viewpoint of economics of the differentiation and interrelationship of areas in a universe of unevenly and imperfectly mobile resources.

This definition avoids the pitfalls of the common definitions of regional economics that we have discussed above. It is analytical rather than classificatory. Regional economics studies all regional problems from a particular viewpoint. The necessary and sufficient conditions for the existence of such problems, *i.e.*, the distinguishing characteristics of such problems, are made explicit in the definition. The existence of scarce resources, their uneven distribution over space, and the imperfect mobility give rise to the *regional* economic problem whose various manifestations regional economics attempts to investigate.

A possible criticism of the definition is that it does not sufficiently stress the "pragmatic, problem-solving orientation of regional economics" and particularly that of urban economics. It has been suggested that this lacuna may be removed by a slight modification of the definition:

> Regional economics is, therefore, the study, from the viewpoint of economics, of the differentiation and interrelationships of areas in a universe of unevenly distributed and imperfectly mobile resources, *with particular emphasis in application on the planning of the social overhead capital investments to mitigate the social problems created by these circumstances.*[11]

However, the addition of the modifying phrase (italicized) does not appear necessary. There is nothing inherent in the subject matter of regional economics to make its orientation any more or any less problem-solving than that of the rest of economic science. Fashions change and centers of interest shift. Ours is an analytical definition seeking to uncover the fundamental binding links of the subject. The modification appears to imply that the unifying links do not demarcate the subject matter of regional economics, which at present concentrates on the study of a part of the field so demarcated. Our position is opposed to this. To us, the current practice of regional economists does not exhaust the boundaries of the subject. An analytical definition not only spotlights current practice but also indicates and suggests lines for future study. Regional economics studies the regional economic problem wherever it occurs. The regional economic problem occurs wherever certain conditions specified earlier are found. Conceptually, there is no other limitation to the subject matter of

11. Professor Meyer has suggested this modification to me. In addition, I am indebted to him for answering my queries and for his comments on an earlier draft of this note.

regional economics. The current interests of regional economists may be appropriately included not in a definition of regional economics but in a discussion thereof.

## REFERENCES

1. M. BECKMAN, "Some Reflections on Lösch's Theory of Location," *Papers and Proceedings of the Regional Science Association*, I (1955), pp. N1–N9.
2. G. H. BORTS, "The Equalization of Returns and Regional Economic Growth," *American Economic Review*, L (1960), pp. 319–347 [Selection 11 of this volume].
3. G. H. BORTS and J. L. STEIN, "Investment Return as a Measure of Comparative Regional Economic Advantage," in W. Hochwald, ed., *Design of Regional Accounts* (Baltimore: The Johns Hopkins Press, 1961).
4. W. ISARD *et al.*, *Methods of Regional Analysis* (New York: John Wiley and Sons, Inc., and the M. I. T. Press, 1960).
5. W. ISARD and J. H. CUMBERLAND, eds., *Regional Economic Planning* (Paris: O.E.E.C., 1961).
6. L. LEFEBER, *Allocation in Space* (Amsterdam: North-Holland Publishing Co., 1959).
7. A. LÖSCH, *The Economics of Location* (New Haven: Yale University Press, 1954).
8. J. R. MEYER, "Regional Economics: A Survey," *American Economic Review*, LIII (1963), pp. 19–54.
9. G. MYRDAL, *Economic Theory and Underdeveloped Regions* (London: Gerald Duckworth & Co. Ltd., 1957).
10. H. S. PERLOFF, *Regional Studies at U.S. Universities: A Survey of Regionally Oriented Research and Graduate Education Activities* (Washington, D.C., 1957).
11. L. ROBBINS, *An Essay on the Nature and Significance of Economic Science* (London: Macmillan & Co. Ltd., 1932).

# *Regional Theory and Regional Models*

Whenever a social scientist tries to utilize a term that has had a long history, he faces an initial dilemma. If the term has evolved as a response to the need for some way of describing an important and continuing element in human existence, it may well be the best way to denote that element. On the other hand, terms that have been widely used tend to take on a variety of connotations, which cluster, as it were, around the central idea. This is particularly true of broadly descriptive terms of categorization. The examples of *class, industry, era,* and *style* all spring to mind. Such words are, in a sense, "empty boxes," which tend to take on the coloration of their contents. Usually, they have been heavily used; sometimes, so much so that the social scientist is forced by his need for precision and clarity in terminology to coin new terms in order to express the central notions without historical overtones.

The word *region* clearly falls into the same group as those above.[1] So widely has the term been used that we are faced with the probability of confusion if we try to employ it in formal models. Yet, paradoxically, it is just this widespread usage that encourages the belief that the region is a useful concept for many analyses in which spatial relationships are taken into account. If the region is ignored, an essential way in which man has subjectively regarded his environment is abandoned. In a social science that is not rich in conceptual foundations, this is not good strategy. If the concept is given some other name or names, the practical difficulties of communication are thereby increased. It is necessary, then, to examine the usage of the word, and to decide whether to use the word to describe whatever concept it is held to symbolize.

A basic subjective awareness of differences from place to place is a widespread human trait. At the same time, the use of relatively few primary characteristics to differentiate between places may indicate why *region* has been a useful and popular idea, enabling the individual to reduce the complexity of the world to a relatively small and comprehensible number of elements, distinct in both location and quality. Rationalization of this type is probably of doubtful validity,

---

1. Extensive discussion of the regional concept is to be found in Hartshorne [3] and [4], and in James and Jones [6]. Consideration of the concept in regional science appears in Isard [5] and in Garnsey [1].

Teitz, Michael B., "Regional Theory and Regional Models," Papers and Proceedings of the Regional Science Association, IX (1962), pp. 35–50.

but it serves to point up the basic fact that the word region is widely used in everyday language, and that there is at least an implicit understanding of its meaning. We might hypothesize that that meaning is such as to give to the word a concrete connotation beyond any that most spatial analysts would wish for. People can name regions—The South, The Far West—better than they can define the word itself. However, such an assertion is intuitive, in the absence of any documented studies on this point. It seems reasonable, though, to say that the word has taken on a variety of meanings that vary from simple areal delimitation to the implication of the existence of a strong and persistent pattern of social and economic behavior over some vaguely understood area.

We wish to use the regional concept as an aid in the description and understanding of the impact of spatial friction and differentiation on human activity. If the region is to be anything more than an arbitrary taxonomic convenience in empirical work, then it must be shown that the concept can be specified minimally with enough uniformity and objectivity to ensure that communication between investigators is possible, and that results can be reproduced and tested. In other words, if we are to use the concept of region in our models, an intuitive notion of that concept is not enough.

But rigorous definition of the region proves to be very difficult. It is necessary to begin by assuming the abstract idea of a space, which amounts to taking as given the very thing that we are trying to describe. But no alternative is readily apparent, and we shall leave the concept of a space incompletely defined, while assuming that it exists.

Once this is done, the problem resolves itself into that of constructing a theoretical framework in which the defining of a variable over a space may lead to a division into subspaces that are useful and meaningful in terms of theory concerning the nature of that space and variable. This latter requirement is a further condition for the employment of the regional concept, a condition that involves the theory of the phenomena with which we are concerned rather than the goodness of the definition of the regional concept that we use to analyze that phenomena.

Two main concerns, then, may be identified with respect to regional models. First, we need a better formal understanding of what is meant by the regional concept; and secondly, we must identify models to which this particular concept can give added power and depth. Naturally, these concerns are not independent. As an adequate regional concept is developed, it should give indications of new types of regional models. And the development of new regional models may insure that the forms of regional concept used in them are, in turn, submitted to tests of completeness and adequacy.

## SET-THEORETIC FOUNDATIONS FOR A REGIONAL CONCEPT

The history of the regional concept is one of argument and disagreement. Following Bertrand Russell's dictum that "the most savage controversies are those about matters as to which there is no good evidence either way,"[2] we will ignore the discussions of existence or nonexistence of regions, and who should look for them and why. And since this reformulation of the concept is to be a formalization also, it is necessary to recognize the sacrifices in richness that must be made, at least to begin with. We shall start by regarding the region simply as some sort of aggregative classificatory device that is used for the purpose of reducing the number of cases with which the investigator of spatial phenomena must deal. By means of this heuristic definition we may find it possible to make use of some simple tools of set theory and classification in order to develop basic notions that will then be applied to the idea of region.

Let it be said, though, that some of the most basic questions will be left unanswered. The abstract idea of a space will be taken as a primitive, for only then is it possible to speak of a *region* of that space. The main objectives will be the partitioning of a space into subspaces, the means of partitioning employed, and the relation of the subspaces to the parent space.[3]

Initially, we consider as a zero dimensional space a finite set of undifferentiated but discrete objects. Call this the set $X$ with elements $x$. The elements of $X$ may be placed in a one-to-one correspondence with the positive integers beginning with 1. If $1, 2, \ldots, n$ are used in this correspondence, we may now say that we have the set $X$, with elements identified as $x_i$, $(x_i \in X; i = 1, 2, \ldots, n)$. The elements are unidimensionally identified and may be thought of as points on a straight line (Figure 1).

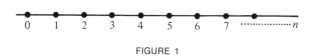

FIGURE 1

Consider a further set of integers, $J = \{0,1\}$. With the set $I = \{1, 2, \ldots, n\}$, we may form the cartesian product set $I \times J$. Call this set $C$; $C = \{(1,0), (1,1), (2,0), (2,1), \ldots, (n,1)\}$.

Select from $C$ some subset $F$ such that

$$F \subset C, \text{and}$$
$$F = \{(i,j); i = 1, \ldots, n; j = 0 \text{ or } 1, \text{but not both}\}.$$

2. Russell [10; p. 109].
3. The following discussion draws upon Halmos [2], Johnson [7], and Kamke [8].

This set, with exactly $n$ elements, $(i, j)$, describes a function, which we call $F$, with domain $I = \{i: i$ an integer; $0 < i \leqslant n\}$, and range $J = \{j: j$ an integer; $0 \leqslant j \leqslant 1\}$. Whether we say that the set $F$ is the function, or whether the function is the means whereby the elements of the domain and range are uniquely paired to form $F$, is not really material at this point.[4] Either expression of the idea of function will do. The elements of $X$ now may be uniquely associated with the ordered pair elements of $F$, and they may be conceived of as being embedded in the plane of a cartesian coordinate system (Figure 2).

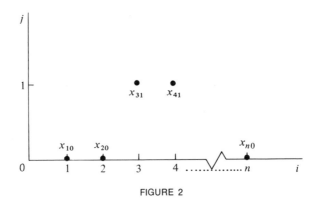

FIGURE 2

The set $X$ may now be written as

$$X = \{x_{ij}: i = 1, \ldots, n; j = 0 \text{ or } 1\}$$

and it is evident that the value of the $j$ subscript depends upon some function $F$ which determines the $n$ ordered pairs, $(i, j)$.

Although it would be very easy at this point to consider the system purely in terms of ordered pairs of integers (or a binary function), the notion of the set, $X$, of undefined objects, is retained because it may be interpreted in terms of a research problem. The set may now be described as a collection of objects, each of which is firstly identified in terms of a dimension, and secondly, characterized by a value of some variable or differentiating characteristic, $j$. As observers of this set we might view its "population" in various ways, each of which would yield a different amount and type of information, and require a differing amount of effort.

    (i) Ignoring all characterization, we have only the undifferentiated but finite $X$.

    (ii) Using the integer characteristic, we may differentiate and

4. See Johnson [7; Ch. 1].

count the elements, $x_i$. Strictly, we now have $n$ subsets of $X$, each containing exactly one element.

$$X' = \{\{x_i\}\}, i = 1, \ldots, n$$

(iii) With the particular binary differentiating function implied by $F$, we may see two subsets of $X$. One of these may be empty; whether this is so will depend on $F$.

$$X'' = \{\{x_{i0} : i \in I\}, \{x_{i1} : i \in I\}\}$$

Obviously, many possible different sets, $F$, could be recognized. In fact there will be as many as there are ways of partitioning $X$ into two subsets, $X_1, X_0$.

It is evident that if the function $F$ gives the partition $\{X_0, X_1\}$, then its inverse, $F^{-1}$, will give $\{\overline{X}_1, \overline{X}_0\}$. In total there are $2^n$ such binary functions, and therefore $2^n$ such partitions. Even with such a simple relation as the binary, defined on an integral domain, the number of resulting possible partitions will grow very rapidly with $n$, although the number of subsets in each partition will be equal to two. Within this total are included all possible ways of classifying the population into two classes by virtue of a single binary differentiating characteristic.

The case of a binary function and integral domain is one which frequently occurs in practice, but the system still needs greater generality to be most useful. Such generalization seems to be possible in several directions. We now examine some of these possibilities.

1. Let the set $J$ expand so that $J = \{0, 1, 2, \ldots, m\}$, $i.e.$, the range of each function $F$ will now be over the integers $0 \leq j \leq m$. The classification remains two-dimensional and the original set $X$ is unchanged. Partitions of the form $\{X_0, X_1, X_2, \ldots, X_j, \ldots, X_m\}$ will now result, with $X_j = \{x_{ij} : i \in I\}$. With each distinguishably different partition there is associated some function that will result uniquely in that partition when defined on the domain variable, $i$. In total there are now $(m+1)^n$ such functions and partitions. As $n$ increases and the permissible values of $j$ increase, the number of partitions will increase rapidly, but the number of non-empty sets in any partition is restricted by the value of $n$. If $n < m+1$ there must be at least $(m-n+1)$ empty $X_j$ in each partition; there may of course be more, but there also must be at least one non-empty set.

2. Just as it is possible to expand the sets $I$ and $J$, so it is also possible to expand the number of sets with which we deal. Instead of differentiating the set $X$ on the basis of counting and a single characteristic, $j$, we introduce a new characteristic, $k$. As an example,

consider the case of $J = \{0, 1, 2\}$, $I = \{1, 2, \ldots, n\}$, and introduce $K = \{0, 1, 2\}$. The scheme may still be represented in two dimensions if the $i$ axis is suppressed, a procedure that is justifiable if we recall that the introduction of $i$ was simply for the purpose of counting and identifying the $x \in X$. The individual elements are now symbolized by $x_{jk}$ and each may take on values of $j$, $k$ in any of nine ways, some of which are illustrated in Figure 3.

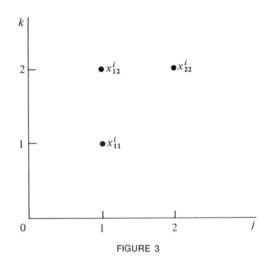

FIGURE 3

In addition to the modes of partition outlined above, it becomes possible to partition by: (1) either $j$ or $k$ alone; (2) by $j$ and $k$; or (3) by some subset of $j$ and/or $k$, as soon as some function set, $F$, is specified. The general form of these types of partition for the case given would be:

$$\{X_{0.}, X_{1.}, X_{2.}\} \text{ or } \{X_{.0}, X_{.1}, X_{.2}\} \tag{1}$$

$$\{X_{00}, X_{01}, X_{02}, \ldots, X_{22}\} \tag{2}$$

$$\{\dot{X}_{0, k=0, 1}, X_{0, k=2}, \ldots, X_{2, k=2}\} \tag{3}$$

With $I = \{1, 2, \ldots, n\}$, $J = \{0, 1, \ldots, m\}$, and $K = \{0, 1, \ldots, p\}$, it may be shown that there are $[(m+1)(p+1)]^n$ possible partitions, and the addition of a new characteristic that takes on $s$ possible values will again increase the number of partitions by a factor of $s^n$.

Note that there is no weighting problem. Each new variable is considered independently of all the others for purposes of partition. The problems of weighting will arise when it is required to compact the data even further, or when it is suspected that the variables are not in fact orthogonal — that they are merely reflecting some other more basic variable. Both of these problems are exceedingly important in theoretical and empirical work, but since their complexity is so great we shall not consider them at present.

3. So far we have generalized within the restriction that the elements of the set $X$ are enumerable. That is, they may be placed in correspondence with the set of natural numbers (positive integers). The sets $J$, $K$, etc., associated with differentiating characteristics also have been restricted in this way, although it is easy to see that we could extend them over the integers, since there is no *a priori* reason for excluding negative values. Though useful for our initial purposes, this restriction excludes some important sets. For instance, the sets of all points on a continuum, such as a straight line or a two-dimensional space, are non-enumerable. Yet these sets are basic to much of the work in regional theory. Some way to include them should be found.

The set of points on a straight line may be placed in correspondence with any continuous subset of the real numbers. Let the set $X$ now be thought of in this way and redefined:

$$X = \{x_i : 0 < i \leq n\}$$

The domain variable $i$, with its set $I = \{i : 0 < i \leq n\}$, which was formerly introduced for purposes of counting and identification of the $x \in X$, is now used purely for identification, since the elements of $X$ are infinite in number. If $J = \{0, 1, 2\}$ as before, a cartesian product set $I \times J$ is infinitely large, as are the numbers of possible partitions and functions.

So long as the $j$ are finite and discrete, we might try to solve the problem by reordering the $i$ so that all $x_i$ with identical $j$ are contiguous. In this way we would still have an infinite number of functions and partitions, but they would all be in the form of monotonic step functions. (See Figure 4.)

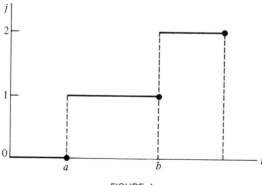

FIGURE 4

15

Each such function specifies the $j$ value associated with any $n_i$ over continuous portions of the domain, $0 < i \leq n$. The function set associated with that of Figure 4 might be written as:

$$F_m = \{(i,j): j = 0 \text{ iff } 0 < i \leq a; j = 1 \text{ iff } a < i \leq b; j = 2 \text{ iff } b < i \leq n\}$$

A difficulty lies in the reordering assumption. If reordering of the $x_i$ is not possible, then there is no succinct way in which we can represent the outcomes. For each of the monotonic step functions there remains exactly one partition, but infinitely many other partitions with other functions also exist. The most we can say about these is that if more than one $j$ value is involved, the function is discontinuous because of the discrete $j$. Thus, if the ordering of the $i$ is immutable, we may distinguish functions associated with partitions on a discrete $j$, and divide the functions into uniform, monotonic and other.

These are some of the general set-theoretic ideas that might be used in attacking the problem of partition and classification. Many questions have not been examined, including those involving continuity and weighting that are of the utmost difficulty. However, the central notions can perhaps be grasped from the discussion.

## A REGIONAL CONCEPT

With the ideas developed so far, it is possible to formulate a notion of region that will be useful in the study of regional models. From the set-theoretic analysis of classification we will draw some preliminary ideas and definitions.

It is necessary to specify some of the basic elements of the idea of region in its widest sense. Underlying all is the notion of simultaneous association and differentiation: some thing (or collection of things) is held to be different in some way from other things, with which it is nevertheless associated. This is not unique to the region—all classificatory activity is involved with the same idea.[5] We may hypothesize that the region for our purposes draws its character from the idea that the things being differentiated are located in some space.

Usually this space will be some model of part of the surface of the earth, in one, two, or three dimensions. But there is no reason why other spaces cannot be used. The space in which location is posited may be of any form; only when the model is applied to some particular study does that form become critical.

5. The correspondance between the terminology for uniform regions and that for classification is shown by W. Bunge in his *Theoretical Geography*.

Four ideas for regional theory seem to be necessary. First, we define the population with which the theory is concerned; that is the equivalent of the set $X$, with elements $x$. Call this set the *population constituent set* or *constituent set*. Its specific nature will depend on the context of the regional theory.

Secondly, we define the space with reference to which the constituent set is located. The space may be regarded either as another set in which the constituent set is embedded, or as a set of relationships among the elements of the constituent set. In either case, we may identify it with the set $I$ in the previous discussion, the elements of $I$ consisting of ordered $n$-tuples and the location being in $n$-dimensional space. Call this set, $I$, the *location set*, and the space involved the *location space*.

Thirdly, we must define the attributes of the constituent set with which we are concerned. For any given attribute or characteristic, $j$, there exists a set of values that that attribute may take on. This set, which we have previously called $J$, may be termed the *attribute set*. Note that it is distinct from the set of attributes.

Fourthly, using these concepts, we will define a *regional system* as a partitioning of some locationally identified constituent set. A *region* then becomes a locationally identified set that is an element of a partition of a locationally identified set. More precisely, a regional system is a particular partition of the constituent set, where that set is placed in a one-to-one correspondence with a subset of the location set. This latter process we shall call "locational identification" of the constituent set, and the result is a set that may be written as

$$X_{HI} = \{x_{hi} : h = 1, 2, \ldots, n; i \in I\}$$

The one-to-one correspondence implies that each constituent is uniquely located. The relevant partition will be formed from a subset of the cartesian product of $H$ and some attribute set $J$, and may be expressed as

$$X_{H \times J} = \{X_{.j} : j = 1, \ldots, m\}, \text{ where } X_{.j} = \{x_{hj} : h \in H\}$$

In this formulation the location subscript has been omitted so that the constituent is identified only by the counting set, $H = \{1, 2, \ldots, h, \ldots, n\}$.

This rather cumbersome procedure seems quite necessary to preserve the distinction between the population under study, the space in which it is located, and the attributes by which it is differentiated. The differentiation process partitions both the population and the location space. But the location space is significant only as it impinges upon the population. It does not necessarily follow that the whole location space is partitioned unless there is a one-to-one relationship between the location set and the constituent set. Where this is not so, the regions formed will not be continuous within the location space, even though that space is itself continuous.

In fact, the concept allows us to throw light on the problem of continuity in regional systems. We make no restrictions on the continuity of the component set — it may be continuous, discontinuous, or punctiform. Similarly, the location set may vary, but only within the restriction that it be placeable in one-to-one correspondence with the constituent set, or have some subset that is so placeable. This restriction is necessary for the constituent set to be locationally identified. Confusion over the apparent continuity of the earth surface, or rather of the surface of the chosen model of the earth, is avoided by defining regional systems as partitions, and allowing a region to consist of constituents at a point, over a set of points, or over a continuous space.

One point needs further clarification with respect to location. In any regional system the locational set is itself a form of attribute defined upon the constituent set. According to the way in which the location set is regarded, so may the final regional system differ. A major problem is whether location is to be treated as an active attribute, whether it should be the source of restrictions on the regions formed. If locational restrictions, such as, for example, some kind of contiguity, are included explicitly in the requirements for constituents of a region, the resulting system may be quite different from one without such restrictions. In the latter case, location is an implicit attribute, and a region is "stratified" whenever it consists of two or more locationally noncontiguous segments having the same attribute value.

At this point it seems useful to connect some of the ideas expressed so far with existing notions of regional theory. We shall examine the concepts of uniform and nodal regions, as these are the two types that have been most extensively discussed.[6] However, there will be given no more than a few indications of the way in which the present framework may encompass them.

The *uniform* region has variously been called *homogeneous* and *formal*. All these names characterize aspects of what is usually meant by the term — an area of some sort of homogeneity with respect to one or more characteristics. The idea here has been extended beyond that of area, but the formal system can easily take account of uniform regions. We go farther by specifying the function that determines the partition that in turn gives rise to the system of regions. Such a function is

6. See Hartshorne [4; p. 140 ff.], and Whittlesey [11].

implicit in any empirical delimitation of a region, although in practice it is not often defined.

As an example, we consider the case of a discrete constituent set, $X$; discrete attribute set, $J = \{0, 1\}$; and continuous location set, $I$, in a two-dimensional space. Thus each constituent is associated with an ordered pair of real numbers from some specified set of such pairs. Given some function, $F$, it is apparent that with respect to $j$, the original population is partitioned into two subsets. It is also evident that if the $x$ are discrete and finite in number while distributed upon a continuous surface, we can always construct a regional division of the location space that will partition them in the same way as they have been partitioned with respect to $j$. Such a division is schematically indicated in Figure 5, in which the subscripts indicate location and the superscript is the value for $j$.

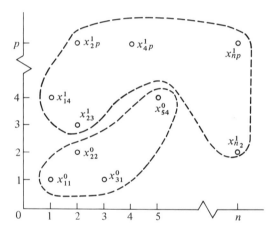

FIGURE 5   Punctiform uniform regions.

The dashed lines in Figure 5 are equivalent to a dashed line in Figure 2 at some value between zero and one. In both cases, infinitely many such lines could be drawn without affecting the information on partition that is given. Figure 2, however, tends to stress the division between the two sets, while Figure 5 also stresses the spatial configuration of the constituent set. Infinitely many regions could be drawn on the map and all could be considered equally valid and uniform in the absence of any constraint requiring the exhaustion of the location space. Boundaries in terms of the location space are arbitrary so long as they enclose the requisite subsets of the constituent set.

Where the constituent set and the location set are both continuous, it may still be possible to define uniform regions under certain conditions. These are analogous to those realized in Figure 4. If

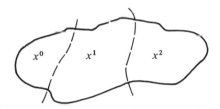

FIGURE 6   Uniform regions based on a continuous constituent set.

all elements with identical $j$ values are contiguous in the location space, the boundary between the subsets will be uniquely determined. Generalized into two dimensions this situation may be described by Figure 6.

By relaxing the contiguity restraint this may be expanded to include the "stratified" case, as in Figure 7. Here the $X_0$ may be regarded as a single stratified region or as two separate regions if location is introduced as an explicit classificatory variable.

If the constituent set, location set, and attribute set were all continuous, $e.g.$ $j = \{J: \ 0 \leqslant j \leqslant 2\}$, an infinite number of regions based upon the attribute $j$ could be defined. In order to reduce the information to manageable form we might resort to some discrete reduction of the $j$ values:

$$0 \leqslant j < 1$$
$$1 \leqslant j < 2$$

This is again equivalent to the basic form of Figure 6, but since we have forced the attribute set into a compressed form, we will call the outcome a *region by compression*. It is, of course, the type of uniform region that is defined by an interval on a contour map.

The *nodal* or *functional* region constitutes the most widely used alternative to the uniform region. Just as we may associate the uniform region with the observation of apparent internal uniformity, so

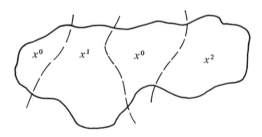

FIGURE 7   Continuous stratified uniform regions.

the nodal region may be associated with internal unity. Unity of organization can encompass a great diversity of elements that are bound together in a systematic way by interconnections, interactions, or flows. Even the lowest order of nodal region is likely to be the outcome of process relationships among the constituents, while for the corresponding uniform region it is probable that the process underlying the distribution of the attribute is in some way external to the constituent set.

A region may be considered nodal if the rationale for grouping together its constituents is one of interconnection. However, there is as yet no hard-and-fast definition of what components of linkage actually constitute a region. At the simplest level we may not distinguish between constituents and nodes; the region would then be a number of constituents linked to each other. If the region is based on a hierarchical functional system, it may be necessary to distinguish between constituents and nodes. In this case the region may consist of:

1. Constituents having the same node; the node defined as not part of the region.
2. Constituents and their node; the node not being a constituent.
3. Constituents and their node; the node a constituent with or without reflexive connection.
4. Constituents and their node; the node may or may not be a constituent.

The variety of possibilities for a single-node region is a portent of the intricacy of higher order nodal regions. We shall not discuss any beyond simple cases.

Consider case (1) above. If the nodal region is to consist of constituents having the same node, then there is no essential difference between it and the simple uniform region. We may define a discrete attribute set in which each element corresponds to some node. The particular regional system will arise from some function set that relates that particular attribute set to the constituent set. Such a region is in fact just as likely to be called uniform as nodal. Consider the example of a region consisting of dairy farms which serve some city. As a "dairy region" it is uniform; as a "milk shed" it is nodal.

Once the node is introduced explicitly as part of the region several complications arise. There is not sufficient space to examine all the possibilities, but it should be pointed out that alternative formulations for a regional system can be given by structuring the constituent set either in terms of individual nodes and constituents or in terms of node-constituent pairs. The latter form especially seems to be amenable to expression in matrix form and allows us to keep the attribute set entirely nonlocational in character.

**21**

## REGIONAL MODELS

We now turn to the problem of models that may be fruitfully identified with the regional concept. That is, we seek models that as part of their analysis of spatial relationships imply functions that partition the population with which they are concerned. Phrasing the question in this way means that we are not involved with models from any particular discipline. Nevertheless, economic models will be the central concern at this stage.

There is no *a priori* reason why any model of nature or of human activity should contain a regional dimension, or for that matter any other particular dimension. But since such activities often imply some degree of movement, we might expect that a spatial variable of some kind would yield insights. The inclusion of a spatial variable does not mean, though, that the model is thereby made "regional."

The distinction between regional and spatial models is made explicit because there has been so much ambiguity and confusion. While both kinds exist and have been used with good results, their basic differences have not been sufficiently recognized and analyzed. Spatial models dealing with the relationships of activities at point locations, usually in two-dimensional space, have been used as the basis of quasi-regional models, and their outputs have been interpreted as having a regional significance. That it may be simpler to construct spatial models that are not regional (in that any regions involved are not part of the output of the model) than to incorporate regions fully, is possibly indicated by the number of nonregional or quasi-regional equilibrium systems for economic activities, in contrast with Lösch's lonely attempt to construct a fully regional equilibrium system.[7]

We have already seen that it is not implicit in the concept that a region be a continuous entity in some locational space. Rather, for even the simple single-variable case, the region may consist of a point, a collection of points, a line, a collection of lines, an area, or a collection of areas. With this in mind, we can consider the rationale for the construction and utilization of a regional model.

If we examine an activity that results in the distribution of some variable over a space, we must ask what kinds of characteristics are likely to make a regional model more useful than some other. The primary characteristic of regional models is the partitioning of the population over which the variables are defined. So we may expect to be interested in those activities having structural qualities that lead to such partition. Similarly, we may look for primary spaces tending to

---

7. Lösch [9; Ch. 8].

make such partitions more clearly visible, perhaps, for example, discontinuous rather than continuous spaces.

Most models of economic activity, whether concerned with a spatial variable or not, have assumed certain characteristics that are necessary for the derivation of marginal conditions for optimization. In order to do this with the tools of the calculus, the assumption of continuity is made at a critical point. Thus, in the theory of consumer demand, the utility function of the individual is assumed to be continuous and differentiable, so that it may be maximized subject to a given income constraint. In the theory of the firm, we assume a continuous cost function and demand function in order to maximize profits. For the purposes of microeconomic theory these assumptions are vital and unquestionable. The awkward problem of economies of scale is not at the center of interest, and the fact that such economies exist and are important has to be assumed away. It was one of the great achievements of Lösch that he could incorporate scale economies into a spatial model in such a way that a partitioning should logically result.

Still there are implicit assumptions in the Lösch model that are brought out when we consider it as a model resulting in regions—the regions in this case being for our simplified purposes the individual market areas resulting at any given level of demand. In terms of the previous discussion it is clear that the population constituent set of the Lösch model is discrete and located by a discrete subset of ordered pairs from the real numbers in a sixty-degree lattice. Lösch used this basic fact to derive the number of consumers, and thereby the demand, that were available for each scale of production.[8] However, he then goes on to derive market-area boundaries in terms of the continuous location space that has been used to identify and locate the constituents. It is on this space that hexagons are drawn and market-area boundaries specified. In terms of his original model there seems to be no reason why these boundaries should be regarded as any more meaningful than arbitrary lines. Since no constituent can locate at any point off the lattice without destroying the whole equilibrium, boundaries outside the lattice points cannot be regarded as unique (see Figure 8).

The Lösch model, examined in terms of the point distribution, leads one to see the connectivity between producers and consumers, and thus to patterns of movement and transport cost under alternative hypotheses (see Figure 9). Under the assumption of straight line connections, the patterns that emerge are very different from those that we tend to associate with the hexagonal system.

8. Lösch [9; Ch. 9].

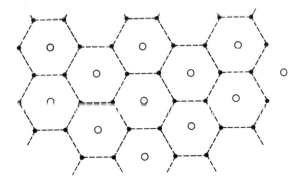

FIGURE 8   Lösch market pattern based on a three-consumer set with indeterminate boundaries.

## CONCLUSION

The ideas outlined in this paper are tentative and only partially developed. They have arisen very much as a response to the deficiencies in existing regional models. Whether this particular structure can lead to added order and power in such models remains to be demonstrated. But with increasing demands for analysis at a regional level, a substantial theoretical basis for regional models is manifestly needed.

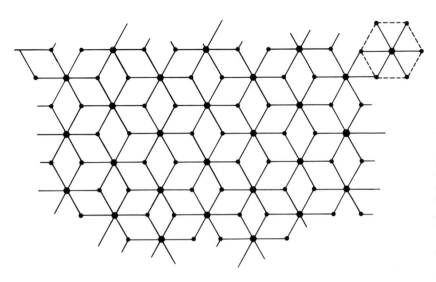

FIGURE 9(a)   Connectivity in a Lösch market network: Smallest market set—three consumers.

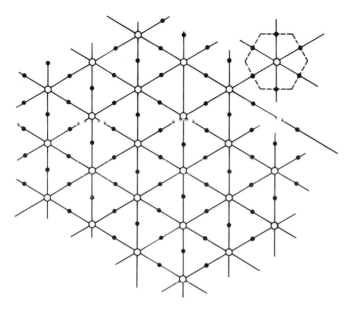

FIGURE 9(b)    Connectivity in a Lösch market network: Market set based on four consumers.

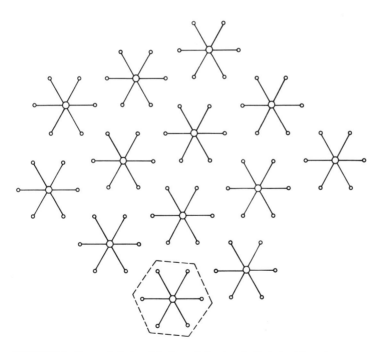

FIGURE 9(c)    Connectivity in a Lösch market network: Market set based on seven consumers.

## REFERENCES

1. M. E. GARNSEY, "The Dimensions of Regional Science," *Papers and Proceedings of the Regional Science Association*, II (1956), pp. 27–40.
2. P. HALMOS, *Naive Set Theory* (Princeton, N. J.: D. Van Nostrand Company, Inc., 1960).
3. R. HARTSHORNE, *The Nature of Geography* (Lancaster, Pa.: Association of American Geographers, 1946).
4. ———, *Perspective on the Nature of Geography* (Chicago: Rand McNally, 1959).
5. W. ISARD, "Regional Science, the Concept of Region and Regional Structure," *Papers and Proceedings of the Regional Science Association*, II (1956), pp. 13–27.
6. P. E. JAMES and C. F. JONES, eds., *American Geography: Inventory and Prospect* (Syracuse, N. Y.: Syracuse University Press, 1954).
7. R. E. JOHNSON, *A First Course in Abstract Algebra* (Englewood Cliffs, N. J.: Prentice Hall, Inc., 1953).
8. E. KAMKE, *Theory of Sets* (New York: Dover Publications, Inc., 1950).
9. A. LÖSCH, *The Economics of Location* (New Haven, Conn.: Yale University Press, 1954).
10. B. RUSSELL, *Unpopular Essays* (London: Allen and Unwin, 1951).
11. D. C. WHITTLESEY, "The Regional Concept and the Regional Method," in James and Jones [6], pp. 19–68.

# PART II ECONOMIC THEORY AND REGIONAL EXPANSION

3

# Location Theory and Regional
# Economic Growth[1]

I

During the past several decades there has been a growing interest in location theory in America. Building on the pioneering works of Thünen, Weber, Lösch, Palander, and others,[2] a number of economists and geographers have extended the analysis to apply to a wide range of problems and have attempted to synthesize location theory with other fields of economics.[3] However, very little work has been done in using the principles of location to analyze the historical growth of regions in America.[4] While economists concerned with location theory sometimes point out the implications of their analysis for the growth of regions, they have not followed up these discrete observations with any systematic analysis. A fundamental difficulty has been that the theory of regional economic growth[5] has little relevance for the development of regions in America. Not only does the sequence of stages outlined by the theory bear little resemblance to American development but its policy implications are also fundamentally misleading.

1. I am indebted for criticisms and suggestions to several of my colleagues at the University of Washington, particularly Philip Cartwright, J. R. Huber, Franklyn Holzman, and Robert Lampman. Dean H. W. Stoke and the Research Committee of the Graduate School at the University of Washington generously provided financial assistance for research, part of which is used in this article.
2. A summary of earlier contributions to location theory may be found in E. M. Hoover, *Location Theory and the Shoe and Leather Industries* (Cambridge, Mass.: Harvard University Press, 1937).
3. In addition to Hoover's valuable study already cited, see his *The Location of Economic Activity* (New York: McGraw-Hill Book Co., 1948). See also Bertil Ohlin, *Interregional and International Trade* (Cambridge, Mass.: Harvard University Press, 1935); National Resources Planning Board, *Industrial Location and National Resources* (Washington, D.C.: Government Printing Office, 1943); and the articles by Walter Isard cited in later footnotes.
4. A significant exception is Walter Isard's "Transportation Development and Building Cycles," *Quarterly Journal of Economics*, LVII (November, 1942), pp. 90–112. See also William H. Dean, *The Theory of the Geographic Location of Economic Activities (Selections from the Doctoral Dissertation)* (Ann Arbor, Mich.: Edward Bros., Inc., 1938).
5. See Section II.

North, Douglass C., "Location Theory and Regional Economic Growth," Journal of Political Economy, LXIII (June, 1955), pp. 243–258.

This paper will attempt to demonstrate the inadequacies of the existing theory of regional economic growth and will advance a number of propositions that may lead to a more useful theory, both for analyzing the historical development of the American economy and for understanding the contemporary problems associated with regional economic growth.

The analytical propositions advanced in this paper, though explicitly oriented to America's development, would apply equally well to other areas that meet the following conditions: (1) regions that have grown up within a framework of capitalist institutions and have therefore responded to profit-maximizing opportunities, in which factors of production have been relatively mobile,[6] and (2) regions that have grown up without the strictures imposed by population pressure.

## II

Both location theory and the theory of regional economic growth have described a typical sequence of stages through which regions move in the course of their development.[7] E. M. Hoover and Joseph Fisher, in a recent essay entitled "Research in Regional Economic Growth,"[8] point out that "there is now a fairly well-accepted body of theory regarding the normal sequence of development stages in a region."[9] This sequence may be outlined as follows:

1. The first stage in the economic history of most regions is one of a self-sufficient subsistence economy in which there is little investment or trade. The basic agricultural stratum of population is simply located according to the distribution of natural resources.

2. With improvements in transport, the region develops some trade and local specialization. "A second stratum of population comes

6. Obviously both profit maximization and factor mobility are relative notions and nowhere perfectly met. However, there is a vast difference between the response of an underdeveloped area where the social and economic structure is not fundamentally geared to capitalist stimuli and the kind of response one can expect in a basically capitalist society. The reluctance of the economic historian to make more extensive use of the tools of the theorist reflects in good part the fact that most of the world's economic history falls outside our first condition and that therefore economic theory is of little use in analyzing a large part of its development. On the other hand, the joint efforts of economic theorists and historians applied to the development of the United States and of some other areas hold out the promise of yielding valuable insights.

7. See August Lösch, "The Nature of Economic Regions," *Southern Economic Journal*, V (July, 1938), pp. 71–78; Hoover, *Location Theory and the Shoe and Leather Industries*, pp. 284–85, and *The Location of Economic Activity*, pp. 187–88.

8. Universities–National Bureau Committee for Economic Research, *Problems in the Study of Economic Growth* (New York: National Bureau of Economic Research, 1949), Ch. V.

9. *Ibid.*, p. 180.

into being, carrying on simple village industries for the farmers. Since the materials, the market, and the labor are all furnished originally by the agricultural populations, the new 'industrial superstructure' is located with reference to that 'basic stratum.' "[10]

3. With the increase of interregional trade, a region tends to move through a succession of agricultural crops from extensive grazing to cereal production to fruit-growing, dairy farming and truck gardening.[11]

4. With increased population and diminishing returns in agriculture and other extractive industries, a region is *forced* to industrialize. "Industrialization means the introduction of so-called secondary industries (mining and manufacturing) on a considerable scale."[12] Typically, the early stages of industrialization are based on the products of agriculture and forestry and include such activities as the processing of food, the manufacture of wood products, and the preparation of textile fibers. If industrialization is to continue, mineral and energy resources become critical.

> As a second stage of industrialization, then, we see [in the regions possessing economically usable mineral resources] such industries as the smelting, refining, and processing of metals; oil refining; chemical industries based mainly on coal, petroleum, potash, salt, and other minerals; and glass and ceramics industries. Where cheap hydroelectric power is available, industries requiring large amounts of cheap power (nonferrous metals refining, ferroalloys, and special steels, artificial abrasives, etc.) are possible, as in Norway, Switzerland, the Tennessee Valley, and the Columbia River Valley.[13]

5. A final stage of regional growth is reached when a region specializes in tertiary industries producing for export. Such a region exports capital, skilled personnel, and special services to less advanced regions.

The role of transport costs has been critical in the advancement through these successive stages of growth. Isard summarizes this effect as follows: "Historically we find that reduced transport rates have tended (1) to transform a scattered, ubiquitous pattern of production into an increasingly concentrated one, and (2) to effect

10. Hoover, *Location Theory and the Shoe and Leather Industries*, p. 284. The second stage of regional growth has been elaborated by Hoover and Fisher to include some further specialization and interregional trade (*op. cit.*, p. 181).

11. The theory of location diverges here from the theory of regional economic growth in stressing the historical pattern of the emergence from feudalism. Since this pattern has little meaning for American development, it is omitted here. However, it will be an important part of my argument that American location theorists have implicitly accepted a good deal of this stage sequence based on the European experience of emergence out of feudalism without recognizing the significant difference between this pattern and the pattern of American development.

12. Hoover and Fisher, *op. cit.*, p. 182.

13. Hoover, *The Location of Economic Activity*, p. 193.

progressive differentiation and selection between sites with superior and inferior resources and trade routes."[14]

## III

When this sequence of stages is placed against the economic history of regions in America, two basic objections arise. (1) These stages bear little resemblance to the actual development of regions. Moreover, they fail to provide any insights into the causes of growth and change. A theory of regional economic growth should clearly focus on the critical factors that implement or impede development. (2) Furthermore, if we want a normative model of how regions should grow, in order to analyze the causes of arrested development or relative decay, then this sequence of stages is of little use and is actually misleading because of the emphasis it places on the need for (and difficulties of) industrialization.[15]

The problems of industrialization will be explored later in this paper when the causes of regional growth are examined. Here we are concerned with the first objection: the lack of correspondence between the stages of the theory of regional economic growth and the economic history of regions in America. A major discrepancy is immediately evident — namely, that America was exploited in large part as a capitalist venture. Settlement in new regions and their subsequent growth were shaped by the search for and exploitation of goods in demand in world markets. The result was a kind of development very different from that implied by the theory of regional development in which regions gradually extended the market from a subsistence economy. From the early joint-stock companies on through the whole westward expansion, a basic objective was to exploit the land and its resources in order to produce goods that could be marketed "abroad" and would bring in a money income. This is in marked contrast to the experience of Europe (which appears to be the model for the early stages of the theory of regional economic growth), where a market-oriented economy emerged only gradually from the predominantly local economies of the manorial system. If a subsistence economy existed in a new region in America, it was solely because of a lack of means of transport, a condition that was swiftly remedied by the concerted efforts of the settlers.[16] This is not to deny

14. Walter Isard, "Distance Inputs and the Space Economy. Part I. The Conceptional Framework," *Quarterly Journal of Economics*, LXV (May, 1951), pp. 188–98.

15. Hoover and Fisher stress the difficulties of achieving an industrial status and maintain that most of the bottlenecks and problems of arrested development occur in moving from an agricultural to an industrial economic base (*op. cit.*, pp. 182–84).

16. More often than not, this concerted effort was directed toward getting the government to provide the necessary internal improvements.

that many homesteaders maintained a subsistence existence but only to affirm that such settlement was not significant in shaping the economic development of the region, any more than the modern subsistence farmer of the back country is shaping the development of contemporary agriculture.

This point may be illustrated briefly from the economic history of the Pacific Northwest.[17] Not only has this region never experienced a subsistence economy, but its markets from the very beginning have often been thousands of miles distant. Even before general settlement, the region was exploited for its furs by the Hudson Bay Company. With the decline of the fur trade and the coming of settlers, wheat, flour, and lumber were quickly developed as exportable commodities. They first found markets in California in the 1840's. With the Gold Rush the demand for both wheat and lumber expanded tremendously, and the region experienced rapid growth based on these two commodities. In 1868 the first wheat shipment went from Portland to Liverpool, and by the late 1870's Pacific Northwest soft wheat had become an important part of the world wheat trade; a fleet of ships sailed from the region by the route around Cape Horn every year. In 1857 the first shipment of flour was made to Japan, and thereafter Pacific Northwest flour found markets in Australia, Hawaii, the Orient, Europe, British Columbia, and California.[18] In each decade after 1850 an increasing percentage of the crop was exported either as wheat or in the form of flour. Before the end of the nineteenth century over half the crop was being exported from the region.

The history of the lumber industry reflects a similar preoccupation with markets foreign to the region. The first lumber shipment went to California in 1847, and during the Gold Rush lumber exports from the Pacific Northwest expanded rapidly. The rate of growth of the lumber industry was directly related to the growth of the markets reached by water (primarily California, British Columbia, and some foreign markets). In 1894 James J. Hill established a forty cent per hundredweight freight rate on lumber sent to Minneapolis on his railroads, and the industry began to compete with the southern pine

17. This brief summary of the development of the Pacific Northwest is condensed from a larger research project that I am currently undertaking. Support for the data presented here may be found in John B. Watkins, *Wheat Exporting from the Pacific Northwest* (State College of Washington Agricultural Experiment Station Bull. 201 [May, 1926]); the Silver Anniversary Number of the *Commercial Review* (Portland, Ore.), July 1, 1915; E. S. Meany, Jr., "History of Northwest Lumbering" (Ph.D. dissertation, Harvard University, 1935); and R. W. Vinnedge, *The Pacific Northwest Lumber Industry and Its Development* (New Haven, Conn.: Yale University School of Forestry, 1923).

18. A substantial amount of the wheat and flour sent to California was exported to Europe.

region for markets in the Middle West. With this rapid growth of markets the industry expanded manyfold. In the first five years of the twentieth century output more than doubled, and thereafter in each successive decade Pacific Northwest fir increased its share of the national market at the expense of southern pine.

The rate of growth of the region has been directly related to these basic exports. Between 1860 and 1920 lumber and flour-milling accounted for between 40 and 60 per cent of the value of the region's manufacturing output. Almost all the rest of secondary industry (as well as tertiary industry) was passive in the sense that it served local consumer needs. Its growth therefore reflected the changing fortunes of the region's exportable commodities.[19] Wheat played a similarly critical role in the development of the region, although by the end of the nineteenth century the agricultural export base had broadened to include a number of other commodities.

This brief account of the development of the Pacific Northwest bears no resemblance to the theory of regional economic growth. There was no gradual evolution out of a subsistence economy. Instead, the whole development of the region from the beginning was dependent on its success in producing exportable commodities. Nor was the Pacific Northwest's history exceptional. Furs and the products of mining were typically the early exportable commodities of western America. Colonial America exported such products as tobacco, rice, indigo, naval stores, ships, and fish. Even the well-worn historical generalization by location theorists that reduced transport rates will transform a scattered, ubiquitous pattern of production into an increasingly concentrated one is not true of America. Many new regions in America developed from the beginning around one or two exportable commodities and widened their export base only *after* transport costs had been reduced.[20] In short, both this generalization of location theorists and the early stages in the theory of regional economic growth appear to be taken uncritically from European experience rather than derived from the economic history of this country.

A basic starting point for reshaping our views on regional economic growth might well be the insights of the late Harold Innis in his studies of the growth of the Canadian economy.[21] Innis' early research

19. This point will be elaborated and qualified in the following section.

20. In the Pacific Northwest the export base (particularly of agricultural commodities) broadened only after the advent of the railroad.

21. See *The Fur Trade in Canada* (New Haven, Conn.: Yale University Press, 1920); *The Cod Fishery: The History of an International Economy* (New Haven, Conn.: Yale University Press, 1940); *Problems of Staple Production in Canada* (Toronto: University of Toronto Press, 1933); and, in collaboration with A. R. M. Lower, *Settlement and the Forest and Mining Frontier* (Toronto: Macmillan Co., 1936).

had convinced him of the crucial importance of the export staple in shaping new economies. His subsequent studies of the growth of these staple exports were always directed toward attempting to understand "how the Canadian economy had been generated and how it had been shaped as a working economy."[22] An analysis of the export staples of the Canadian economy became the basis for understanding the character of that country's economic development. Moreover, it provided real insights into the political and social institutions of the country.

The term "staple" refers to the chief commodity produced by a region. It is customarily thought of as describing products of extractive industry. Since my concept of the export commodities of a region may include products of secondary or tertiary industry as well, I shall use the terms "exportable commodities" (or services) to denote the individual items and "export base"[23] to denote collectively the exportable commodities (or services) of a region. In young regions, typically dependent on extractive industry, my exportable commodities and Innis' export staples are synonymous.

Settlers in new regions typically experimented with a number of different crops before discovering one that was economically feasible.[24] The success of an industry in producing an exportable commodity can be understood in terms of the principles of location theory.[25] The development of an exportable commodity reflected a comparative advantage in relative costs of production, including transfer costs. Distributive transfer costs have served to limit the extent of the export market.

22. W. A. Mackintosh, "Innis on Canadian Economic Development," *Journal of Political Economy*, June, 1953, p. 188. This article provides an excellent summary of Innis' views.

23. The use of the term "base" has become popular among urban land economists and city planners in the concept of the urban economic base, which refers to those activities of a metropolitan community that export goods and services to other areas. For a history of the development of the concept see Richard B. Andrews, "Mechanics of the Urban Economic Base: Historical Development of the Base Concept," *Land Economics*, XXIX (May, 1953), pp. 161–67.

24. The experiments with silkworm culture in the Southern colonies are a famous case in point.

25. For our purposes it is convenient to follow Hoover's breakdown of costs into procurement, processing, and distribution costs (see *The Location of Economic Activity*, pp. 7–9, 15–115). While processing costs reflect factor-input coefficients and factor prices, procurement and distribution costs depend fundamentally on transfer costs.

Isard has done a great deal of work attempting to introduce the problems of space into economic theory through the concept of distance inputs (the movement of a unit weight over a unit distance). The price of a distance input is the transport rate and, as in the case of capital inputs, a reduction in price has both a scale and a substitution effect. Distance inputs are conceived to be simply another factor of production whose price is the transport rate and whose optimum combination with other factors can be determined by the principles of substitution (see his "Distance Inputs and the Space Economy," *op. cit.*).

From the viewpoint of the region, the demand for the exportable commodity was an exogenous factor, but both processing and transfer costs were not. Historically new regions bent every effort to reduce these costs in their concerted drive to promote their economic well-being. The ceaseless efforts of new regions to get federally subsidized internal improvements, state aid for canal construction, federal and state aid for railroads, and river and harbor improvements were a part of the continuous effort of each region to reduce transfer costs to better the competitive position of its exports.[26]

As regions grew up around the export base, external economies developed which improved the competitive cost position of the exportable commodities. The development of specialized marketing organization, improved credit and transport facilities, a trained labor force, and complementary industries was oriented to the export base.

The concerted effort to improve the technology of production has been equally important. Agricultural experiment stations, state universities, and other local research groups become service adjuncts to export industries and conduct research in technological improvements in agriculture, mining, or whatever manufacturing comprises the region's export base.

The purpose of this concerted effort is to enable the region better to compete with other regions or foreign countries for markets. In new regions highly dependent on extractive industry, these external economies and technological developments tend to more than counteract diminishing returns in the staple product.[27] As a result, these efforts tend to reinforce a region's dependence on its existing staples rather than promote changes in the export base. This conservative bias is further reinforced by the role of capital. Capital is typically imported into new regions in the development of the export staple industries. Indeed, until a region develops sufficient income to provide a substantial share of its own investment capital, it must rely upon outside sources. External suppliers of capital tend to invest primarily in existing export industry rather than in new, untried enterprises.[28]

26. Such efforts have not been confined to pressure-group activity but have erupted into political movements. The Grangers and the Populists were fundamentally concerned with a number of economic measures that would, for example, improve the position of American wheat on the world wheat market or provide the western miner with a better market for his silver.

27. In the case of mining this statement probably would not hold.

28. This outside capital often comes in waves associated with (or in anticipation of) substantial reductions in costs or increases in demand. As a result the growth of regions tends to be uneven. This whole subject of the growth of regions is dealt with in more detail in Section V.

## IV

The following section will deal with the way in which regions grow; first, however, we must explore the significance of the export base in shaping the whole character of a region's economy.

At the outset, export industries must be clearly distinguished from "residentiary industries."[29] The term "residentiary" is used to designate industry for the local market which develops where the consuming population resides. In order to determine the market area of each industry more precisely than can be done by *a priori* classification, the "location quotient" developed by Hildebrand and Mace[30] is employed. The location quotient measures the concentration of employment in a given industry in one area (the "subject economy," which for our purposes is the region) with another area (the "benchmark economy," which for our purposes is the nation).

> Formally the location quotient is the numerical equivalent of a fraction whose numerator is employment in a given industry in the subject economy relative to total employment in the subject economy and whose denominator is employment in the given industry in the benchmark economy relative to total employment in the benchmark economy. *A priori* a location of 1.00 means no greater relative specialization in the subject economy than in the benchmark economy, for the particular industry. In each industry values significantly below 1.00 indicate much greater relative specialization in the benchmark economy; or if well over 1.00 much greater relative specialization in the subject economy.[31]

29. The term "residentiary industry" was first used by P. Sargent Florence in National Resources Planning Board mimeographed releases. Rutledge Vining subsequently employed the concept in "Location of Industry and Regional Patterns of Business Cycle Behavior," *Econometrica*, XIV (January, 1946), pp. 37–68.

30. George Hildebrand and Arthur Mace, Jr., "The Employment Multiplier in an Expanding Industrial Market: Los Angeles County, 1940–47," *Review of Economics and Statistics*, XXXII (August, 1950), pp. 341–49.

P. Sargent Florence developed the concept of a coefficient of localization. He first computed a "location factor" for each industry by computing the ratio of the percentage of employment in the given region found in the given industry to the corresponding percentage for the nation as a whole. If all industries were perfectly evenly distributed among regions, the location factor would be unity. "The coefficient of localization for a given industry is obtained by computing the weighted average deviation from unity of the location factors for all regions, the weight for a local region being the proportion of total national employment found in that region. This measure divided by two varies between zero and unity" (Vining, *op. cit.*, pp. 40–51). Completely even geographic distribution would give a coefficient of zero, while increasingly greater concentration of industry in a region would give a coefficient approaching unity. Although this method is somewhat different from that of Hildebrand and Mace, the result is the same.

31. Hildebrand and Mace, *op cit.*, p. 243. In their study of Los Angeles County these authors varied the subject and benchwork economies. Using the United States as the benchmark economy, they used successively the twelve western states, the eleven counties of southern California, and Los Angeles County as subject economies. Then using the eleven western states as the benchmark economy, they used southern California and Los Angeles County as subject economies, and finally used Los Angeles

Thus industries producing for export will show values significantly above 1.00.[32]

We are now in a better position to examine the role of the export base in shaping the economy of the region.

Clearly the export base plays a vital role in determining the level of absolute and per capita income of a region. While the return to factors of production[33] in the export industries indicates the direct importance of these industries for the well-being of the region, it is the indirect effect that is most important. Since residentiary industry depends entirely on demand within the region, it has historically been dependent on the fate of the export base.[34] Vining's analysis indicates that employment in residentiary industry tends to bear a direct relationship to employment in export industries. The median figure for employment in residentiary industry in individual states was approximately 55 per cent of the total employment.[35]

The export staple plays an equally vital role in the cyclical sensitivity of the region; it acts as the "carrier" in diffusing changes in the level of income from other regions to the subject region. Furthermore, the sensitivity of the region to fluctuations depends on the income elasticities of the export staples. Clearly regions that specialize in a few products with high income elasticities will have more violent fluctuations in income than more diversified regions.[36]

---

County relative to southern California. As a result, they were able to delimit precisely the extent of the market for each export (while exports out of the country would increase the location quotient, they would not of course be isolated by this technique).

32. Hildebrand and Mace allowed for differences in demand functions, which might make some residentiary industry appear with a location quotient above 1.00. They came to the conclusion that 1.508 was the boundary line in their study (*ibid.*, p. 246).

This location quotient is not too well adapted to use in agriculture. There I have used a coefficient of specialization in which the numerator is the region's physical volume of production relative to the physical volume of production of the agricultural goods for the nation. The denominator is the region's absolute population relative to the nation's absolute population. While such a coefficient has some obvious limitations and must be used with care, it is more adaptable to the available data than the one discussed above.

33. Obviously the disposition of nonwage income to residents of the region or outside the region is important here. It will be further considered in the next section.

34. This statement requires both substantiation and careful qualification. This article is primarily concerned with the historical development of the American economy, and here the statement needs little qualification. The fortunes of regions have been closely tied to their export base. However, it is conceivable that a region with a large influx of population and capital might simply "feed upon itself" and thereby account for a substantial share of its growth. Moreover, in older "mature" regions, economic activity may become so diversified as to make the export base less significant. The question will be dealt with in the next section.

35. Vining, *op. cit.*, p. 49.

36. For further discussion of this subject see Vining, *op. cit.*

When we turn to the role of exports in shaping the pattern of urbanization and nodal centers,[37] we are on ground that has been more thoroughly explored by location theorists and geographers.[38] Again, however, the pioneering work has been done by German location theorists who have extended the implications of each stage of economic growth to embrace the logical pattern of urbanization that would ensue.[39] Since these stages do not fit the American development, the pattern of American urbanization likewise differs in many respects from the German models. However, it is beyond the scope of this article to explore the whole question of urbanization and the export base. We may note in passing the observations of August Lösch that in such areas as Iowa, with a rather even distribution of production of agricultural staples, the distance between towns increases with their size.[40] In contrast, cities in the English coal districts are the same distance from each other irrespective of size.[41]

While discussion of the spatial distribution of urban areas would take us too far afield, the role of the export base in shaping the growth of nodal centers deserves some attention. Nodes grow up because of special locational advantages that lower the transfer and processing costs of exportable commodities. Nodal centers become trading centers through which exports leave the region and imports enter for distribution throughout the area. Here special facilities develop to implement the production and distribution of the staples. Subsidiary industries to service the export industry, as well as specialized banking, brokerage, wholesaling, and other business services, concentrate in these centers and act to improve the cost position of the export.[42]

The character of the labor force will be fundamentally influenced by the export industries. The types of skills required, the seasonality

37. The concept of nodes is one that has been extensively used by geographers. The term refers to *sites* that have strategic transfer advantages in reference to procurement and distribution costs and therefore become processing centers. Such advantageous points are limited in number and tend to develop into major metropolitan areas. For further discussion of nodes see Hoover, *The Location of Economic Activity*, pp. 119–30.

38. For a summary of recent developments in this area see Walter Isard, "Current Development in Regional Analysis," *Weltwirtschaftliches Archiv*, LXIX (September, 1952), pp. 81–91.

39. An excellent summary of the German contributions is contained in Isard's "The General Theory of Location and Space Economy," *Quarterly Journal of Economics*, LXIII (November, 1949), pp. 476–506.

40. Lösch, *op. cit.*, p. 75. In this article Lösch advances an interesting theoretical model of spatial location.

41. *Ibid.*, p. 75. A summary of the development of concepts of spatial organization may be found in Isard's "Distance Inputs and the Space Economy," *op. cit.*

42. These specialized facilities provide economies in addition to the general economies of urban concentration resulting from such things as fire and police protection, lower utility rates, and a specialized labor force. For further discussion of these aspects of urban concentration see Ohlin, *op. cit.*, pp. 203–4.

and stability of employment, and the conditions of work will shape the social attitudes of the working force.

As already noted, the political attitudes of the region will be largely directed toward improving the position of its export base. The extent of such activity is too well known historically and too obvious in the contemporary American political scene to require extended discussion.

## V

Previous sections of this paper have examined the significance of the export base for a region's economy. I have tried to indicate the primary role that such exports have played historically, but I have not yet touched on the critical question of the causes of the growth of a region. It is evident that this growth is closely tied to the success of its exports and may take place either as a result of the improved position of existing exports relative to competing areas or as a result of the development of new exports. However, a major question that must first be examined is whether a region must industrialize if it is to continue to grow. Such a necessity has been a major tenet of the theory of regional economic growth. Moreover, industrialization has been regarded as a difficult stage to achieve, so that it is the source of problems of arrested regional development. Hoover and Fisher stress three factors that make this transition difficult: (1) the need for greatly improved transportation facilities, which call for large-scale capital investments; (2) the need for intensification of the geographic division of labor; and (3) the fact that industrial technology is novel to an agricultural region.[43] If these statements are correct, then the implications for our analysis are clear. At some point regions must shift from an extractive to an industrial export base, and this shift will be fraught with difficulties. However, the contention that regions must industrialize in order to grow, as well as the contention that the development of secondary and tertiary industry is somehow difficult to achieve, are both based on some fundamental misconceptions.

The importance of industrializing is based upon the notion that, with increased population and diminishing returns in extractive industry, the shift to manufacturing is the only way to maintain sustained growth (measured in terms of increasing per capita income). This argument has been buttressed by evidence such as that gathered by Dr. Louis Bean correlating per capita income with percentage of

43. *Op. cit.*, p. 182. Hoover and Fisher go on to point out that "further difficulty arises from the fact that when a non-industrial region reaches a limit of growth it is likely to retrogress or decay" (*ibid.*, p. 184).

the labor force engaged in primary, secondary, and tertiary occupations by states for 1939.[44] Bean's figures purport to demonstrate that increased industrialization leads to higher per capita income, and he goes so far as to say that "a 10-point [per cent] increase in industrial progress in the east and south . . . apparently tends to add $100 to $150 (1939 prices) per capita and in the western states substantially more."[45] In fact, Bean's statistics do not prove this, and the policy implications of such generalizations may be misleading and dangerous.

We may note first of all that his correlation is not very impressive. There were eleven states in which the percentage of the labor force in primary occupations was above the national average whose per capita income either exceeded the national average or was close enough to the average so that annual variations could well place it on one side or the other. Indeed, had the correlation been made for postwar years, it would have been substantially different.[46]

Furthermore, money-income data significantly understate the real income of the farmer,[47] because of the great variety of goods and services produced on the farm that require cash payment in the city.[48]

However, the real source of error has resulted from a basic misunderstanding of the nature of the economy. A state whose export base consists mostly of agricultural products may have a low percentage of its labor force in primary activity and a high percentage in tertiary occupations and *yet* be basically dependent upon agriculture for the high per capita income it enjoys. It is the agricultural export staples that provide the high income that enables the state to support a substantial level of services. In such a case both the secondary and the tertiary activities are "residentiary" and can survive only because of the success of the basic agricultural export staples. In short, a percentage shift in such a state from primary to secondary and tertiary employment does not necessarily reflect a shift away from dependence on agriculture to dependence on manufacturing and services. Instead, it may reflect the simple fact that farmers are receiving high incomes for their staple crops and therefore buy more goods and services from residentiary industry.

44. *Studies in Income and Wealth,* VIII (New York: National Bureau of Economic Research, 1946), pp. 128–29.

45. *Ibid.,* p. 137.

46. See "State Income Payments in 1950," *Survey of Current Business,* August, 1951, p. 18.

47. There is also evidence to indicate that money incomes are disproportionately understated.

48. See Margaret Reid, "Distribution of Non-money Income," *Studies in Income and Wealth,* Vol. XIII (New York: National Bureau of Economic Research, 1951). See also Jacob Viner, *International Trade and Economic Development* (Glencoe, Ill.: Free Press, 1952), pp. 63–73. Professor Viner provides a number of trenchant criticisms of Bean's argument.

This brings us to the related question of the difficulty of industrialization. The implication of the preceding paragraph is that a substantial amount of secondary industry of the residentiary variety will develop automatically as a result of high incomes received from the exportable commodities. Nor is this the only kind of manufacturing that can be expected to develop. We may distinguish four different kinds of manufacturing that will develop:[49]

1. Materials-oriented industries which, because of marked transfer advantages of the manufactured product over the raw material, locate at the source of the latter. Among the industries in this category are sugar-beet refining, flour-milling,[50] and lumbering.[51] Such industries may develop further stages of vertical integration until transfer cost advantages become equalized. Such industry is typically part of the export base.

2. Service industries to the export industry. Foundries and establishments that make machine tools, specialized agricultural implements, and logging and lumbering equipment are illustrations.

3. Residentiary industry producing for local consumption.

4. Foot-loose industries, where transfer costs are not of significant importance in location. A great many such industries develop purely by chance in some location.[52]

While foot-loose industries have typically developed by chance, the other three types of secondary activity develop naturally because of locational advantages in a society responsive to profit-maximizing stimuli. There is nothing difficult about the development of such industries. The difficulties arise when promoters seek to develop in a region industries which simply are unsuited for the area and which can therefore be maintained only under hothouse conditions.[53]

The argument may be advanced that the kinds of industry de-

49. This classification is similar to that of E. J. Cohn, Jr., in *Industry in the Pacific Northwest and the Location Theory* (New York: Columbia University Press, 1954), pp. 42–44.

50. However, milling-in-transit privileges may modify this materials orientation.

51. See National Resources Planning Board, *op. cit.*, Ch. VI, for a further account of such industries.

52. For further discussion of such industries see National Resources Committee, *The Structure of the American Economy*, Part I: *Basic Characteristics* (Washington, D.C.: Government Printing Office, 1939), p. 36.

53. This does not mean that there is no room for appropriate public policy that may create the social overhead benefits that will make certain industries feasible. I can do no better here than to quote Viner: "There are no inherent advantages of manufacturing over agriculture, or, for that matter, of agriculture over manufacturing. It is only arbitrarily in fact that the line separating the two can be drawn. The choice between expansion of agriculture and expansion of manufactures can, for the most part, be left to the free decisions of capitalists, entrepreneurs and workers. To the extent that there is need for government decision, it should be made on rational grounds, in the light of considerations of costs and comparative returns from alternative allocation of scarce national resources, human and material" (*op. cit.*, p. 72).

scribed above do not constitute industrialization. How much and what kind of secondary industry must a region possess to be termed "industrialized"? By 1950 census classification, the state of Oregon had almost 24 per cent of its labor force in manufacturing, which was only slightly under the United States average (25.9 per cent) and exceeded the United States average in durable goods (16.7 per cent as compared with the national average of 13.8 per cent). It was well ahead of the neighboring states of Washington and California, despite the fact that these two states had a variety of manufacturing industries, in contrast to Oregon's specialized dependence on the Douglas fir lumber industry. Is such a state industrialized? Implicit in the concept appears to be the notion that industrialization is somehow tied up with steel and the capital goods industries. However, historically, the locational pull of coal and iron ore has shaped the development of the steel-producing centers, which in turn have attracted and concentrated heavy industry.[54] While locational influences in the steel industry have been changing significantly in the last half-century with the growing importance of scrap and the changing composition of inputs,[55] nevertheless, the possible areas for the development of efficient large-scale steel production[56] and, therefore, of capital goods industry are severely circumscribed. A more useful concept of industrialization for our purposes is a region whose export base consists primarily of finished consumers' goods and/or finished manufactured producers' goods.

We may summarize the argument up to this point as follows: (1) There is no reason why all regions must industrialize in order to continue to grow. (2) A great deal of secondary (and tertiary) industry will develop automatically either because of locational advantages of materials-oriented industry or as a passive reflection of growing income in the region resulting from the success of its exportable commodities. (3) The concept of industrialization is an ambiguous one that needs further clarification if it is to be useful.

Since the growth of a region is tied to the success of its export base, we must examine in more detail the reasons for the growth, decline, and change in the export base. Clearly, the decline of one exportable commodity must be accompanied by the growth of others, or a region will be left "stranded."[57] Among the major reasons[58]

54. National Resources Planning Board, *op. cit.*, p. 162.
55. Walter Isard, "Some Locational Factors in the Iron and Steel Industry since the Early Nineteenth Century," *Journal of Political Economy*, LVI (1948), pp. 213–17.
56. The extensive utilization of scrap makes possible small-scale steel production as a residentiary industry wherever the local market achieves sufficient size.
57. The cut-over region in the Great Lakes area is a case in point.
58. For further discussion on shifting industry see National Resources Planning Board, *op. cit.*, pp. 92–104.

for the decline of an existing exportable commodity have been changes in demand outside the region,[59] exhaustion of a natural resource,[60] increasing costs of land or labor relative to those of a competing region,[61] and technological changes that changed the relative composition of inputs.[62] A historically important reason for the growth of new exports has been major developments in transport (in contrast with more cost-reducing improvements in transport, which may reinforce dependence on existing exports). Such developments have often enabled a region to compete with other regions in the production of goods that were previously economically unfeasible because of the high transfer costs.[63] Growth in income and demand in other regions[64] and technological developments[65] have also been important. The role of the state and federal government in creating social overhead benefits has created new exports in many regions,[66] and the significance of war in promoting industries that may either continue or leave a residue of capital investment for peacetime use has also been important.

A region may expand as a result of increased demand for its existing exportable commodities, whether due to an increase in the income of the market area or to a change in taste. An improvement in the processing- or transfer-cost position of the region's staples vis-à-vis competing regions will likewise promote growth.

Historically, in a young region, the creation of a new export or the expansion of an existing export has resulted in the influx of capital investment both in the export industry and in all the kinds of passive and supporting economic activity described above. Meier has described this process for the Canadian economy in the first decade of the twentieth century, when increased world demand for wheat not only led to an expansion of warehousing, transport, public utilities, and construction in the prairie provinces, but also, by increasing income, augmented the demand for secondary products and thereby induced investment in a host of other industries.[67] As a result

59. Such as the decline in the demand for beaver hats, which affected the fur trade.

60. Exemplified by the Great Lakes lumber industry.

61. The most famous example is the decline in the New England cotton textile industry.

62. Such as the case of steel cited above.

63. The whole history of canal and railroad development contains innumerable illustrations of such developments (see Isard, "Transportation Development and Building Cycles," *op. cit.*).

64. The growth in demand for wheat in England and on the European continent in the last half of the nineteenth century is a famous example.

65. The development of the petroleum industry is a typical illustration.

66. The development of hydroelectric power in the Pacific Northwest and the resultant development of the aluminum industry is an example.

67. G. M. Meier, "Economic Development and the Transfer Mechanism," *Canadian Journal of Economics and Political Science*, XIX (February, 1953), pp. 1–19. M. C. Daly

the growth of a region will, in all likelihood, be uneven, coming in spurts of increased investment rather than proceeding at an even pace.

Increased capital investment in the export industry will go toward achieving optimum size of the enterprise, increased mechanization of the processes, and further development of the specialized services to the export. The source of capital will play an important part in the region's growth. Typically, the capital in young regions comes from outside. Profits (and some other nonwage income) flow out of the region. To the extent that the export base is profitable, a part of this income will be reinvested in the expansion of this base.

With the growth of population and income, indigenous savings will increase. Both indigenous savings and the reinvested capital can pour back into the export industries only up to a point, and then the accumulated capital will tend to overflow into other activity. As described above, some will go into residentiary industry and industries subsidiary to the export; but it is also very likely that some will go into locationally "foot-loose" industries, which may start out to serve only the region, but which can expand into export industries.

At this point a region is no longer young. The social overhead benefits that have been created through political pressure or as a part of the pattern of urban development and the development of a trained labor force and indigenous capital make it far easier to develop new exports. Whether such industries were originally residentiary and, by gradually overcoming transfer-cost disadvantages, became export industries, or were originally foot-loose industries not significantly affected by transfer costs, the result is to broaden the export base. As such a region matures, the staple base will become less distinguishable, because its production will be so varied.

We may expect, therefore, that the differences between regions will become less marked, that secondary industry will tend to be more equalized, and indeed, in economic terms, that regionalism will tend to disappear.

## VI

The purpose of this paper has been to re-examine location theory and the theory of regional economic growth in the light of the historical development of regions in America and to advance some

has attempted to work out a geographic multiplier between "localized" and "nonlocalized" industry, using data for Britain for the years 1921–31 ("An Approximation to a Geographic Multiplier," *Economic Journal*, L [June–September, 1940] pp. 248–58. See also Hildebrand and Mace, *op. cit.*

propositions that may lead to a new theory of regional economic growth.

It has been argued that the stages outlined in the theory of regional economic growth bear little relationship to the character of American development and more specifically do not focus on the crucial elements that will enable us to understand that growth. Furthermore, the traditional theory has policy implications that may be fundamentally in error.

The first stage of subsistence has been relatively unimportant, and, to the extent that it existed at all, it was because means of transport were lacking rather than because of a nonmarket orientation. In Europe a subsistence or a village economy with local markets was built into the social and economic structure for centuries. In America subsistence was only a frontier condition to be overcome as rapidly as means of transport could be built.

The second stage of the theory is based on a gradual widening of the market area with improved transport and the development of a second stratum to service the basic agricultural stratum. Far from moving through such a gradual progression American regions, as soon as any transport permitted, developed goods for export often to markets thousands of miles away. The early town centers were located not only so as to service the agricultural stratum but so as to implement the export of the region's staples. The prosperity of the region depended on its success in competing with other areas producing the same staple exports. Therefore, the region's economic and political efforts were oriented toward the reduction of processing and transfer costs. The struggle for internal improvements by the West, the agrarian pressure for inflation and cheaper credit, and the campaign for free coinage of silver were fundamentally economic movements. Their objectives included increasing the supply of capital, eliminating real or fancied transport discrimination, reducing interest rates, and improving the market for silver, however much they may also have been concerned with social justice.

The third stage of regional growth has been described as the gradual shift from extensive to intensive farming. While it is true that rising land values promoted such a shift, there were many other reasons for a shift in the staple base. New means of transport, changing demand, new technological developments, changing cost relationships vis-à-vis competing regions, government subsidization of social overhead benefits, and war have all been important.

The shift from an agricultural to an industrial base has been looked upon as the difficult, but indispensable, step for sustained economic growth. It is a major argument of this paper that such a step may be neither necessary nor desirable and that the evidence customarily advanced to support this argument proves nothing of the sort. There is nothing to prevent population and per capita income from growing in a region whose export base is agricultural. Moreover, there is nothing difficult about developing secondary and tertiary industry in such a region. Indeed, it will develop automatically, often to such an extent that analysis of the region in terms of distribution of employment will lead to the conclusion that it is an industrial region.

The final stage has typically been conceived to be the mature regional economy exporting capital, skills, and specialized services to less well-developed regions. While this may be true for some regions, it is unlikely to be a final stage for all. Indeed, one would presume that some sort of balanced relationship would emerge among regions as transfer costs become less significant and income differentials tend to be ironed out by long-run factor mobility.

The major propositions that emerge from this paper are:

1. For economists' purposes the concept of a region should be redefined to point out that the unifying cohesion to a region, over and beyond geographic similarities, is its development around a common export base. It is this that makes it economically unified and ties the fortunes of the area together. This tends to result in the interdependent development within the region of external economies and unified political efforts for government assistance or political reform. The geographer has emphasized the distributive functions of the nodal centers of a region, but the role of the nodal center in providing external economies for the export industries has been equally important.

2. The success of the export base has been the determining factor in the rate of growth of regions. Therefore, in order to understand this growth, we must examine the locational factors that have enabled the staples to develop.

3. The importance of the export base is a result of its primary role in determining the level of absolute and per capita income in a region, and therefore in determining the amount of residentiary, secondary, and tertiary activity that will develop. The export base has also significantly influenced the character of subsidiary industry, the distribution of population and pattern of urbanization, the character of the labor force, the social and political attitudes of the region, and its sensitivity to fluctuations of income and employment.

4. In a young region dependence on staples is reinforced by the concerted efforts of the region's residents to reduce processing and transfer costs through technological research and by state and federal government subsidization of social overhead benefits, as well as the tendency for outside suppliers of capital to reinvest in the existing staple base.

5. Some regions, because of locational advantages, have developed an export base of manufactured products, but this is not a necessary stage for the sustained growth of all regions. A great deal of secondary and tertiary industry will result from the success of the export base. This residentiary industry will, in all likelihood, provide for widening the export base as a region develops.

6. The growth of regions has tended to be uneven. A given increase in demand for the region's exports (or a significant reduction in processing or transfer costs) has resulted in a multiple effect on the region, inducing increased investment not only in the export industry but in all other kinds of economic activity as well.

7. As a region's income grows, indigenous savings will tend to spill over into new kinds of activities. At first, these activities satisfy local demand, but ultimately some of them will become export industries. This movement is reinforced by the tendency for transfer costs to become less significant. As a result, the export bases of regions tend to become more diversified, and they tend to lose their identity as regions. Ultimately, we may expect along with long-run factor mobility more equalization of per capita income and a wider dispersion of production.

J. C. STABLER

# Exports and Evolution: The Process of Regional Change

## THEORIES OF REGIONAL DEVELOPMENT

While interest in the theoretical aspects of the location of economic activity dates back approximately one hundred and fifty years to the work of Johann Heinrich von Thünen, attempts to construct a theory that would explain the process of subnational development are of relatively more recent origin.[1] In recent years the question of quantitative and qualitative change through time has received increasing attention at all levels. Those interested in regional development have had at least three sources from which to draw inspiration. One was the well-developed body of location theory; another, international trade theory; and yet another, the empirical studies[2] and observations[3] of structural change facilitated and partially caused by technological progress. Two distinct theoretical frameworks have emerged. One, largely attributed to the work of Edgar M. Hoover[4] and frequently referred to as the "stages" theory, is an extension of location theory

1. Development and/or growth have been used to mean: (1) a rise in regional per capita income, (2) an expansion in the volume of regional output, or (3) both of these. It is useful to recognize that one does not necessarily accompany the other in direction of change. Expansion (or contraction) of an activity depends on the competitive advantage offered at alternative locations, while per capita income is determined by the relationship between the rates of change in regional income and population. In this study, growth and development will be used interchangeably to mean an increase in the volume of output *and* an increase in per capita income. Other instances involving change will be discussed in terms of specific characteristics.

2. See Allen G. B. Fisher, "Capital and the Growth of Knowledge," *Economic Journal* (September, 1933), pp. 379–89; *The Clash of Progress and Security* (London: The Macmillan Company, 1935); and "Production, Primary, Secondary and Tertiary," *Economic Record* (June, 1939), pp. 24–38; and Colin Clark, *The Conditions of Economic Progress* (London: The Macmillan Company, 1940).

3. For a summary of the work in this field produced by the writers of the German historical school of economic thought see Bert F. Hoselitz, "Theories of Stages of Economic Growth," *Theories of Economic Growth*, Bert F. Hoselitz, ed. (New York: The Free Press, 1960).

4. See Edgar M. Hoover, *Location Theory and the Shoe and Leather Industries* (Cambridge, Mass.: Harvard University Press, 1937); *The Location of Economic Activity* (New York: McGraw-Hill Book Co., 1948); and, with Joseph L. Fisher, "Research in Regional Economic Growth," *Problems in the Study of Economic Growth* (New York: National Bureau of Economic Research, 1949), pp. 175–88.

Stabler, J. C., "Exports and Evolution: The Process of Regional Change," Land Economics, XLIV, No. 1 (February, 1968), pp. 11–23.

combined with generalizations derived from observed structural changes following the introduction of improved technology. The alternative approach, known as the "export base" theory, is the result of work initiated by Douglass C. North[5] and is an extension of location theory combined with aspects of international trade theory that are useful for subnational analysis.[6]

The stages theory posits regional development primarily as an internal evolutionary process.[7] In the first stage of its economic history the region's inhabitants are concerned almost exclusively with providing the necessities for existence. Population is distributed in accordance with the resource base necessary to support a self-sufficient subsistence economy.

5. Douglass C. North, "Location Theory and Regional Economic Growth," *Journal of Political Economy* (June, 1955), pp. 243–58 [Selection 4 of this volume]; "The Spatial and Interregional Framework of the U.S. Economy: An Historical Perspective," *Papers and Proceedings of the Regional Science Association* (1956), pp. 201–09; "Agriculture in Regional Economic Growth," *Journal of Farm Economics* (December, 1959), pp. 943–51; *The Economic Growth of the United States: 1790 to 1860* (Englewood Cliffs, N.J.: Prentice-Hall, Inc., 1961); and *Growth and Welfare in the American Past: A New Economic History* (Englewood Cliffs, N.J.: Prentice-Hall, Inc., 1966).

6. Other variants of the export base theory exist. It has been used by Harold A. Innis and other writers to analyze Canadian national development. See Harold A. Innis, *The Fur Trade in Canada* (New Haven, Conn.: Yale University Press, 1920); *Problems of Staple Production in Canada* (Toronto: University of Toronto Press, 1933); *The Cod Fishery: The Study of an International Economy* (New Haven, Conn.: Yale University Press, 1940); and, with A.R.M. Lower, *Settlement and the Forest and Mining Frontier* (Toronto: The Macmillan Company, 1935); Kenneth Buckley, "The Role of Staple Industries in Canada's Economic Development," *Journal of Economic History* (December, 1958), pp. 430–50; A. W. Currie, *Canadian Economic Development* (Toronto: Thomas Nelson and Sons, 1963); W. T. Easterbrook and Hugh G. J. Aitken, *Canadian Economic History* (Toronto: The Macmillan Company, 1963); W. A. Mackintosh, "Economic Factors in Canadian History," *Canadian Historical Review* (March, 1923), pp. 12–25; and "Innis on Canadian Economic Development," *Journal of Political Economy* (June, 1953), pp. 185–94; G. M. Meier, "Economic Development and the Transfer Mechanism: Canada 1895–1913," *Canadian Journal of Economics and Political Science* (February, 1953), pp. 1–19; Melville H. Watkins, "A Staple Theory of Economic Growth," *Canadian Journal of Economics and Political Science* (May, 1963), pp. 141–58. This approach has also been widely used in the analysis of urban areas to describe economic structures, estimate the ratio of employment in "export" to "residentiary" activities and as an aid in forecasting future growth potential. For some of the pioneer studies see, for example, M. C. Daly, "An Approximation to a Geographic Multiplier," *Economic Journal* (June-September, 1940), pp. 248–58; Homer Hoyt, "Homer Hoyt on the Development of the Economic Base Concept," *Land Economics*, (May, 1954), pp. 182–86; George Hildebrand and Arthur Mace Jr., "The Employment Multiplier in an Expanding Industrial Market: Los Angeles County, 1940–47," *Review of Economics and Statistics* (August, 1950), pp. 341–49. The concept has been extended and improved by, among others, Werner Z. Hirsch, "Interindustry Relations of a Metropolitan Area," *Review of Economics and Statistics* (August, 1959), pp. 360–69; and Charles M. Tiebout, *The Community Economic Base Study*, Supplementary Paper No. 16 (New York: Committee for Economic Development, 1962).

7. While interregional trade is not ruled out, it arises as a result of change *generated* within the region and is not, as in the export base theory, the vehicle by which the impetus for development is provided.

The initial step in the development process is a particularly difficult one and two critical conditions must be met. The first involves a reduction of transfer costs. Probably the best way to accomplish this, in a primitive economy, is by improving the transportation network. Lower transfer costs make it possible to trade with other areas. By shifting the region's resources into that use (those uses) which provides the greatest competitive advantage, the second condition is satisfied and a basis for trade is established. An increase in per capita income follows. Increased income stimulates some local industry, *i.e.*, the village production of a few very basic goods and services. But as population grows, in order to provide a constantly rising standard of living, land use must become increasingly intensive. This is sufficient to provide a rising standard of living for some time.

Eventually, however, a point is reached when the second major step in the development process must be taken if economic progress is to continue. This step becomes necessary because, as per capita income grows, people reach a point beyond which additional income is not used primarily to purchase agricultural products but is increasingly utilized to acquire manufactured goods. Thus a growing aggregate demand is shifted to industrial, and away from agricultural regions. The first phase in this step includes processing of the region's food and raw material products. This, however, does little to sustain progress and the second phase, the intensive utilization of regional and imported mineral resources, must be entered. Critical factors necessary for advancement into this phase are good transfer facilities and the presence of metallic and power resources. The rate at which this step can be completed often depends on the availability of capital, organizational ability, and certain skills from outside areas. The last phase of the process is completed with the emergence of those tertiary activities characteristic of an advanced industrial economy. With the completion of this phase the region exports capital, finished products, skilled personnel and specialized services to less developed regions. Failure to make the transition to an industrial base places the region outside the main stream of economic progress.[8] If this happens, population pressure develops as the growth of opportunity slows and living standards fall behind those in developing areas. Emigration occurs but not fast enough to bring living standards into equality.[9] Furthermore the nonindustrialized region is drained of its younger, more energetic population as emigrants are largely drawn

8. "Under present and foreseeable conditions, however, it remains true that if a region is to increase both in total and per capita real income — which is our concept of growth — it must eventually industrialize. Industrialization means the introduction of so-called secondary industries (mining and manufacturing) on a considerable scale." Hoover and Fisher, "Research in Regional Economic Growth," *op. cit.*, p. 182.

9. Hoover, *The Location of Economic Activity*, pp. 189–90.

from this group.[10] In general, stagnation and decay are the penalties for failing to develop a manufacturing base.

In many ways this theory is descriptive of the national development of Great Britain vis-à-vis the rest of the world.[11] An adequate resource base, coupled with a technological lead that was not seriously challenged until after the pattern was essentially completed, permitted that country to constantly shift its resources into more intensive uses. The rest of the world, failing to keep pace with British technology, lagged by other comparative measures as well. The transfer of British capital and skill to other areas and subsequent development in these areas strengthened the conclusion that failure to industrialize meant a perpetually inferior economic status. However, even in the heyday of free trade and laissez-faire, the *nations* of the world resembled closed economies much more than *regions* of a national market economy, and to base the theory of regional development in an open economy on the pattern experienced in a system of partially closed economies may not be entirely valid.[12]

North's initial work in this area was written partly to protest both the stages theory's inability to explain the development process in the North American context and its policy implications, which he termed "fundamentally misleading."[13] In North America many (if not most) regions were initially developed because their natural resource base provided a direct incentive for capitalist exploitation. Each region began its economic history in the framework of a market society. The subsistence stage was entirely absent. An external demand for the region's resources or products was the major stimulus which generated settlement and development.

In North's framework, capital is attracted to any region promising favorable profit opportunities in the amount necessary to create whatever requirements are needed (including transfer, processing and service facilities) to exploit the resource. Income received from the sale of the export will induce some further investment in population-serving or residentiary activities — the extent of which depends on whether the resource is exploited under labor intensive or extensive conditions and the resulting income distribution. With a highly unequal distribution (such as arises within the framework of plan-

10. Hoover, *ibid.*, p. 190.

11. See T. S. Ashton, "The Industrial Revolution in Great Britain," and J. D. Chamber, "Great Britain Becomes the Workshop of the World, 1820–1880," both in *The Experience of Economic Growth: Case Studies in Economic History*, Barry E. Supple, ed. (New York: Random House, 1963).

12. John Friedmann, "Poor Regions and Poor Nations: Perspectives on the Problem of Appalachia," *The Southern Economic Journal*, (April, 1966), pp. 465–73.

13. North, "Location Theory and Regional Economic Growth," *op. cit.* [Selection 3, p. 29 of this volume].

tation agriculture) development of residentiary activity will be limited. With a more equal distribution much more development will be encouraged.[14] However, continued growth of the region is directly a function of the expansion of its exports. Expansion of the export sector(s) may occur because of "the improved position of existing exports relative to competing areas or as the result of development of new exports."[15] If the initial export has required large investments in transfer facilities and "other types of social overhead" then "external economies are created which facilitate the development of other exports."[16] However, the transition to a manufacturing base "may be neither necessary nor desirable."[17] Thus, according to North's analysis, the policy implications of the stages theory are misleading.

In focusing on the growth-generating capacity of industries producing for "external" markets, North has certainly called attention to one of the major determinants of regional development. However, changing technology and the income elasticity of demand for the region's product(s) are also important considerations, especially over a longer period of time. Thus both theories concentrate on important aspects of subnational growth, but each is only a partial explanation of the complete process.

The size of the area in question also has a major bearing on the importance of what phenomena are most important in generating growth. As Charles Tiebout has pointed out, the world exports nothing, but world per capita income has risen.[18] Obviously, improving technology has been fundamentally responsible for this increase. On the other hand, to take the opposite extreme, it is the unusual business enterprise that grows without selling external to itself. North has suggested that for purposes of economic analysis the region should be defined in terms of a common export base.[19] This

14. North, "Agriculture in Regional Economic Growth," *op. cit.*, pp. 945–46. North presented this article as an elaboration of the argument presented in the article reproduced as Selection 3 of this book.

15. [See Selection 3, p. 40.]

16. North, "Agriculture in Regional Economic Growth," *op. cit.*, p. 946.

17. [Selection 3, p. 46.] This quotation continues, "... There is nothing to prevent population and per capita income from growing in a region whose export base is agricultural." But in his later article elaborating his original statement (see footnote 14), this position is modified somewhat by the following statements "Regions that remain tied to a single export commodity almost inevitably do not achieve sustained *expansion*." (Italics mine.) But, "... the successful production of agricultural (or indeed most extractive) commodities for sale without the region can be and under certain conditions has been the prime influence inducing economic *growth* ...." (Italics mine.) See also Vernon W. Ruttan, "Discussion: The Location of Economic Activity," *Journal of Farm Economics*, (December, 1959), pp. 952–54.

18. Tiebout, *The Community Economic Base Study*, p. 75, and "Exports and Regional Economic Growth," *Journal of Political Economy* (April, 1956), p. 211.

19. [Selection 3, p. 00].

idea certainly has merit if regional specialization and interregional trade is to be given proper place in the analysis of subnational growth. But, while this approach appears useful, especially for investigating the early development of a region, there is no reason to expect additional export industries to emerge whose boundaries are coincident with the old as the area matures. In any case, at the practical level, the delimitation of the region is often dictated by the availability of information compiled according to administrative or political jurisdictions. And often the analysis of a region is necessarily an analysis of the factors contributing to the development of such a subdivision.[20] This may not be the handicap it is sometimes thought to be. If regional research is to be undertaken with the possibility of action contingent on the findings, the area defined will logically be that of the jurisdictional unit involved.[21]

In the analysis that follows, an attempt will be made to synthesize the more important aspects of the two theories. First, however, it may be useful to restate some of the established concepts of location theory in what may be a more useful form. The framework for location analysis has usually been developed in such a way that it facilitated determination of what individual activities would locate at specific places in an established environment. It would be more useful in the study of regional development if the further growth-inducing characteristics associated with various types of locational attraction were made more explicit.

## LOCATION THEORY

In an economy governed by market forces the decision of where to locate is, or rationally should be, one of choosing that site at which the sum of all costs incurred by the individual enterprise is as low as possible for servicing the market or markets in which the product is sold. A number of factors are important in determining where this minimum cost location will be for any enterprise, and of course the

20. For a general discussion of the various ways a region may be defined, the following articles provide some interesting insights: Henry W. Broude, "The Significance of Regional Studies for the Elaboration of National Economic History," *Journal of Economic History* (December, 1960), pp. 588–96; Joseph L. Fisher, "Concepts in Regional Economic Development," *Papers and Proceedings of the Regional Science Association* (1955), pp. w1–w20; John R. P. Friedmann, "The Concept of a Planning Region," *Land Economics* (February, 1956), pp. 1–12; Forest G. Hill, "Regional Aspects of Economic Development," *Land Economics* (May, 1962), pp. 85–98; and Rutledge Vining, "The Region as an Economic Entity and Certain Variations to be Observed in the Study of Systems of Regions," *Papers and Proceedings of the American Economic Association* (1949), pp. 89–104.

21. Hoover and Fisher, "Research in Regional Economic Growth," *op. cit.*, p. 179.

degree of emphasis assigned specific factors will differ between industries.

In general, all profit-oriented activities will be concerned with total costs associated with assembling their inputs, combining these inputs in the desired manner, and distributing the resultant output. But depending on the specific technique used in producing each product, the characteristics of the product, and the nature of the market, natural and institutional factors exert varying degrees of influence on those making location decisions. Nor are these influences static. Rather, they are subject to change as the technique used in the production process is altered; as the nature of the institutional environment is modified; and as the pattern of final demand shifts as a result of increasing (or decreasing) per capita income and its distribution, changes in the age structure of the population, the mobility of the population, and for other reasons.

But though the influence exerted on any particular activity can often be observed to change over the course of a few decades (and even years in some instances) the general considerations themselves are much more durable. These considerations are the factors determining input and output access, and the influence they exert can be shown to explain the location of all but a minor amount of activity subject to market forces.[22] In general, most location decisions are the result of one of the following conditions: input access is the major consideration; output access is the major consideration; or because neither input nor output access alone exert a dominant influence, *i.e.*, both are of approximately equal importance. This grouping is examined below with representative examples given of activities that have responded to these influences in the recent past.

## I.  Input-Oriented Activities

**A.  Resource area exerts major influence**  The location of a substantial amount of economic activity is explained by the distribution of natural resources, either because the activity is technologically tied to the resource input or because costs are minimized by a location in the resource area. Many, though not all, activities grouped in the primary industries are included in this category as are some of those in the tertiary industries.

Of the technological ties the most obvious example is presented by the influence which the geologically determined location of mineral

22.  This general approach is used by Harvey S. Perloff *et al.*, *Regions, Resources and Economic Growth* (Baltimore, Md.: The Johns Hopkins Press, 1960) in their analysis of the influence of natural resources on differential rates of regional growth. See Chs. 6 and 7 in particular.

resources exerts on mining and drilling activities. Since mineral deposits are usually found at points, rather than over extensive areas, location possibilities are restricted to a finite number of specific points.

In a similar manner the location of other primary industries are tied by the geographically determined location of biotic and land resources[23] to areas where the resource is found in suitable quantity or quality rather than in points. For a number of reasons, however, agriculture is influenced less, as an industry, by the location of natural resources than are other primary industries. For example, only some agricultural sectors are direct users of land inputs, and even where land inputs are used, greater possibilities exist for the substitution of other factors for the natural input than is the case with the other primary industries. Still the locations of many direct users of land inputs are closely associated with specific land types (field and special-ty crops). In the tertiary group a number of recreational activities are oriented to a particular resource type or area, *i.e.*, sport hunting and fishing, scenic tours, and skiing. But even when such a technological tie exists, some locational choice is provided by the comparative costs associated with alternative areas or sites and/or the use of alternative products. And because of these differential costs the existence of a high-grade resource does not insure its development.

**B.   Interindustry relationship exerts major influence**   In addition to activities technologically tied to a natural input, a sub-stantial number of others find input access the primary locational consideration. Linkages of this type are formed because transfer costs associated with moving the (major) input exceed the sum of any processing cost differential that may exist at alternative sites plus transfer costs on the product (smelters, sawmills, the finish feeding of livestock, aluminum reduction, and iron production), because the input may be perishable (food processing),[24] or because a substantial saving is realized when technologically separate operations are carried out at the same time and place (the fuel costs saved when steel rolling and shaping mills locate where the output of the blast furnace can be used without reheating).

Since most of these ties are with inputs received from primary industries, such activities usually locate in resource areas. However, the tie is with the output of another industry and only incidentally with any geographic area.

**C.   Transportation network creates favorable access areas**
The nature of the transportation system joining resources, produc-

23. Land is defined to include its natural fertility, topography, and climatic charac-teristics.

24. The input to some food processing activities may be both perishable and more costly to transport in the unprocessed state.

tion centers, and markets sometimes creates, apart from any natural advantage, favorable input access locations. Thus, when an input of secondary importance (from the point of transfer costs) is separated by some distance from the major input source, the volume of outbound traffic may be considerably greater than that carried on the return trip. In this case low back-haul rates on the major input may make competitive production possible at the site of the minor input. (Steel production at Duluth, Minnesota is an example.) Of greater importance, perhaps, are trans-shipment points. All factors necessary in the production of particular products are in some instances first assembled at such points. And total transfer costs associated with production at trans-shipment points are often less than or equal to total transfer costs realized at alternative production locations.[25] Thus, some ocean ports and rail heads have become important production centers.

**D.   Other favorable input access locations**   A final group of input-oriented activities is one whose major input is not a raw or semi-processed material. Instead, it may be labor inputs that constitute the major portion of production costs. For a location of this type it is necessary that the real costs of the labor input be low enough to offset any transfer cost differentials that might exist at alternative locations. In the case of unskilled or semi-skilled labor, such locations may be found where part of the potential labor force is unemployed because of the industrial structure of the region (mining and heavy industry, which provide relatively few jobs for female workers), where employment is seasonal (some agricultural and recreation areas), and in regions that are for some reason depressed in comparison with the rest of the country. (Apparel-producing industries frequently utilize such labor input areas.) In the case of highly skilled labor, a new firm may locate in the vicinity of already established producers if training new employees at alternative locations is sufficiently expensive.[26] And finally, the critical input may be neither material nor labor but access to ideas (the fashion garment industry) or communication (brokerage and speculative activities).

## II.   Output-Oriented Activities

**A.   Population distribution exerts major influence**   Opposite the input-oriented industries are those whose optimal location is at the market for their product. Since final demand represents a significant share of total transactions, many of these location patterns

25. Hoover, *The Location of Economic Activity*, p. 39.
26. Hoover, *ibid.*, pp. 111–13.

approximate the distribution of population. For a large percentage of these industries, contact with the buyer is of major importance either because the product is budgetarily insignificant to him and he will not travel far to acquire it (routine personal and community services and most individual items sold at retail), or it must be produced where it is used (homes and streets). For these activities transfer costs and operating costs at locations removed from their market are not location-determining considerations. It could be said that a technological tie, similar to that which binds extractive industries to a resource, links these industries with population.

Other output-oriented activities which are influenced by population distribution are those that produce a product that is so bulky, heavy, or perishable that transfer costs on the output exceed the sum of differential processing costs plus transfer costs on inputs that are not available locally (fresh eggs, beer, soft drinks, and bakery products).

While these activities are population-oriented, the relationship is not linear, because in some cases scale economies require a minimum-sized market in order to produce at all. Therefore, larger population concentrations tend to produce more of these goods and services per capita because the scale economies are satisfied for a larger number of activities. Further distortion is introduced by differences in per capita income and tastes that may reflect differences in age structure, ethnic background, climatic conditions, and so on.

**B. Interindustry relationship exerts major influence**  The industries that are output-oriented, but only coincidently associated with population distribution, provide an input to other industries.[27] This input may be provided by business service or trade outlets. Again, frequent face-to-face contact is often required, and transfer costs as well as any differential operating costs are of minor significance in determining location. However, economies of scale may also be a consideration, and the spatial association of these activities with industries providing their market is weighted in favor of larger industrial concentrations.

The market-oriented industries that produce a product input for other industries are those whose transfer costs on the output are high enough to offset any differential processing costs plus input transfer costs (tin-can producers are an example).

## III.  Input and Output Access Exert Strong Influence

**A. Industrial complex exerts major influence**  As more intermediate stages are formed in the production process, a group of

27. Activities providing inputs to government may be considered as subject to the same influences to the extent that market forces determine their location — *i.e.*, it is not a direct result of deliberate government policy designed to disperse industry or distribute it more evenly.

activities is created that is increasingly further removed from both natural inputs and final markets. They are the producers of intermediate products whose inputs are received from industry and whose output is sold to industry. (Primary and secondary metals, metal fabricating, rubber products, and the chemical products industries are examples.) Total transfer costs are obviously minimized by a location that provides maximum access to both suppliers and buyers — *i.e.*, an industrial complex location. External economies may be important, communication with suppliers and customers is facilitated, and a large adaptable labor pool is available. Total costs are thus minimized by a location that provides maximum interindustry access, and the most industrialized regions have a much higher percentage of employment in these industries than of either population or total-industry employment.[28] Moreover, the relative importance of intermediate industries has grown, and the attraction of existing industrial areas has been strengthened.

## B.   Market potential modifies influence of factor location

SCALE ECONOMIES MODIFY LOCATION PATTERN.   The industries in this group produce a finished product and are, therefore, concerned with regional population distribution and/or market potential. However, economies of scale are important enough to exclude all but the very large markets as possible locations. In addition, inputs are composed mainly of intermediate industrial products on which transfer costs may be substantial and frequent contact with suppliers important. The resultant location tends to be in the largest regional market that offers adequate input access and reasonable access to the remainder of the market. (The automobile and farm implement industries are examples.)[29]

CRITICAL INPUT MODIFIES LOCATION PATTERN.   These activities produce a product in which at least one input is critical, fixed, and scarce while output transfer costs are substantial (the dairy and horticulture industries). Such activities seek locations as close as possible to market concentrations that provide the minimum input requirements (often substantial factor substitution is necessary — *i.e.*, fertilizer used on soils that are naturally relatively poor). Such conflicting influences produce a location pattern that is, under one set of circumstances, market oriented (most population centers are provided with locally produced dairy products) and under another,

28. Perloff *et al.*, *op. cit.*, pp. 395–96.
29. Perloff *et al.*, *ibid.*, p. 459. Also see Joe S. Bain, "Economies of Scale, Concentration and the Condition of Entry in Twenty Manufacturing Industries," *American Economic Review* (March, 1954), pp. 15–39; and H. Edward English, *Industrial Structure in Canada's International Competitive Position* (Montreal: The Private Planning Association of Canada, 1964).

input oriented (the regional concentrations of dairy farming in the Great Lakes area and northwest Europe).[30]

## IV. Input and Output Access Exert Little Influence

Industries that produce a product made of high-value, low-weight inputs and whose output is valuable but not fragile, bulky, or perishable are not significantly influenced by transfer costs. If production costs exhibit little regional variation, the location of these activities cannot be systematically classified. Production of some electronic products is an example. Some research activities are also spatially unfettered.

## SYNTHESIS

Most regions in market economies enter the commercial framework by exploiting some natural resource,[31] but because these are not evenly distributed, and their existence directly determines the location of a certain amount of economic activity, the pattern of development will not be uniform. The greater the number of natural advantages found in close proximity the better are the development prospects of that area, because the "location" of an activity means that the volume of productive effort has expanded. However, natural conditions differ considerably in their growth-generating potential and the extent of development is dependent on the composition of natural conditions as well as their abundance.

In the first instance, assuming that sufficient demand exists to make a region's natural assets attractive for capitalist exploitation, and that factors are relatively mobile and responsive to differential stimulus, the extent of development can be predicted from the production function(s) of the locating activity(ies).[32] The number of workers required, their spatial concentration, and the income received are considerations of major importance; these are the criteria that strongly influence the volume and type of residentiary activity that will follow. The more workers, the more concentrated they are, the higher the average income and the more even its dis-

30. The bulkier, heavier fluid milk tends to dominate in market areas and the lighter, less perishable, more valuable derivatives in input areas.

31. This statement seems consistent with both Hoover and North.

32. It would seem to make little difference for long-range development prospects, whether the region was empty or inhabited by a group of subsistence farmers, as long as population pressure did not exist. In fact under certain conditions the discovery of a new resource or technique could even overcome the stagnating effect of population pressure.

tribution, the greater will be the volume and variety of induced residentiary activity.[33] The type and amount of transport facilities and basic social investment required are also dependent on the type of product produced by the locating industry.[34] But after the establishment of the initial activity, expansion will be limited once an equilibrium has been reached — *i.e.*, when there is no further incentive for regional or "outside" investors to increase the volume of exports per unit time or the capacity of residentiary sectors.[35] Beyond this, expansion in the volume of activity will depend on a number of conditions, some endogenous to the region and some exogenous. These are primarily population growth, changes in taste, new discoveries and/or depletions, changes in technology, linkage effects, and the historical sequence of development.

To consider some of these in more detail, a region will experience an increase in the volume of activity if the demand curve for its export shifts out.[36] This may occur for a number of reasons: (1) because per capita income in the exogenous sector is rising (historically, largely because of improving technology) and the income elasticity of demand for the export is high; (2) because, even if its income elasticity of demand is low or negative, the increase in demand associated with a growing population is greater than the decrease due to a rising level of per capita income; (3) because of depletion or exhaustion in other areas producing the same item; (4) because improved transfer facilities have lowered total delivered costs, making marginal producers in other areas unable to compete; or (5) because technology has found new uses for the export.

Or the region will experience an increase in volume of activity if technological improvements are made in the production of the export. This will lower production costs and allow a downward movement along the demand curve (provided the demand curve is not completely inelastic) and permit more output to be produced per unit of input, thus increasing regional (and national) per capita income.[37] Again, there will be an increase in the volume of activity if

33. Some of these points are discussed by Robert E. Baldwin, "Patterns of Development in Newly Settled Regions," *Manchester School of Economics and Social Studies* (May, 1956), pp. 161–79; and by Watkins, "A Staple Theory of Economic Growth," *op. cit.*, pp. 144–45.

34. North, "Agriculture in Regional Economic Growth," *op. cit.*, p. 946.

35. For a discussion of "leakage" effects (payments to factor owners outside the region) on the amount of induced residentiary activity see Watkins, *op. cit.*, pp. 145–46.

36. For an increase in the output of the export to occur it is necessary that factor supply curves be somewhat elastic–assuming constant technology.

37. Extreme differences between regional and national market structures could modify the extent to which each participated in the gain from improved technology. If the export was produced and sold under monopolistic conditions it would be possible for the region's inhabitants to reserve most of the benefits for themselves. On the other

the technology of the initial activity is such that linked activities are attracted to its location.[38] The greater the amount of linked activity attracted to the region, the greater the volume of total expansion. This will occur when the suppliers of the initial activity's inputs are output-oriented or the buyers of its output are input-oriented. Or this increase will occur when new exports are developed. This may happen when new discoveries are made in the region; improved technology creates a demand for resources (or potential products) available in the region but not previously exploited (or produced); improved transfer facilities allow potential exports to compete in markets where they previously could not; or a former residentiary industry grows into an export industry. Also, if technological improvements are made in other sectors of the economy, the cost of imports will be lowered and this will raise real income and increase regional market potential.

Any of the above conditions that result in an expansion of the export sector or an increase in regional per capita income will usually induce an additional expansion in the residentiary sector.[39]

In addition, it should be mentioned that various constraints such as a critical shortage of water, an unfavorable climate which prevents the region from producing at least part of its own food supply, or a cultural pattern that is opposed or indifferent to economic progress, may limit the potential expansion of the region and/or confine it to the production of specific items.[40]

It is readily observable that various combinations of the above criteria may be grouped in such a manner as to insure a continuous expansion in the volume of regional activity, population, and per capita income. There is little evidence to indicate that evolution to a manufacturing base is necessary for continued progress in every case.[41] However, it must be recognized that regions that do develop

---

hand, if the region's export was produced and sold under highly competitive conditions, while its imports were purchased in monopolistic markets, most of the gain might be realized in other regions.

38. Watkins, *op. cit.*, p. 145.

39. For a more complete discussion of the factors causing nonbasic (residentiary) to basic (export) employment variations see Gerald Sirkin, "The Theory of the Regional Economic Base," *Review of Economics and Statistics* (November, 1959), pp. 426–29.

40. Tiebout, "Exports and Regional Economic Growth," *op. cit.*, p. 164.

41. The state of Washington represents a subnational area where population and per capita income has increased for at least a half century. Per capita income has constantly remained above the national average even though the economic structure is organized primarily around the extraction and processing of natural resources. See the comparative data in Perloff *et al.*, *op. cit.* For a discussion of the development of this area see Edwin J. Cohn, Jr., *Industry in the Pacific Northwest and Location Theory* (New York: Columbia University Press, 1954); Richard L. Pfister, "External Trade and Regional Growth: A Case Study of the Pacific Northwest," *Economic Development and Cultural Change* (January, 1963), pp. 134–51; and James N. Tattersal, "Exports and

such a base have several advantages because the number of output-oriented and interindustry-oriented activities that are attracted to the region widen the base and enhance the possibility of continuous expansion. With growing national wealth, the high income elasticity of demand for manufactured goods and personal services continuously stimulates both the export and residentiary sectors of an industrial region.[42] The capacity for developing such a base has historically been favored by the ability to attract an activity that would induce an extensive amount of linked industry to locate in the region, for other reasons than the presence of a variety of natural resources. The capacity of major iron and steel producing centers to generate these linkage effects has been very great.[43] And the past attraction of this industry to locations where water and large, high-grade coal and iron deposits are found together or where they can be brought together cheaply (usually by water transportation) goes far to explain the concentration of manufacturing industries in today's mature market economies.[44] High linkage effects have also been generated at good ocean port locations where the assembly of inputs, transfer cost advantages, and market potential have combined to create a favorable environment for the continuous growth of manufacturing and other activity.

Finally, the historical time in which the nation enters the development process is important, because technological advance has generally given industry a greater locational freedom.[45] But the potential growth of the region is influenced by both the historical timing of national development and the sequence in which the region enters the national development process. Since location decisions are always made "at the margin"—in the context of the traditional "givens" of economic analysis—the importance of sequence is emphasized.[46]

Economic Growth: The Pacific Northwest 1880–1960," *Papers and Proceedings of the Regional Science Association* (1962), pp. 215–34.

42. This does not mean that every region developing an industrial base is assured unending success. For an analysis of a once-dynamic industrial region that has ceased to keep pace see Edgar M. Hoover, "Pittsburgh Takes Stock of Itself," *City and Suburb: The Economics of Metropolitan Growth*, Benjamin Chinitz, ed. (Englewood Cliffs, N. J.: Prentice-Hall, Inc., 1964); and Pittsburgh Regional Planning Association, *Economic Study of the Pittsburgh Region* (Pittsburgh: University of Pittsburgh Press, 1963).

43. The significance of oligopolistic pricing policies, *i.e.*, basing point, should not be overlooked as a factor influencing the spatial concentration of industry.

44. Walter Isard, "Some Locational Factors in the Iron and Steel Industry Since the Early Nineteenth Century," *Journal of Political Economy* (June, 1948), pp. 203–17; and Michael Chisholm, "Tendencies in Agricultural Specialization and Regional Concentration of Industry," *Papers and Proceedings of the Regional Science Association* (1963), pp. 157–62.

45. See Chisholm, *op. cit.*, p. 161, for a discussion of this process.

46. Harvey S. Perloff with Vera W. Dodds, *How a Region Grows: Area Growth in the U.S. Economy* (New York: Committee for Economic Development, Supplementary Paper No. 17, 1963), p. 26.

Today's location decision is made in an environment shaped by all the marginal decisions of the past, and the existing spatial framework may be quite different from that which would emerge if the same decisions were to be made today.[47]

This should not be taken to imply that policy should be directed toward encouraging industrialization in all regions. To do so would mean that natural and institutional advantages in various areas of the national economy would not be taken full advantage of and consequently the potential standard of living would be compromised. But while regions cannot be expected to develop at the same rate nor to follow the same pattern, it is possible for factor returns to be equalized if sufficient mobility exists—and this is one of the principle virtues of an open economy. Policy directed toward enhancing mobility and encouraging the expansion and diffusion of technology will do more for the welfare of the entire population than one which fosters development in non-optimal locations even though it may mean a decline in both population and the volume of economic activity in some areas.[48]

47. Chisholm, *loc. cit.*
48. See Perloff and Dodd, *op. cit.*, Ch. 10.

ML. GREENHUT

RHUT

*Needed—A Return
to the Classics in Regional
Economic Development Theory\**

## I

Export base theory speaks in terms of a region's comparative advantage which leads to the sale of goods which directly or indirectly provides resources to the commodity-exporting region. The inflow of resources, in turn, makes possible further development to the end that multiple gains are attributable ultimately to the original export.[1] This export base theory has origins in the trade theories of Ricardo and Mill, the location theories of Ohlin, Lösch, and Isard, and the community development theories of Hoyt. The stock of resources, both natural to the region as well as those obtained by it from trade, serves as a base for its economic growth.

It is significant that the region's export base is not a datum. That is to say, the base changes with time, as currently produced private and social goods help bring forth new goods that change the base. Equally notable is the fact that measurements of the export base on community and intranational levels are not well defined. Approximate methods, such as the location quotient, are frequently used to identify the export base.[2]

Changeability of base and inadequacy of data for measuring the base are partly responsible for the inability of economists to predict accurately the future position of a community or region on the basis of its present structure. But even if the base were constant and data readily available to distinguish clearly between exports and locally

*The author would like to thank J. Buchanan, M. Colberg, and W. Laird for valuable comments on this paper.

1. D. C. North, "Location Theory and Regional Economic Growth," *Journal of Political Economy*, LXIII (June, 1955), pp. 243–58 [Selection 3 of this volume].

2. G. H. Hildebrand and A. Mace, "The Employment Multiplier in an Expanding Industrial Market: Los Angeles County, 1940–4," *Review of Economics and Statistics*, XXXIII (August, 1950), pp. 341–9; Federal Reserve Bank of Kansas City Study, "The Employment Multiplier in Wichita," *Monthly Review Tenth Federal Reserve District*, No. 9 (September 30, 1952), pp. 241–9, and M. L. Greenhut, "Comments on Economic Base Theory," *Land Economics*, XXV (February, 1959), pp. 71–4.

Greenhut, M. L., "Needed—A Return to the Classics in Regional Economic Development Theory," Kyklos, XIX (1966), pp. 461–478.

consumed goods, a vital theoretical shortcoming would still prevail. It is the purpose of this paper to analyze the theoretical significance of the export base and to evaluate the development policies which relate to it.

## II

That export sectors of high productivity may be found to exist along with economic backwardness has been pointed out by Chenery.[3] Among other reasons for this seemingly ambivalent state, resistance to social change is often noted.[4] But whatever the reason, it appears that in some cases comparative advantage in high productive sectors *is* conducive to rapid growth, while in others it *is not.*

Hochwald[5] observes that the South had a substantial amount of cotton, tobacco, sugar, and rice exports but that either it exported the capital funds it received in payment or its imports were more of a luxury-good order than the type which could facilitate development of "residentiary" industries. Accordingly, the export income of the region contributed little to the broadening of its economic base. What, we may ask, would have happened if Southerners had neither invested their capital funds abroad nor imported luxury goods but instead had received back in trade requisite raw materials and equipment? Possibly, many would argue that agricultural production is not high-value output and the South would have lagged anyway, especially when compared to regions that possessed comparative advantage in some secondary or tertiary industries.

The growth of a region, we suggest, however, is independent of the category of the region's exports. The mere fact that a region's comparative advantage lies in high-value products, such as electronics output or vacations, does not give it advantage *ceteris paribus* over a region whose comparative advantage is rooted in agriculture. The essential element of importance in so far as concerns trade is not the kind of sector in which the advantage lies but the degree or extent of the advantage.

Consider, for example, an underdeveloped nation lacking in raw

3. "Comparative Advantage and Development Policy," *American Economic Review*, LI (March, 1961), pp. 18–51.

4. See E. E. Hagen, *On the Theory of Social Change* (Homewood, Ill.: Irwin and Co., 1962); W. Nichols, "Southern Tradition and Regional Economic Progress," *Southern Economic Journal*, XXVI (June, 1960), pp. 187–98; and R. E. Baldwin, "Patterns of Development in Newly Settled Regions," *Manchester School*, XXIV (May, 1956), pp. 161–79.

5. W. Hochwald, "Interregional Income Flows and the South," pp. 320–48, in *Essays in Southern Economic Development*, M. L. Greenhut and W. Tate Whitman, eds. (Chapel Hill, N.C.: University of North Carolina Press, 1964).

material resources and skills, but possessed of favorable climate and beaches. The mere condition of comparative advantage in a high-value product does not signify potentially rapid growth. Or, if we may exaggerate our point: a region unfortunately lacking in resources and skills will, by the law of comparative advantage, still be possessed of some comparative advantage. So, if of all things its comparative advantage lies in the electronics field, we would have on hand a poorly endowed nation and people with a comparative advantage in a rapid growth industry; significantly, the gain would not be attributable to great skills in the given activity but inabilities elsewhere. This region, as our next section will show, may well continue to lag.

## III

With free exchange rates and trade, every country must evidence a comparative advantage in something. However, the existence of comparative advantage, though helpful to any region, is not by itself sufficient to assure rapid economic growth, and the principle holds *even if the advantage lies in high-valued goods.* This is an important point to understand, especially because its full implications can be over-looked.

Let Region or Country I be a very poor underdeveloped nation while Region II is highly advanced. The comparative advantages of the Regions in products A and B are implicitly shown in this Table.

*Output Per Unit of Resource Input*

| COMMODITY | COUNTRY I | COUNTRY II |
|-----------|-----------|------------|
| A | 1 | 20 |
| B | 1 | 10 |

By well-known principles, Country I will export B while Country II exports A. The exact terms of trade will depend upon reciprocal demand and supply conditions.

Let us assume that the supply of commodity A in II is somewhat limited in relation to total world demand. That is to say, producers in II are unable to supply all of the world's needs for A and still have any resource factors available for the production of B. This assumption means that specialization is complete in II. Terms of trade, as a consequence, will be less than the opportunity/cost ratio of 2–1 in II, for otherwise resources will be devoted to the production of B as well as A, which possibility we have already ruled out by assumption.

We shall assume that terms of trade are established at 1.8 A to 1 B. This relation means that Country I can trade 1 unit of B for 1.8 units of A while Country II trades 1.8 units of A for 1 of B. Country I, therefore, gains 0.8 for each resource unit devoted to B, and II gains 0.2 A per unit of resource by specializing in and trading A for B.

Suppose A is a rather simple textile product and B is some specialized tool or die. The underdeveloped region, which we assume by the table is I, would be the one producing the technologically advanced good. (Manifestly other regions may be imagined to be engaged in the production of B. In turn, the advanced Country II, because of a comparatively great advantage in A, may be visualized as producing vast quantities of this particular kind of good. Observe further that, by terms of trade, Country I appears to be in a very favorable position. But before we carry this idea too far, one last preliminary is in order.

The assumption of a terms of trade relation of 1.8 A to 1 B suggests that there exists a marginal exporting region, say Country III, that is producing A and B, and that the underlying opportunity costs in that country are set at this particular ratio. Also implicit to our terms of trade assumptions is the likely condition that Country II is able to produce such a comparatively large part of the world demand all by itself that not many other nations—in fact, none that differ sharply from II—are called on to produce A. This is why the terms of trade settle *near* the comparative cost level of Country II rather than requiring as producers of A some Country IV or V whose opportunity costs approach that of I. On the other hand, we may conjecture from our terms of trade assumption the likelihood that Country I and neighboring countries are unable to supply all or even a substantial part of the B that is demanded, for otherwise the terms of trade would tend to approach the 1 to 1 opportunity cost level of I. What can we now say about the overall development and potential growth of Countries I and II?

First of all, II is a much more advanced nation than I, assuming of course, that resource units are defined identically or nearly identically and that the relations posited for products A and B are descriptive of most activities in the two countries. Second, the underdeveloped country, by our assumptions, is producing the high-valued product. Third, the underdeveloped country gains relatively more from trade than the developed nation, though manifestly if we select a smaller than 1.5 to 1 ratio the converse would hold. This relation points to the principle that if the relative efficiency of a region, developed or underdeveloped, when compared to the last best producing region (*i.e.*, the marginal supplying region) is slight, the region's overall economic gain from trade is much less than that obtained by regions whose relative efficiency is great. This situation holds regardless of whether the relative efficiency is in high- or low-valued goods. Of course, if a region's greatest relative efficiency is found in activities for which only sharply limited demands prevail (so that much of its production must center in those goods in which it has only a slight relative efficiency) that region will, *ceteris paribus*, be in a rather unfortunate position. It is essentially *in this context* that we find an advantage for regions possessed of relatively great efficiency in high-value-added products, for often the demand for such products is comparatively great when related to potential supply.

Fourth, not many nations appear to be so highly skilled as I, relatively speaking, which can produce B with facility comparable to A. Fifth, no matter how favorable and unlimited the relative advantage, the absolute level of efficiency is of even greater importance. But let us expand on this last point.

Recall from our basic example the idea that earning a substantial return from export trade does not, by itself, compensate for general resource inadequacies and cultural drawbacks. Rather, the region's internal structure is likely to be much more helpful than its export base in appraising its growth potential. As our example suggests, even a region that exports high-valued goods under extremely favorable terms of trade may be underdeveloped, and face grave obstacles to growth. A comparative advantage in low-valued lines, such as textiles, that reflects abundant resource endowments and great output capacity may well be ideal even though the degree of relative advantage in terms of trade may be quite small, assuming in addition that all other things — such as social costs, future growth of industry, cultural prospects, etc. — are equal.

The export base, we therefore assert, is not likely to be the best, or in fact even a good guide to understanding the economic development of a region,[6] unless the region be small in size (*e.g.*, a community) and the export base represents the major portion of the economy.

---

6. Florida has long had a high-valued export base and its terms of trade may well have been favorable many years ago with the limited supply of vacations available in the state. Nonetheless, it took almost four decades after its vacation attributes were first made prominent for the state to really move forward economically, and then its economic development was probably attributable to industrial location advantages rather than to its export base. See M. L. Greenhut and M. R. Colberg, *Factors in the Location of Industry in Florida* (Tallahassee: Florida State University Studies, 1961).

The lack of statistical correlation between the ratio of agricultural population and the level of income in interregional (not international) economies is especially germane to this point. Thus Perloff noted, in his "Interrelations of State Income and Industrial Structure," *Review of Economics and Statistics*, XXXIX (November, 1957), pp. 162–71, that the ratio of employment in the industrial and service sectors is an inadequate guide to state income levels in the high-income United States. The same kind of findings also appear in S. E. Harris, ed., *The Economies of New England* (Cambridge, Mass.: Harvard University Press, 1952).

Indeed, the unfortunate and widespread belief that the export base is extremely important—and even more vital, the unfortunate theoretical extension from it that the kinds of activity that constitute the export base manifest the economic development potential of the area—have helped promote the abandonment of classical economic principles, not only in theory but with respect to development policy. In place of the classical guideline, one finds today a miscegenation of plans. The next section of this paper shows why the lexicon of planners reflects the errors that are related to ideas about the export base. However, before we examine these errors, we must generalize our previous illustration.

Our example of gains from trade can be expanded to include $m$ commodities and $n$ countries, and, in fact, it can be designed to show the stability conditions and trade patterns of nations. Such extension and related details would be page- and time-consuming, however, and for the purposes of this article quite unnecessary. Instead, we are able to accomplish the objective simply by selected references to prevailing literature.

On the basis of Samuelson's original paper on gains from industrial trade,[7] Kemp shows that the utility preference function of people who trade with each other must lie above the counterpart function under autarchy. This position will hold at all points because Kemp conceives of charging lump-sum taxes against those who gain the most from trade and providing subsidies to those who otherwise would have fewer goods after trade than before (*i.e.*, without) trade[8]. He derives the relation $p'Z' - w'a' \geq p'Z^0 - w'a^0$ to compare after-trade conditions with before-trade conditions, where $p'$ is the price vector after trade, $Z'$ the consumption vector after trade, $w'$ the related factor price vector, $a'$ the related factor input vector, and where the superscript $^0$ indicates autarchy.[9] The validity of the relation may be established in three parts: First, recall the output gains that are attributable to comparative cost advantages. Then, note that because a production vector $(\bar{Z})$ distinguished from a consumption vector $(Z)$ would reach its maximum at $(\bar{Z}'; a')$, the related consumption $p'Z'$ under the competitive equilibrium must be greater than or equal to $p'Z^0$ in Kemp's equation. Finally, observe that in the absence of trade the values of the production vector $\bar{Z}^0$ would be the same *under the competitive equilibrium* as its corresponding consumption vector $Z^0$; moreover the production vector $\bar{Z}^0$ must carry values which are

7. Paul A. Samuelson, "The Gains from International Trade," *Canadian Journal of Economics and Political Science*, V (May, 1939), pp. 192–205.

8. Murray C. Kemp, "The Gains from International Trade," *The Economic Journal*, LXXII (December, 1962), pp. 803–19.

9. *Ibid.*, p. 805.

directly related to the factor input vector $a^0$; so, the right side of Kemp's equation approaches zero in the competitive equilibrium and under autarchy. Because $Z'$ includes the zero or positive gains of trade, and because the vectors are weighted similarly, the left-hand side of Kemp's relation must be equal or greater in value than the right-hand side. Manifestly, the maximum consumption price vector ($p'Z'$) with trade, compared to without trade ($p'Z^0$) depends ultimately not on the value ($p'$) of the product, but on the quantity of products ($Z$). Kemp's formulation, therefore, suggests that the gains from international or interregional trade depend on the degree of the comparative advantages possessed by a nation and not the type of good for which the advantage exists.

In his later article, Samuelson[10] acknowledges the validity of Olsen's[11] contention that the total utility acquired by a people after trade may be less than that which prevailed (or would prevail) under autarchy. However, though the respective consumption possibility frontiers, when redesignated as utility surfaces or collective indifference curves, can intersect, it is clear that there are points along the curve that reflect a larger or equal total of all goods than that which would be available to consumers under autarchy. In effect, the gains from trade can suffice to enable those who derive advantage to bribe those who otherwise lose, a bribery that would make those who would have lost at least indifferent to trade; but the losers cannot bribe the gainers into repealing all trade. Samuelson notes that "trade will *not necessarily maximize* the real income or consumption and utility possibilities *of any one* country...."[12] However, the fact that it *can improve* the nation's position makes the export base *one* determiner of national well-being.

The connection that exists between the export base and total utility does not, in any case, lessen the significance or value of our caveats. Instead, their repetition is justified and we remind the reader that: (1) the gain from trade is not designated by the kinds of products exported and imported, though, of course, the base does suggest the kind of industry and relative development that prevails; (2) the gain from trade, even when visualized correctly, does not establish in itself a valid yardstick for determining (or predicting) economic growth; nor, as we shall now see, does it serve as the basis for advocating an unbalanced versus a balanced or other government-determined growth policy.

10. "The Gains from International Trade Once Again," *The Economic Journal*, LXXII (December, 1962), pp. 820–34.

11. Erling Olsen, "Undenigshandelns Gevint," *Nationaløkonomisk Tidskrift*, Haeft 1/2 (Argona, 1958), pp. 76–9.

12. "The Gains from International Trade Once Again," *op. cit.*, p. 829.

## IV

In a series of articles a few years ago,[13] it was noted that some economies have developed in accordance with the sector growth theory of economic development that one may glean from location theory,[14] while others have witnessed a pattern of growth apparently conforming to the export base theory, which leans on the high value added-export base idea. It was agreed that the resolution of the kind of theory that is most applicable to and descriptive of a given region's development depends ultimately upon whether the region is open or closed. If it is open (for example, a vacation-type island which suddenly is discovered to the southeast of the New York City–Philadelphia–Washington, D.C. complex), we might find that economic activity would jump directly into the tertiary stage of activity. Much like the early development of the United States, the export base of the island would be of great importance — provided we amend the export base concept to conform to our arguments of Section III. Closed economies, such as in the United States between 1900 and 1940, it was said, would follow a different pattern; they must grow, and grow by sector stages.

Perhaps implicit to these articles, depending upon point of view, is the further idea that small segments of a developed economy, such as the cities in the economy, reflect growth principles that in many ways are counterparts of those relevant to large underdeveloped countries. Tiebout points out that the export base is important to a city because, among other things, foreign "income multiplier" feedbacks are unimportant (in fact irrelevant), and, in addition, if the area we are concerned with is extremely small, practically everything produced is exported. Manifestly, much the same thought can be extended to an economy such as the United States in the early nineteenth century or some underdeveloped nation of today. The small or underdeveloped region is often an open economy, and the export base is important to it.

The idea that the export base may be significant to small or underdeveloped regions and to intranational regions has value only in so far as we direct our attention to (a) the degree of advantage stemming from reciprocal demands and supply and (b) the internal structure that develops coterminously with the initial economic growth of the

13. See North, *op cit.*, C. M. Tiebout, "Exports and Regional Economic Growth," *Journal of Political Economy*, LXIV (April, 1956), pp. 160–4; D. C. North, "A Reply," *ibid.*, pp. 165–8; C. M. Tiebout, "Rejoinder," *ibid.*, p. 169.
14. For example, see E. M. Hoover, *The Location of Economic Activity* (New York: McGraw-Hill Book Co., 1946), pp. 187–95. In a similar key were the findings of Colin Clark, *The Conditions of Economic Progress* (London: Macmillan and Co., 1941), pp. 51 ff., which stressed the ratio of employment in primary, secondary, and tertiary industries.

region. Unfortunately, many theorists have followed the temptation to stress the industry-type in the base, this in disregard of the principles set forth in Section III.[15.]

The willingness to select between industry types or sectors most beneficial to growth reflects the implicit belief that underdeveloped countries cannot rely on the law of comparative advantage, for this law and the classical workings of a market economy would either take too long a period of time to bear fruit, or else they are, in fact, inapplicable to the subject kinds of economies.[16] More specifically, and considering the latter point only, a very small economic market would permit only single or few plant industries, and if modern technology requires a multiple plant-large size firm in order to gain economies of scale, an "unbalanced" industrial growth is said to be necessary.[17] In an even more general reference, we might suggest that a planned economy is said to be required since classical markets require a near infinite demand relative to technology in order to bring about classical market results, and this condition does not hold today. Alas, the grain of truth in these thoughts is often miscast.

For almost two centuries now, economic theory has convincingly displayed the theorem that if production is feasible in a capitalistic economy it must be efficient.[18] If the production of some good is un-

15. G. Myrdal, *Economic Theory and Underdeveloped Regions* (London: Gerald Duckworth and Co., 1957); R. Nurkse, *Problems of Capital Formation in Underdeveloped Countries* (Oxford: Blackwell and Mott, Ltd., 1953); A. O. Hirschman, *The Strategy of Economic Development* (New Haven, Conn.: Yale University Press, 1958); P. Rosenstein-Rodan, "Problems of Industrialization of Eastern and Southeastern Europe," *The Economic Journal*, LIII (June, 1943), pp. 205–16. In contrast, Hisao Nishioka, "On the Industrialization of Underdeveloped Regions," *Occasional Papers No. 3, The Economic Institute of the Aoyama Gakuin University* (July, 1965), esp. p. 10, begins with the observation that the intranational regional economy is an open economy and, accordingly, that the extent of secondary and especially tertiary industrial development is not an adequate guide to the region's growth. (And see note 6 for support of this position.) With an open economy, the export base becomes more important, but here rather than stress industry type within a sector, Nishioka argues for the development most natural to the people and the resources of the region in question.

16. If solely the pure competition framework is contemplated, the consumer satisfaction-productive efficiency conclusions of classical economics do appear to be a long way off. The writer suggests, however, that a different approach to classical theory (see his *Microeconomics and the Space Economy* (Chicago: Scott-Foresman and Co., 1963) would be more reasonable and that in light of it our classical results would not be seen to be so remote as to justify their abandonment and replacement by planning.

17. J. Sheahan, "International Specialization and the Concept of Balanced Growth," *Quarterly Journal of Economics*, LXXI (May, 1958), pp. 183–97; and, for a broad discussion of pros and cons, see F. Machlup, "Disputes, Paradoxes, and Dilemmas Concerning Economic Development," in *Essays on Economic Semantics* (Englewood Cliffs, N. J.: Prentice Hall, Inc., 1963), in particular pp. 289–93.

18. In note 16 we referred to findings that suggest that under limited demand and advanced technology, an oligopolistic economy results, but that if collusion is prevented and free entry maintained, the economy tends to be efficient. We shall try to justify this vital idea in the present note.

economic because demand is inadequate (as is indeed often postulated by growth theorists who favor the planned growth of a selected industry), nothing short of a new demand, *ceteris paribus*, can fill the gap. To be sure, we may change demand (let us say add government demand to private demand) with the effect of gaining the given production in place of alternative production. Observe, however, that all we are accomplishing is, again, putting a selected production in place of another. And, as we have already seen, this idea does not produce advantage when applied on the level of international trade. That the same principle holds on the closed economy level, *i.e.*, in the absence of special considerations such as military preparedness, should be equally clear.

Any planned substitution for the industrial development that naturally would come about must be recognized for what it really is: an acceptance of the idea that political leaders and intellectuals know better than the people the type of goods that should be produced and the type of wants that should be satisfied. The way the decision is effected will determine the degree to which consumer supremacy, individualism, and capitalism are relegated to a lower order of importance, or else replaced entirely by another authority. In substance, the real power behind economic development and the real force of growth is not the export base, by sector and type, but the basic ad-

---

At the very outset to our discussion, let us first recall the thesis advanced by Dewey that within any market area plants of optimum size arise as a result of, let us say, the rationalizing process. (See his "Imperfect Competition No Bar to Efficient Production," *Journal of Political Economy*, LXVI (February, 1958), pp. 24–33. Note, however, that though the plant may be of optimum size, the total demand throughout the economy might be insufficient to permit enough plants to exist, so that, in turn, the firm is unable to obtain all possible scale economies (external and internal). The effect then would be as if production in each market area were at the lowest cost point of the long-run average cost (L.R.A.C.) but that the L.R.A.C. under view were not the lowest one possible. This result would seem to follow naturally from our assumptions, for if demand were greater more market areas would exist, more plants per firm would be possible, and costs would be reduced accordingly. In other words, the conception of market areas and oligopoly appears to indicate optimum cost of manufacture in each market area (the rationalizing process), but on the surface does not seem to assure the lowest possible L.R.A.C. curve. Because of page limitations, the outline of our proof of optimality in size *and* cost must, perforce, be spotty. Let us suggest the outline of our proof as follows:

Suppose the level of the L.R.A.C. curve is not optimal. Then, returns *in the industry* —for risk and uncertainty—must be insufficient compared to the returns in other industries, and the production of the subject product would not be profitable. (Incidentally, this conclusion is the direct counterpart of that we have long accepted for the purely competitive economy.) The effect and reality of the oligopolistic economy is simply that demand is either too small to warrant production or it is large enough to make production worthwhile relative to other alternatives. No planning for unbalanced industry growth, etc., substitutes for this, unless we accept the dictum that demand is or can be made greater in a planned economy than in the market economy, and this, of course, would be an entirely different argument than that germane to this note.

vantages (*i.e.*, underlying efficiency) actually underscoring the investments of the economy, whether or not these investments are privately or publicly initiated and controlled. The real issue in economic development is whether the government should alter and how it should alter consumer demand toward the end of gaining a different production than that called for by a free market.

When viewed in the proper context, the policies and solutions for the regional economic development of underdeveloped countries reflect essentially the same question as that applicable to developed countries; how much and to what extent do we permit government to alter consumer preference? Assuming full employment in primary, secondary, and tertiary industries, we suspect not only that government interference often produces sufficient demand in place of insufficient demand for a particular output, thereby eliciting the efficient production of the desired but otherwise unproduced good, but that it also leads with equal frequency to the inefficient overproduction (increasing costs) of some other good, or, of course, the nonproduction of some good(s). To be sure, planners may sometimes forecast future developments surprisingly well, so that in effect they lead a society to a faster long-run growth than may result from consumer decisions,[19] but the only proper—and safe—context for planned growth, we maintain, is to operate within the arena of consumer choice, not against it, as the section that follows will argue.

## V

We do not contend that government should be oblivious to the growth process, for we accept the time-worn idea that if the private sector could have started economic growth without help from government it would have done so in the long period of underdevelopment that existed before growth theorists began to argue their respective cases. But we do believe that government should confine its interferences to those that facilitate private activity rather than pursue the large scale programs of intervention implicit in the balanced or

---

19. One reviewer suggested that some economists may argue that, by sacrificing advantage now but with proper vision of the future, planners might secure advantage later on. To illustrate, suppose that in 1900 static advantage comparisons suggested that the Bahamas could best be developed by establishing a fertilizer export base. But if a planner could then have predicted that tourism would become a high income elasticity service, the society could have derived long-run advantage by developing vacation facilities instead of the fertilizer industry. There is, of course, truth to this possibility. However, as was further suggested, the planner may err and the short run may be more important than the long run. In fact, if the short run developed chaotically because of stress on industries that the consumer and labor force could not yet support, the long run might witness a failure to reach the level it otherwise would have attained.

unbalanced theories of growth that are so prevalent today. Our objections to interventions that replace one kind of activity by another, in the guise of either unbalanced or balanced growth theory or some offshoot, are many:

1. A balanced or unbalanced growth theory or any other of its kind tends to ignore the specific differences that prevail between nations, such as, for example, the shortage of enterprisers one may find in, say, Laos and Thailand, compared to Brazil and Mexico.[20]

2. The balanced growth theorists, for example, emphasize the idea that a set of investments (not one) is needed, and that this set would be most readily forthcoming under balanced growth; in addition, they contend, a proper balance between all sectors must be maintained.[21] The unbalanced growth theorists argue that key wants once satisfied lead to more wants, or, shall we say, that substantial expansion in one investment sector uncovers the need for substantial investment elsewhere.[22] But each school thereby ignores a fundamental requirement for rapid, smooth growth, namely, the need for economizing the scarce factors of production.[23]

3. The economizing process is natural to competitive society. In contrast, balanced growth theory has led many countries in South Asia and North Africa to ignore comparative advantage in stressing sector type (*e.g.*, ultramodern airports) while unbalanced growth has led others, such as in Eastern Europe, to stress the "big push" and to "overshoot" in belief that imbalance induces new investment and rectification over time.

4. Planned industrial growth is likely to violate fundamental location principles. Consider in this regard such legislation as the original Area Redevelopment Act in the United States and its more recent modifications, and the latest Depressed Areas Act in Great Britain. These statutes are designed to develop selected regions within a national economy by locating manufacturing industry within them. The alternative possibilities of improving agricultural output or improving the outward mobility of population are relegated to a lower order of importance.

In a discussion on this point, Nishioka observes that the "intro-

---

20. A. M. Lipton, "Growth in Underdeveloped Countries," *The Economic Journal,* LXXII (September, 1962), pp. 641–59, points out, some nations may require one path, while others may profit from the alternative path. Thus the quantity and quality of untapped resources, the customs and mores of the people, the available supply of entrepreneurship, the tax system, the reserves of foreign exchange, etc., will all help dictate the best course to follow.

21. W. A. Lewis, *The Theory of Economic Growth* (London: Allen and Unwin, 1955), p. 283.

22. Hirschman, *op. cit.,* p. 93.

23. Lipton, *op. cit.,* p. 651.

duction of industries does not necessarily bring employment for the unemployed," because only the type of labor that suits the subject industries may be employed and often this kind of labor must be brought in from elsewhere.[24] He goes on to observe that to match industries with the human and natural resources of the depressed areas involves bringing into the region precisely the same kind of industries already located there which, in fact, are partly responsible for the regional decline, or the planner must ignore the fundamental factors of industrial location. Indeed, we might add the proviso that these objections either apply or else we must presume an inefficient-ineffective economic system such that private entrepreneurs could not identify for themselves the latent advantages of a depressed area. In turn, one would have to stipulate that only government officials are possessed of this expertise.[25]

It is, of course, true that many regions do possess advantages that have not yet been utilized largely because agglomerating economies are required and these advantages depend upon some substantial prior industrial development. In other words, the location theorist might visualize a region possessed of resource advantages that have not been tapped because, besides resources, industrial location often requires agglomerating advantages.[26] This Weberian component of industrial location signifies that some regional industrial development automatically produces further industrial development. So, in a pattern similar to pump priming, it may be argued that when government induces a new location in an underdeveloped area it will reap cumulative returns as auxiliary industry and other locations tend to develop over a period of time. But would not the argument apply that the main task of government is to establish a framework of authority and an institutional base within which industry and economic activity flourish? By providing a stable monetary and fiscal base, by raising the cultural level of its people (and regions), by enlightening its citizens as to the requirements of and gains from industrial development, the basis necessary for growth can be established and in the process a growth will be witnessed that is attributable to comparative advantages.[27] Whatever mistakes arise would then be natural to free enterprise rather than in addition to this particular system of economic relations.

24. *Op. cit.*, p. 12.
25. Before World War II, the depressed area policy of Great Britain stressed the relocation of labor; after the war, the government bureaucrat became an agent behind industrial relocation.
26. Walter Isard is a leading exponent of this view. See his *Location and Space Economy* (New York: John Wiley & Sons, Inc., 1956), pp. 173–88, 256–85.
27. And see the author's "Industrial Development of Undeveloped Areas in the United States," *Land Economics*, XXXVI (November, 1960), pp. 371–9.

5. We aver, accordingly, that the true role of the state is to eliminate cultural barriers, to simplify and improve the tax base, to help develop the skills of its people, to establish institutions and generate information conducive to new activity or entrepreneurship, and even to adjust saving/income proportions. The proper distribution of savings among investment projects, we believe, will follow the lines most appropriate and natural to the country at hand, and the burden of proof should rest on those who advocate interference with consumer preferences.[28] All interferences, other things being equal, should be confined to those that would be deemed acceptable in any capitalistic economy.

## VI

As Nutter has shown,[29] the ray along which a nation grows, especially the numerical designation of this growth, can be affected by government. Thus, a government may emphasize products for which the largest reduction in costs could be expected. Moreover, an austerity approach to its products to emphasize quantity rather than quality will cause the measured growth rate to rise. Indeed, by altering the ratio of consumption to income, a government may cause production frontiers to move outward more than otherwise would be the case. But, significantly, the nonneutrality of our growth measures does not make austerity and related programs desirable, and a noticeable impact on the consumption-savings ratio can be affected within the less regimented free enterprise system.

By raising the net profit-wage ratio via corporate and other taxes, or, more generally, by raising the savings to consumption ratio, a greater capital investment in the near future may be brought about, with the effect that the production frontier is extended outward more rapidly than might otherwise have been the case. This kind of policy can be best supported under political conditions that demand as rapid a short-run growth as possible. It is imperative, however, that we should not confuse interferences of the indicated kind with the planners' selection of this or that industry or this or that sector as the

28. The two sides of economic development first presented in the Rosenstein-Rodan paper ("Problems of Industrialization of Eastern and Southeastern Europe," *op. cit.*), namely, (1) the optimal savings/income ratio and (2) the distribution of investments, should, in our view, be reduced to the first.

We might further observe here that Jacob Viner, in his *International Trade and Economic Development* (London: Oxford University Press, 1953), p. 50, objects to the emphasis would-be planners place on industry over agricultural development. Viner argues that an increase in income stems from an increased productivity of labor, and this may arise in agriculture as well as in manufacturing.

29. G. Warren Nutter, "On Measuring Economic Growth," *The Journal of Political Economy*, LXV (February, 1957), pp. 51–63.

basis for growth; the former interference is compatible with free choice and the latter is not. To sum up our arguments:

The open-economy, export base theory applies to cities in a developed country, to intranational regions, and to underdeveloped countries. But this theory does not apply in the form so often given it by growth theorists;[30] rather, it applies in the classical form of comparative advantage, such as we presented in Section III of this paper. For large developed countries we typically have on hand a closed — not open — economy. Here, the export base is quite unimportant; nonetheless, classical comparative cost and general competitive market theory are completely applicable. We contend, therefore, that placing heavy stress on industry types and on the extent and variety of investments in the system amounts to a substitution of the "planners handbook" for the underlying body of classical theory. Because we have shown that compliance with comparative cost advantages, not with industry sector or type, optimizes the position of the open economy; because the market economy, based as it is on opportunity costs, aptly conforms to and characterizes the closed economy; because whatever production takes place in the market economy must be efficient, the only general problem for the typical economic region is to make the internal structure ready for the take-off. In the language of the location theorist, agglomerating economies, besides requisite cultural forces, must be present in order for the maximum possible industrial expansion to take place.

How it may be asked, does one provide a region with agglomerating economies? Here our answer must be that the role of government is chiefly to facilitate economic activity by improving the financial, legal, and business institutions that service the economy, and by promoting formation of the social capital necessary for growth. In a related manner, government should help maintain full employment by means of a monetary and fiscal policy that reflects the preference patterns of consumers and workers. Given the assumption of full employment for the economy marked by planned growth and for the one characterized by natural growth, the only growth advantage allowable for the former over the latter — apart from the bias of measurement[31] — would have to be explained in terms of the consumption-saving pattern. Manifestly, the ratio in question is a matter of voter choice, so if rapid short-run capital development is of vital importance, the otherwise unplanned society can have this feature as well. In the ultimate sense, the fundamental force behind economic growth is the state of the arts, the culture, or, let us say, the internal structure of the region.

30. Among others see North, *op. cit.*, and Hildebrand and Mace, *op. cit.*
31. Nutter, *op. cit.*

**79**

# Toward the Application of Dynamic Growth Theory to Regions[1]

## 1. INTRODUCTION

A gaping desideratum exists in the theory of regional economic development. This may be stated best in the vernacular: "Can a region lift itself by its own bootstraps?" Is a region within a larger economy capable of strictly endogenous, self-sustained growth? In 1956, a very thoughtful and stimulating debate between Douglass C. North[2] and Charles M. Tiebout[3] revolved around this very question. The uncertain outcome of that controversy was clearly due to the uncertain status of this fundamental question. North contended that the level of economic activity in a region is a multiple of that region's export activities and thus the growth and development of a region is a function of the growth and development of its export sector. Tiebout, on the other hand, contended that this view was too simple, that other factors could in fact cause a region to grow autonomously — apart, that is, from the growth of its export sector. This issue is further confused by a rather paradoxical analogy between "regions," "nations," and the "world," as Meyer has recently observed: "It is quite obvious, moreover, that an economy can exist without exports and can grow without a growth of its exports, as must be true for the world economy taken together."[4]

It is the intention of this paper to develop this question in terms of some necessary conditions implied by an investment model. Once these conditions are established we shall explore certain theoretical and empirical hypotheses prompted by the use of the theory in regional economic analysis. This will involve, among other things, the relation of the theory to economic base-type studies. Lastly, we shall

1. Research on this paper was made possible with funds provided by Resources for the Future, Inc. (Hartman) and by Hatch 211, W-81 regional project "The Economics of Water Transfer" (Seckler).

2. [8, 9]. North's article [8] is reprinted as Selection 3 of this volume.
3. [11].
4. Meyer [7; p. 32].

Hartman, L. M. and Seckler, David, "Toward the Application of Dynamic Growth Theory to Regions," Journal of Regional Science, VII, No. 2 (1967), pp. 167–173.

conclude with some observations on the possibility of a broader theory of regional economic growth — a theory that incorporates the mechanistic formulations of the investment model with the variety of other elements involved in the process of structural change.

## 2. A REGIONAL GROWTH MODEL

The *sine qua non* of economic growth is the act of investment. Investment ultimately determines both the supply of and the demand for commodities. Growth theory propositions represent a solution to the problem of determining the rate of investment that will bring supply and demand into equality. In a closed economy that rate is determined in conjunction with the marginal propensity to save *à la* Harrod-Domar. In an open economy, such as a region, the problem is much more difficult. For here one not only must enter import and export "leakages" into the system, but the whole question of a savings-determined "equilibrium" rate of growth becomes hazy. In the following simplified model no attempt is made to specify an "equilibrium" rate of growth.

We begin with the ordinary regional accounts equation:

$$Y_t = C_t + I_t + E_t - M_{c_t} - M_{k_t} \tag{1}$$

where $Y_t$ = income, $C_t$ = consumption, $I_t$ = investment, $M_{c_t}$ = imports of consumer goods, $E_t$ = exports net of imports of goods used in export production (= local value added), and $M_{k_t}$ = imports of capital goods used in the production of regionally purchased output, all at time $t$.

Consumption is a homogeneous function with slope = $b$.

$$C_t = bY_{t-1} \tag{2}$$

Imports of consumption goods are a constant fraction of consumption.

$$M_{c_t} = cC_t \tag{3}$$

Exports are autonomous.

$$E_t(\text{autonomous}) \tag{4}$$

Domestic investment is induced by the change in consumption net of imports of consumer goods, and the change in exports. (Investment should be a function of the change in income rather than consumption, but the simplification is permissible here.)

$$I_t = K[(C_t - C_{t-1} - M_{c_t} + M_{c_{t-1}}) + (E_t - E_{t-1})] \qquad (5)$$

Substituting (2) into (5) we get

$$I_t = K[b(1-c)Y_{t-1} - b(1-c)Y_{t-2} + E_t - E_{t-1}] \qquad (5a)$$

Imports of capital goods are a constant fraction of investment.

$$M_{k_t} = mI_t \qquad (6)$$

Substituting (2), (3), (4), (5a), and (6) into (1) we get:

$$Y_t = E_t + (1-m)K(E_t - E_{t-1}) + b(1-c)[1 + (1-m)K]Y_{t-1} \qquad (1a)$$

$$- [b(1-c)(1-m)K]Y_{t-2}$$

Solving (1a) we arrive at the general difference equation of regional income.[5]

$$Y_t = \frac{E_t}{1 - b(1-c)} + \frac{K(1-m)}{1 - b(1-c)} (E_t - E_{t-1}) + a_1(x_1)^t + a_2(x_2)^t \qquad (7)$$

## 3.  CONCLUSIONS FROM THE MODEL

Conclusions from the model can be developed verbally without becoming involved in the mathematical manipulation. The first four equations formulate familiar regional income relations—a regional income identity, a propensity to consume, a propensity to import, and autonomous exports. This part of the model indicates that as exports increase or decrease regional income will increase or decrease by some multiple where the traditional multiplier is reduced by the import leakage. Equation (5) formulates investment as a function of changes in consumption, and (6) of the propensity to import investment goods. These two relations specify the amount of investment in capital facilities required to produce any increase in consumption or exports and the amount of capital goods that would be imported. From Equation (1) we see that investment is a component of regional income. Following the logic of period analysis, an autonomous

5. For an excellent introduction to difference equations and growth models, see Baumol [1; Part 5].

increase in exports requires an increase in investment, which results in an increase in income; and via the consumption multiplier, Equations (1) and (2), it has a multiple effect on income. The increase in income induces further investment in the following period, Equation (5) again, and through this effect (the accelerator) the initial autonomous increase in exports generates an increase in income greater than just the multiplier. It is intuitively plausible that the autonomous increase in exports could set off a period of induced growth where investment increases income, increases in income induce investment, and so on.

Combining all the equations in (1a) gives a statement of current period income as a function of exports, changes in exports, and lagged income. Thus, income could be derived by periods from this statement, given exports by periods and initial income magnitudes, $Y_{t-1}$ and $Y_{t-2}$. The solution statement (7) derives income for *any* period as a function of initial conditions, autonomous exports, and parameter values. Using the solution equation for the regional model, we can follow well-defined paths of analysis by Samuelson [10], Hicks [4], Baumol [1], and other eminent growth theorists.

The growth path of regional income is composed of two factors: first, the autonomous growth path described by the first two elements of Equation (7) and second, the endogenous "self-sustaining" path described by the last two elements of Equation (7). The first element of Equation (7) is the familiar export multiplier, and the second element formulates the accelerator–multiplier effect on income due to incremental changes in exports. The last two elements are left in a general form where $x_1$ and $x_2$ are roots of the quadratic equation and $a_1$ and $a_2$ are constants depending on the parameters $b$, $K$, $c$, $m$ and initial conditions, i.e., $Y_0$, $Y_1$. The question now is this: will the regional economy follow a growth path prescribed exclusively by the autonomous factors, the first two elements, or will it be capable of sustaining a path greater than this, as prescribed by the last two elements?

Since $a_1$ and $a_2$ are positive constants, elementary algebraic operations indicate the last two elements will show positive growth only when the roots $x_1$ and $x_2$ are greater than unity. The solution for the roots is obtained in terms of the parameters, so the conditions for positive growth can be derived from them. Samuelson [10] has shown, in terms of our notation, that the relation $b' \geqq 4K/(1+K)^2$ for relatively large values of $b$ and $K$ (for example, if we restrict $b \leqq 1$, then $K$ must always be greater than $l$) delineates parameter values for positive growth.[6] We can see from this relation that as $K$ gets larger $b$ can

---

6. In Samuelson's model the counterpart to equation (1a) is: $Y_t = [1+\alpha]1+\beta Y_{t-1} - \alpha\beta Y_{t-2}$ and the solution reads: $Y_t = 1/(1-\alpha) + a_1(x_1)^t + a_2(x_2)^t$. The autonomous

get smaller and still maintain equality. However, this requires fairly large values, *e.g.*, with $b = .60$, $K$ must equal 4.5. If we now introduce our import leaks, the relation becomes $b(1-c) \geqq 4K(1-m)/[1+K(1-m)]^2$ and consequently $b$ and $K$ must be correspondingly larger. In the above example, if $c = m = .5$, then $b$ must be 1.2 and $K = 9$, which is obviously unrealistic.

The intuitive "gist" of this model is fairly straightforward: that regions may not be able to generate endogenous growth because income effects are leaked out to other regions. In the model the possibility of self-generating growth is posed as empirically determinable depending upon the empirical magnitude of the propensity to consume, the capital-income ratios, the proportion of capital imports, and the proportion of consumption imports.

## 4. STATES OF A REGIONAL ECONOMY

As we have seen, the first two elements of Equation (7) measure the regional income effect of autonomous growth in exports and the last two elements measure the induced investment effects, which may or may not lead to a period of endogenous regional growth. Let us examine briefly the implication of the equation for the actual behavior of a regional economy. These implications will be relevant to the traditional economic base study approach, which we will take to include the economic base ratio multiplier and the input-output multiplier.[7]

Many different states of a regional economy might be envisaged

element in his equation is 1, corresponding to the $E_t + K(1-m)(E_t - E_{t-1})$ in our equation. Since the autonomous element enters in as a component of the $a$'s, inclusions of a time variable in the autonomous part of the equation means that initial values of these variables must be specified to determine the $a$'s. Also, differing values will affect the rate of change of income due to their effect on $a$'s.

7. We imply that the first component of Equation (7), $Y_t = E_t/[1-b(1-c)]$, is an equivalent statement to $Y_t = \lambda E'_t$, where $\lambda$ is an economic base or an input-output export multiplier and $E'_t$ is gross export revenue, in contrast to $E_t$ which we have defined as local value added to exports. An intuitive proof of the equivalence of these statements can be derived from a simplified input-output model. Consider a four-sector regional economy with sectors (1) basic, (2) secondary, (3) household, and (4) export-import, where all of sector (1) output is export; (1) purchases from (2), (3), and (4); (2) purchases from (3) and (4); and (3) purchases from (2) and (4). The solution to this model reads: $X_3 = \lambda E'_t$, where $X_3$ is total income to households, $E'_t$ is gross value of exports and $\lambda = (a_{31} + a_{32})/1 - a_{23}a_{32}$ ($a_{ij}$'s are input-output coefficients). The expression $1 - a_{23}a_{32}$ is equal to the Equation (7) term $[1-b(1-c)]$ or it is one minus the propensity to consume local goods. The expression $(a_{31} + a_{21}a_{32})$ is the total regional income generated by one dollar of exports, so that $E'$ times the expression gives the total net income from exports, which equals $E_t$ of Equation (7). Thus, $\lambda E'_t = E_t/[1-b(1-c)]$, which is what has been implied. The input-output model in the above example was taken from Hartman [3].

in terms of Equation (7). However, three states will be examined for illustrative purposes. A regional economy could be in (1) a stationary state, (2) a state of endogenous growth, and (3) a state of export expansion, with the further condition that its parameters were of a magnitude where endogenous growth was impossible.

In state (1) Equation (7) would read

$$Y_t = E_t/[1 - b(1 - c)],$$

*i.e.*, regional income would simply be exports times the export multiplier and the remainder of the components of income would be zero. In state (2) the equation would read

$$Y_t = E_0/[1 - b(1 - c)] + a_1(x_1)^t + a_2(x_2)^t,$$

where $E_0$ is a constant and the income effect from investment in export expansion has dropped out. For state (3) the equation would read just as it is initially and, eventually, the last two elements would damp out to zero, so the equation would read

$$Y_t = E_t/[1 - b(1 - c] + K(1 - m)/[1 - b(1 - c)](E_t - E_{t-1})$$

and, thus, the longer run components of regional income would be the export multiplier and the combined multiplier-accelerator effects on the period-to-period changes in exports.

Since the economic base type multipliers are designed to estimate only the first element in Equation (7), this approach to regional income projection is potentially vulnerable to several kinds of errors, depending on the initial and terminal states of the regional economy. Obviously, if the region is in state (2) and goes through a period of endogenous growth the simple economic base type multiplier approach would be in complete error in deriving the causes of growth and the consequent projection. If the economic base type multiplier were measured from a region initially in state (1) with a projected terminal state (3), then the projection would be off by the amount of $K(1 - m)/[1 - b(1 - c)](E_t - E_{t-1})$.

The outcome of these considerations is that income for a regional economy in a state of change may contain elements of induced investment income and also income from autonomous investment. The economic base approach is one of static equilibrium, and the dynamic investment components of income are not accounted for in the estimation of multipliers nor in the projection of income. On this point it is interesting to note that economic base multipliers estimated for the same region at two different points in time may be significantly different.[8] Some of these differences are undoubtedly accounted for by both induced and autonomous investment components. For example, a region starting on a big expansion of exports may experience considerable induced investment, which then damps out. Some historical study of recent income changes for a region would give some basis for judging if investment components of income would be significant or not, *i.e.*, whether the static equilibrium condition of the base study approach were satisfied.

## 5. TWO QUESTIONS

This use of growth theory prompts two large questions that we cannot pretend to answer but which we can at least ask.

First, as previously noted, this model yields no solution to an equilibrium growth path as is found in the traditional Harrod-Domar formulations. The reason for this is very simple: equilibrium growth paths for closed economies in these models are set by an exogenous factor—the supply of savings. But it is obvious that the supply of saving in a region is endogenous. Savings flow into and out of regions quite freely in response to investment opportunities. Regions, moreover, may go into net debt or credit positions for indeterminate, but very lengthy, periods of time. There is therefore no clearly defined "warranted rate of growth" for a region. In this respect the model is more akin to the early Samuelson work than to that of Harrod, Domar, and Hicks. What endogenous factors one ought to look for and what a desirable, maintainable, growth rate of a region would be are researchable questions of extreme importance.

Secondly, and more empirically, this analysis casts serious doubt upon the suitability of a geographic region as the unit of analysis. We have seen that the more closed a region is the more likely it is to grow endogenously. Thus, the important fact about regions from this point of view is "closure." It would be a fruitful task to attempt to find closed subregions of the national economy—that is, regions that export and import the bulk of their trade to each other—and see if these subregional complexes behave in the manner predicted. This theory clearly implies that if such complexes do exist, then the aggregate economy is composed of a set of rather independently fluctuating components. It is not, of course, necessary that these

8. See reference to a study of Wichita, Kansas, in Isard [6; p. 201]. Multipliers measured for five-year periods showed considerable variation. This variation was attributed to fluctuation in employment in the aircraft industry. However, growth theory indicates there would be components of induced investment causing variation if employment (income) in the basic industry was varying.

elements be in any sense geographically contiguous. The relations between such regions—what makes them an "entity"—are trade relations. A complex made up of Colorado and California, or one of New York and Illinois, might be a more appropriate unit of analysis than geographically determined regions such as the Northeast or the Southwest. The analysis casts some doubt, for example, on the value of studies such as that of the Missouri River Basin.

## 6.  STRUCTURAL CHANGE

North[9], in his closing statement to the debate with Tiebout, correctly identified the real controversy as a question over short-term growth vs. long-term growth. North was concerned with growth over two decades; whereas Tiebout had a more abbreviated time path in mind.

Let us rephrase this long-term vs. short-term distinction in terms of Equation (7). Import-reducing activities merely raise the level of income, whereas activities that raise the rate of growth of exports raise the growth of income. If, say, an economy were growing at a zero rate and some new industry located there, the level of income would increase; but after the impact of this new industry was absorbed by the system, it would settle down to a zero growth rate. An activity that permanently raised the growth rate of exports, however, would permanently raise the growth rate of income. This conclusion is true, except in the case where the new industry so lowers $c$ or $m$ as to map the economy into explosive growth domain.

However, no model of regional growth will be adequately explanatory without a theory of structural change as implied in changing import levels. Hirschman has used the concept of a "threshold," where domestic production replaces imports, for sectors forward and backward linked to a basic industry in developing countries.[9] A threshold is a level of imports where domestic production becomes economically feasible or where basic industry output reaches a level that induces the growth of processing facilities. Implied in a threshold is a level and also a rate of growth, since the decision to locate would be an expectational one based on future capital earnings potential. Duncan [2] has arranged some empirical data to identify population concentrations that will support various kinds of service activities. He also uses the concept of a "threshold;" in this case it would be the population level to provide the market potential for the particular service activity. These data suggest that regions or trade centers may exper-

9. [5; Ch. 6].

ience considerable reduction of imports during certain stages of growth.

## 7.  CONCLUSIONS

The major conclusions of this paper concern the conditions for endogenous growth potential in a region. Some further conclusions and questions were posed. They indicate (1) that the economic base type approach to regional growth theory may be completely in error if actual regions exist where endogenous growth is possible; (2) that any theory of regional income determination must consider both autonomous and induced investment components; (3) that "warranted" rates of growth cannot be specified by traditional growth theory for open regions; and (4) that economic base approaches are incomplete without a theory of structural change.

## REFERENCES

1. W. J. Baumol, *Economic Dynamics* (New York: The Macmillan Company, 1964).
2. O. F. Duncan, "Service Industries and the Urban Hierarchy," *Papers and Proceedings of the Regional Science Association*, V (1959), pp. 105–120.
3. L. M. Hartman, "The Input-Output Model and Regional Water Management," *Journal of Farm Economics*, XLVII (1965), pp. 1583–1591.
4. J. R. Hicks, *A Contribution to the Theory of the Trade Cycle* (New York: Oxford University Press, 1950).
5. A. O. Hirschman, *The Strategy of Economic Development* (New Haven, Conn.: Yale University Press, 1958).
6. Walter Isard et al., *Methods of Regional Analysis* (New York: John Wiley and Sons, Inc., and M.I.T Press, 1960).
7. J. R. Meyer, "Regional Economics: A Survey," *American Economic Review*, LIII (1963), pp. 19–54.
8. D. C. North, "Location Theory and Regional Economic Growth," *Journal of Political Economy*, LXIII (1955), pp. 243–258.
9. ———. "A Reply," *Journal of Political Economy*, LXIV (1956), pp. 165–168.
10. P. A. Samuelson, "Interactions between the Multiplier Analysis and the Principle of Acceleration," *Review of Economics and Statistics*, XXII (1939), pp. 75–78.
11. C. M. Tiebout, "Exports and Regional Economic Growth," and "Rejoinder," *Journal of Political Economy*, LXIV (1959), pp. 160–164 and 169.

# PART III   DEVELOPMENT POLE THEORY

7

# Note on the Concept
# of "Growth Poles"*

C. Cassel[1] has presented the model of an economy with balanced growth and without changes in the proportions between the flows. Population grows; total production increases in the same proportion as population; the relationship between the flow of producer goods and the flow of consumer goods is constant; the propensities to consume and save, the coefficients of production and work time remain the same. Real capital increases in exact proportion to production and consumption; real income per capita remains constant; the index of the general price level and relative prices do not change. In brief, "the economy in one period is the exact replica of the economy of a preceding period; quantities are simply multiplied by a certain coefficient."[2]

Similarly, Joseph Schumpeter has constructed a growth system where, in contrast to the stationary system, population, production, and capital increase from period to period in exactly the same proportions; where products, services, and currency all follow the same course; where flows increase without changes in structure and without fluctuation.[3]

We know that static equilibrium and a stationary system are logical postulates appropriate for showing changes and for classifying types of changes. Similarly, growth without change of proportions or fluctuation (which is the precursor of contemporary modalities of balanced growth) is a tool that can be used to understand and classify the structural changes, fluctuations, and progress (eventually regress) that accompany every observable growth.

Yet not one single observable growth pattern of an economy is described by the model that has just been characterized.

*Translated by Linda Gates and Anne Marie McDermott. Perroux, François, "Note sur la Notion de 'pôle de croissance'," Economie Appliquée (1955).

1. G. Cassel, *Theoretische Sozialoekonomie* (Leipzig, Fourth Edition, 1927; First Edition, 1918).

2. J. Tinbergen and J. J. Polak, *The Dynamics of Business Cycles: A Study in Economic Fluctuations* (Chicago, 1950), p. 126, quoted by W. Kraus, "Multiplikator, Akzelerator, Wachstumsraten und Konjunkturzyklen," *Weltwirtschaftliches Archiv*, LXXIII (1954), p. 84.

3. F. Perroux, "La pensée économique de Joseph Schumpeter," (Introduction to the French translation of *Theorie der wirtschaftlichen Entwicklung*, Dalloz, 1935); "Les trois analyses de l'évolution et la recherche d'une dynamique totale chez J. Schumpeter," *Économie Appliquée* (April-June, 1951).

One of the aspects of structural change is the appearance and disappearance of industries, the variable proportion of the flow of total industrial production within these diverse industries in successive periods, and the varying rates of growth for different industries measured over one period or over successive periods.

Another aspect that shows structural changes in a national economy is the diffusion of growth of an industry, or of a group of industries. The appearance of a new industry and the growth of an existing one result initially from prices, flows, and expectations. Over longer periods of time, the products of an industry or of a group of industries are so completely transformed as sometimes to be hardly recognizable when compared to their original shape; these call for new inventions, which, in turn, give birth to new industries.

The bitter truth is this: growth does not appear everywhere at the same time; it becomes manifest at points or poles of growth, with variable intensity; it spreads through different channels, with variable terminal effects on the whole of the economy.

Examining this method of growth makes explicit and scientifically workable a view that has already been presented in several theoretical elaborations,[4] a view set forth as a result of observing countries with retarded growth,[5] yet which is equally apparent in the politics of modern states.[6]

4. J. Schumpeter explains by innovation, that is, by the creation of new industries on a broad scale, the Juglar cycle as well as the large Kondratieff cycle. J. Maurice Clark points out the role of strategic factors in the short run, and there is apparently no reason for not observing their influence in periods that include several cycles. On the contrary, it is important to distinguish between structural changes (proportionate and connected) observable in the short run (in two or four phases) and the structural changes observable over a century.

5. The method advocated is appropriate to so-called underdeveloped countries. In a number of these countries, capitalistic industries (today the centers of exploitation by oil magnates) are implanted in economies large parts of which remain at the level of the natural economy or craftsman's economy. The whole of the economy is not yet articulated by systems of prices, flows, and expectations. It becomes so articulated by the creation of several growth poles, connected by the methods of transportation, which made up little by little the substructure of the market economy. Geographical and economic isolation of the growth poles, in these cases, clearly brings to light the obstacles to the propagation of cyclical expansions and contractions which affect "imported" capitalistic industries; this isolation also shows systemic changes (types of organization) and structural changes, which permits us to describe them as the movements of a national economy.

6. The method opens the way to growth politics practiced as much by Soviet Russia as by the free world; these politics would be ill-suited to the analysis of general equilibrium or to abstract models of combinations of the global flows. We have in mind the creation of industrial poles in the Urals, in Russian Asia, as well as the politics of "industrial complexes," a recommended politics and one which has already been instituted in Africa. One of the schemas characteristic of the operation is this: a center of extraction of raw material is connected to a center of energy production and thence by communication routes to transportation and transformation centers. What was often obtained from successive foundations in the past, by projects or plans seeking

We shall consider: (1) the motor* industry and growth; (2) the complex of industries and growth; and (3) the rise of growth poles and growth of national economies.

## MOTOR INDUSTRY AND GROWTH

In observable growth over periods of time, attention is attracted by certain industries.

Sooner than others, they become developed in forms that correspond to those of modern large-scale industry: the separation of individual factors of production from each other; the concentration of capital under one single power; the technical division of labor and mechanization.

During certain periods these industries have growth rates for their own products higher than the average growth rate for industrial production and for the product of the national economy.

Their rate of growth, at first accelerated during a succession of periods, reaches a limit, after which it undergoes a relative decline.[7] Beyond the accidental reasons, there are general reasons for this rhythm. The technical progress of a new enterprise is ordinarily followed, for a time, by lesser progress. Demand for the product becomes less elastic. Speculation, if it has been sparked by the enterprise, is extinguished or lessened and moves elsewhere.

Observation of the industries that offer these characteristics poses two questions:

1. Is it possible to construct analytically the effect exercised by a motor industry on another industry?

2. How does the action of the motor industry affect the entire output of the economy?

1. Under general competitive equilibrium the optimization of output for the economy is a result of the maximization of profit for each individual firm. The profit of each individual firm is a function of its output and of its purchase of services (inputs).

their coordination experimentally, is now undertaken by the formation of a complex pole. (The amateur of lame metaphors would perhaps say: the separated parts of the motor, instead of seeking the law of their adjustment, are put together at the same time.) In any case, it is indeed a motor that we are talking about. The complex pole calls for new creation, disturbs areas, and changes the structure of the environment it brings to life.

*Editor's note: "L'industrie motrice"* signifies an industry that is a driving force in the economy.

7. Cf. the series studied by Simon Kuznets, *Secular Movements of Production and Prices* (Boston, 1930), "Retardation of Industrial Growth," Chapter IX, in *Economic Change* (New York, 1953); *Toward a Theory of Economic Growth*, contribution for the second centennial of Columbia University (1954).

Under these conditions, each firm maximizes its own profit by appropriate decisions, taking account of the price, which is the only indicator by which the firm's decisions are related to those of other firms; firms are interdependent through price alone.

The situation is quite different where the profit of a firm is a function of its output, of its inputs, and of the output and inputs of another firm.[8] In this second situation, the two firms are no longer connected to each other by price alone; they are also connected by output and inputs; that is, because these elements depend on technique and its changes, the firms are connected by the technique used by each of the firms and their changes.

That is one of the recent definitions of *external economies*.

If we compare an industry to a firm, what has been said of the interrelations between firms can also be said of the interrelations between industries. If we eliminate the concept of industry and retain only a group of firms, the application of external economies is immediate.

Profits, instead of being formed by decisions of each firm relative to its output and input, are *induced* by the output and input of another firm. Insofar as profit is the driving force of capitalistic expansion and growth, the impetus no longer results from research and from the acquisition of profit by each individual firm, which is connected to others by price alone, but rather from research and the acquisition of profit by individual firms, each of which experiences the consequences of the level of output, of the level of input, and of techniques practiced by the others. Thus non-Paretian relationships are introduced.

This change suggests two important consequences for an understanding of growth: (1) It shows how short-term expansion and long-term growth of large groups of firms can be brought about.[9] (2) It points out the difference between the type of investment whose volume and nature are determined according to the potential revenue obtained by a single firm that does the investing and the investment whose volume and nature are or would be determined by taking into account profits and other secondary advantages.[10, 11]

8. Tibor Scitovsky, "Two Concepts of External Economies," *Journal of Political Economy* (April, 1954), p. 143 ff.

9. Growth of an industry (Scitovsky, *ibid.*, p. 149) can induce profits: — in industry B, which buys products produced by industry A; — in industry C, whose product is complementary to the product of industry A; — in industry D, whose product is a substitute for the products used by industry A; — in industry E, whose product is consumed by individuals whose incomes are augmented by the growth of industry A.

10. According to the general theory of the balance of small units in a system of complete competition, the optimum investment is realizable only if each unit can make additional investments that are perfectly divisible. Only on this condition can the investor balance the marginal return and the marginal cost of the additional invest-

2. How does the action of the motor industry affect the entire output of the economy?

The birth of a new industry is always the fruit of expectation. An agent or several agents present a brand-new situation to each other; they deem it possible; they assume the risks of its realization. The project depends on the scope of their economic horizon,[12] and is made precise in a plan, or more exactly in several alternative plans, which are subject to corrections in the course of subsequent periods. To the extent that these plans are, or become, compatible with the plans of the other agents[13] in a group, expectation becomes creative.

If all the factors used were idle and if creation imposed no loss to any other sector, the product of the industry would effect a clear increase in the entire output of the economy over the course of the preceding phase.

If all the factors used in the growth process are furnished by means of "replacement," with amortized resources being replaced by more productive funds, work forces being withdrawn to make way for qualitatively superior work forces, and no loss being imposed otherwise on the sectors foreign to the ones in which the replacement is being effected, the entire output of the economy still experiences a clear increase.

If a function of the factors used is taken from pre-existing systems with losses of productivity in certain of their sectors, the net increase in total output is the algebraic sum of the gains and losses in productivity.

Once the new industry is introduced into the economy its action on total output, from period to period, can be followed analytically by distinguishing: 1) its own participation in total output (the dimension

ment; and—the conditions of divisibility being realized for all the other variables upon which he must base his decision—only thus can he equalize his marginal cost and the price. We know quite well that today the condition of perfect divisibility is not met. It may be a question of a private investor (for an additional blast-furnace) or a public investor (for a canal, a railroad, or a bridge). In any case, if he applied the general theory of equilibrium, the investor would abstain or act irrationally from the economic standpoint. It is said that he does not abstain and that his decision, though irrational from the point of view of individual income, can be very rational with respect to collective productivity. So it is every time that profits induced in a network are added to the profits of that network or used to compensate for the network's own losses. (One might say, by way of generalization, that this happens each time that advantages induced in a whole are added to the advantages in a particular sector or used to compensate for the losses in that sector.)

In observable growth periods, investors act, indeed, as if the theory of general equilibrium of micro-units were strict and incomplete, and their attitude is often justified economically with regard to the system and with a dynamic outlook for the succession of events.

11. Scitovsky, *ibid.*
12. Number of variables, length of expectation.
13. Producers and consumers.

of its product in the total output); and 2) the supplementary product which, from period to period, it induces in its environment. Because a new industry does not generally appear alone and expansion in new industries in fact overlaps, the increase in the total output is a function: a) of the levels of the additional products themselves of the new industries taken as a whole; and b) of the levels of the additional products induced by the new industries taken as a whole.[14]

Yet these connections viewed retroactively through output, input, and technique are not sufficient to account for the historically observed facts. The appearance of one or of several industries changes the "atmosphere" of a period and creates a "climate" conducive to growth and progress. These are metaphors, words; however, they indicate significant links, which can be submitted for analysis. Innovation introduces different and supplementary variables into the economic horizon and the plans of the agents and groups of dynamic agents: it has a destabilizing effect. Innovation well-executed by certain agents serves as a valuable example for others and gives rise to imitations, which are themselves creative. Finally, successful innovation, in giving rise to a surplus of inequalities among the agents who are aware both of each other's activities and of the results of these activities, intensifies their will for *relative* gain and *relative* power.

Since each dynamic economic balance is connected to a dynamic social balance, an accumulation of disturbances in the first has repercussions in the second. Innovations in the workings of the economy call for innovations in the structure of the economy; more precisely, changes in the technical and economic characters of *functions* give rise to changes in the juridical and political characters of the *institutions*. Because these influences are not exercised uniquely, nor even retrospectively, in these sequential relationships, a unique, constant, and necessary sense is not found. In the course of a period, face to face with a constellation of innovations, all the agents capable of creative expectations are stimulated and involved. It may concern a determined series of operations during a relatively short period: it is "canal fever," "railroad fever," or "gold fever." Or it may be a question of a large number of new operations, even if the diffusion of their complete effect is slow or very slow: these are (to use the usual expressions which we now know to be imperfect) "industrial revolutions" or "agricultural revolutions."

The analysis, it will have been observed, although giving ear to the central intuition where innovation and routine are opposed, is very different from the analysis offered us by J. Schumpeter. Schum-

14. The effects of condensation of industrial creations and transformations become intelligible over a period of time.

peter concentrates his attention unilaterally on the role of private entrepreneurs, and especially on the role of the big private entrepreneurs; but public powers and their enterprises can no more be forgotten than the small innovations of adjustment. Schumpeter bases his reasoning on a stable stationary equilibrium whose observable analog would be furnished by cyclical contraction in a country with developed capitalism or by stagnation of the economies anterior to capitalism. The analysis supported here, however, admits fundamentally that there is *no real situation* to which the stable stationary equilibrium corresponds and that a stable stationary equilibrium is only a device for marking and classifying changes and instabilities. Finally, Schumpeter elaborates on his theory for a system of complete or nearly complete competition; the analysis at hand integrates the numerous forms of monopolistic competition in the largest sense of the word (monopolies, oligopolies, and combinations of the two).

The analysis thus opens to the concept of the cluster of industries.

## THE CLUSTER OF INDUSTRIES AND GROWTH

In saying "cluster of industries," we do not have in mind simply the presence of several industries in communication with each other through Paretian or non-Paretian connections; we want to introduce three elements into the analysis: (1) the key industry; (2) the non-competitive system of the cluster; (3) the occurrence of territorial agglomeration.

1. Here is an industry that has the quality, when it increases its output (and productive inputs), of increasing the output (and inputs) of another or of several other industries. Let us, for the moment, call the first the motor industry, and the second the affected industry (or industries).[15]

The motor industry can increase its output in order to put its fixed capital to the best and greatest use, that is, in order to operate at increasingly lower points on its cost curves. When it has attained its optimum output, if it is not a monopolist that maintains its price, it can proceed to new reductions of price, which will induce new increases of output in the affected industries. It is in the motor industry's interest to do precisely that, if account is taken of the consequences that such an increase of output and price reduction will provoke. The increase of output by motor industries can thus result from the anticipation of the effects engendered on the affected industries, or, if there was any hesitation or sluggishness on the part of

15. We retain here only the effects which have just been defined.

the heads of the motor industries, from encouragement given by the state, in the form of subsidy, for example.

The quality that we have examined exists in variable degrees from one motor industry to the next: let us call the key industry the one that induces in the totality of a system, such as, for example, a national economy, an increase in total output much greater than the increase in its own output.

That is to say, we cannot draw up once and for all a list of key industries according to their technical and exterior characteristics. Industries that produce multiple complements, such as raw materials, energy, and transportation, are surely cut out to become key industries, but in order for them to take on this character, other conditions must also be met.

The key industry concept, essentially relative, is a tool of analysis which, in each concrete case, calls for the precise definition of the affected system, of the period considered, and of the connection between the motor industry and the affected industry. The decisive factor is that in every structure of an articulated economy[16] there exist industries that constitute privileged points of application of the forces or dynamics of growth. When these forces bring about an increase in the output of a key industry, they bring about a powerful expansion and growth of a larger system.

2. Often, the system of the cluster of industries is by itself "destabilizing," because it is a combination of oligopolistic forms.

We are familiar with numerous types of industrial systems which, even when their static equilibrium can be constructed theoretically, appear very unconvincingly stable when one considers them in an active state and under conditions not too far removed from reality.

Partial monopoly can very convincingly impose an agreement on small satellite firms or participate in them by using its accumulated reserves. The duopolist that has large capacity and low cost can act likewise toward a duopolist with weak capacity and high prices. In the tacit agreement, the parties' respective positions are not determined once and for all, any more than they would be in a group formed around a leader. Oligopolistic struggle, conflicts of elimination, conflicts with the intent to subordinate one party to another, and eventual agreement are all possible and, in fact, frequently observed consequences of these situations. The "destabilizing" effect of each of these systems taken by itself is a practice in growth when, over a long period, the dominant firm increases the productivity of the industry and realizes an accumulation of efficient capital greater than that which

16. Where the systems of flow, price, and expectations are developed.

would have resulted from an industry subjected to a more competitive system.

Still these industrial systems do not by themselves reveal the instability of a cluster of industries each of which is in an oligopolistic system and acts as both supplier and consumer to each other.[17] Let us imagine the relationship between an industry producing a raw material in a system of partial monopoly and of an industry that produces steel in a system of partial monopoly, the latter habitually absorbing most of the product of the former. Let us attach these industries to transport industries benefiting from a monopoly and to a state which, by its purchases as well as by its interventions, exercises an effect on the preceding industries. We arrive at a rich collection of indeterminates and of dynamic instabilities of prices and quantities. Even if a regulating politic is pursued by the big firms, groups, and public powers, modifications of the juncture and of the relationship of forces give rise to changes. The conflict or cooperation in the projects of large units and of their groups as coordinated and arbitrated by the state acts directly on prices, output, and inputs.

It is the action resulting from these forces that brings about the expansion and growth of the affected systems.

3. Territorial agglomeration adds its specific consequences to the nature of the activity (key industries) and to the noncompetitive systems of the cluster.[18]

In a complex industrial pole that is geographically agglomerated and in a period of growth, one notes the effects of an intensification of economic activities because of proximity and human contacts. Industrial urban agglomeration produces consumers whose consumption patterns are diversified and progressive compared with those of rural agricultural environments. Collective needs (housing, transportation, public services) emerge and become affiliated. Location incomes are added to business profits. In the course of production, types of producers arise, such as entrepreneurs and qualified workers; industrial frameworks are formed; they influence each other, create their individual traditions, and eventually participate in a collective spirit.

To these effects of intensification are added the effects of interregional disparities. The complex industrial pole, geographically agglomerated, modifies not only its immediate geographical environment but, if it is sufficiently powerful, the entire structure of the

17. *Cf.* François Perroux, *Cahiers de l'I.S.E.A.*, Série D, No. 8, *Matériaux pour une analyse de la croissance économique*, Livre I, Ch. II: "Les Phénomènes dans un pole industriel: La Ruhr."

18. On all these points numerous examples concerning the Ruhr are given in the *Cahiers de l'I.S.E.A.* cited in note 17.

national economy where it is situated. As the center of accumulation and agglomeration of human resources and of fixed and definite capital, it brings into being other centers of accumulation and agglomeration of human means and fixed and definite capital. When two of these centers are brought into communication with each other by means of material and intellectual interchange, extensive changes are noted in the economic horizon and in the plans of the producers and consumers.

Growth of the market in space, when it is the result of communication between industrial poles, and more generally between activity poles, territorially agglomerated, is just the opposite of equally distributed growth. It is effected by concentration of means at growth points in space from which exchange beams then radiate; changes in technique, political vicissitudes, and trends in currents of worldwide traffic between major poles can favor or disfavor territorially agglomerated poles. The concentrations of men and of fixed and definite capital accompanied by the inflexibility of the installations and of the structures which accompanied the initial development of the pole all make their consequences felt once the decline begins; the pole which used to be an area of prosperity and growth becomes a center of stagnation.

Historians and geographers, even if they do not use the terms "motor industries" and "growth poles," are familiar with these realities. To adopt the type of analysis we are proposing would seem, therefore, to refuse several unjustified limitations imposed on us by the customary theory which gives preference to the phenomena of the market and price.

Once this new analysis is adopted, the history of national economies and the theory of their development must be taken up again from their origin. We will confine ourselves here to pointing out only the most general consequences of the change of perspective.

## GROWTH OF THE POLES AND GROWTH OF NATIONAL ECONOMIES

The national economy in growth no longer seems to us merely like a politically organized territory on which a population lives, nor like a group of factors of production whose mobility is nonexistent at the borders.

The national economy presents itself to us as a combination of relatively active systems (motor industries, poles of geographically agglomerated industries and activities) and of relatively passive industries (affected industries, regions dependent on geographically agglomerated poles). The first induces the phenomena of growth on the second.

The changes henceforth imposed in order to evaluate the comparative *dimensions* or *economic power* of nations are evident. But two consequences fundamental to the analysis of economic growth must be pointed out.

1. There is today (and there was previously under other forms) a conflict between the economic areas of large economic units (firms, industries, poles) and the politically organized areas of the national states. The first do not coincide with the second; their growth depends on imports, exports, supply centers, and markets outside the national territory. Because large economic units are the instruments of prosperity and consequently the arms of power for the national state, there is frequently a combination of private and public power in the administration of these large units; a struggle between these large capitalistic and "national" units on a global scale results in forms of imperialism both private and political, exercised by nations that are economically "real" and "active" upon nations that are economically "apparent" and relatively "passive."[19] The Marxist dialectic which points out the conflict of the forces of production and the institutional forms captures part of the attention we ought to devote to another dialectic also active in the modern world, which is defined by the conflict of areas of growth engendered by growth poles and politically organized territorial areas.

2. As long as national and nationalistic politics continue to exist in a world where they are surpassed by technique and by the deployment of economic life, waste is fostered, which constitutes a curb on growth, even in the absence of violent conflicts. Each state is forced to exploit, for the exclusive or principal benefit of its own nation, those poles which it disposes of in its own territory and those which it has acquired outside its boundaries. The state uses part of the limited means at its disposal in manpower, real capital, and monetary capital in order to exclude its partners from the advantages it claims to derive from the exclusive possession of growth poles.[20] From this action spring the struggles of quasipublic oligopolies that can threaten prosperity and peace. The elimination or reduction of these practices is not the least of the numerous advantages of a politics of harmonious growth on a global scale.

19. *Cf.* Maurice Bye, "La grande unité interterritoriale et ses plans," *Cahiers de l'I.S.E.A.*, Série F, No. 2 (1955).
20. Or strategic junctions of traffic.

# Interregional and International Transmission of Economic Growth

## "GROWING POINTS" AND LAGGING REGIONS

To complete our survey of inducement mechanisms, we shall examine in this chapter how growth can be communicated from one region or one country to another. In this inquiry we may take it for granted that economic progress does not appear everywhere at the same time and that once it has appeared, powerful forces make for a spatial concentration of economic growth around the initial starting points. Why substantial gains may be reaped from overcoming the "friction of space"[1] through agglomeration has been analyzed in detail by the economic theory of location. In addition to the locational advantages offered by *existing* settlements others come from nearness to a *growing* center where an "industrial atmosphere" has come into being with its special receptivity to innovations and enterprise. It was largely the observation of the latter connections that suggested to Marshall the concept of external economies.[2]

Whatever the reason, there can be little doubt that an economy, to lift itself to higher income levels, must and will first develop within itself one or several regional centers of economic strength. This need for the emergence of "growing points" or "growth poles"[3] in the course of the development process means that international and inter-regional inequality of growth is an inevitable concomitant and condi-tion of growth itself.

1. This term was used by Robert M. Haig in "Toward an Understanding of the Metropolis," *Quarterly Journal of Economics*, LX (1926), pp. 184–5.

2. A good survey of Marshall's views and of other contributions to this subject is in Eric A. Lampard, "The History of Cities in the Economically Advanced Areas," *Economic Development and Cultural Change*, III (Jan., 1955), pp. 81–137, particularly pp. 92–101.

3. "Pôle de croissance" is the term used for both regional and sectoral growth leadership in the expanding and instructive French literature on the subject. See for example F. Perroux, "Note sur la notion de 'pôle de croissance'", *Matériaux pour une analyse de la croissance économique*, Cahiers de l'Institut de Science Economique Appliquée, Série D, No. 8 (1955) [Selection 7 in this volume]; J. R. Boudeville, "Contribu-tion à l'étude des pôles de croissance brésiliens," Cahiers, Série F, No. 10 (1957).

*Hirschman, Albert O., "Interregional and International Transmission of Economic Growth" as found in* The Strategy of Economic Development *(New Haven, Conn.: Yale University Press, 1958), pp. 183–201.*

Thus, in the geographical sense, growth is necessarily unbalanced. However, while the regional setting reveals unbalanced growth at its most obvious, it perhaps does not show it at its best. In analyzing the process of unbalanced growth, we could always show that an advance at one point sets up pressures, tensions, and compulsions toward growth at subsequent points. But if all of these points fall within the same privileged growth space, the forces that make for transmission of growth from one country, one region, or one group of persons to another will be singularly weak.

The ability and tendency of growth to round itself out for a long time within some subgroup, region, or country while backwardness retains its hold elsewhere has often been noted. If the tendency manifests itself along clearly marked geographic lines, the result is the division of the world into developed and underdeveloped countries and the split of a country into progressive and backward regions. On the other hand, progress and tradition may dwell in close spatial proximity simply by fastening on different human groups and economic activities that exist side by side; this state of affairs, often encountered in developing countries, has been aptly termed "dualism" and has already been examined in our earlier analysis of the industrialization process.

With respect to different social or income groups a similar phenomenon may be noted: once one group has shown its readiness to acquire new wants and its ability to afford the products satisfying them, it will be catered to by a multitude of firms all tailoring their output to the type of per capita buying power and to the size of the market that have been revealed. It takes innovators like Ford and Giannini to strike out beyond this charmed circle, just as it seems to take a special kind of boldness to establish a new basic industry or to perceive the development potentials of the more backward regions of a developing country.

Thus investors spend a long time mopping up all the opportunities around some "growth poles" and neglect those that may have arisen or could be made to arise elsewhere. What appears to happen is that *the external economies due to the poles, though real, are consistently overestimated by the economic operators.*

The reason for this tendency—perhaps implicit in the phrase "nothing succeeds like success"—must be sought in the realm of social psychology. The progressive sectors and regions of an underdeveloped economy are easily overimpressed with their own rate of development. At the same time, they set themselves apart from the less progressive operators by creating a picture of the latter as lazy, bungling, intriguing, and generally hopeless. There seems to be a cliquishness about progress when it first appears that recalls the same phenomenon among adolescents: the girls who menstruate and the boys who shave have an acute sense of their superiority over those who cannot yet claim such achievements. The tendency to magnify the distance that separates one group or region from another shows up in the derogatory use of the term "indio" in some Latin American countries to designate whoever is economically or socially one's inferior. Similarly, the average Italian, in whose country economic progress has long been closely associated with latitude, is always ready to declare that Africa begins just south of his own province.

Thus the successful groups and regions will widely and extravagantly proclaim their superiority over the rest of their country and their countrymen. It is interesting to note that to some extent these claims are self-enforcing. Even though the initial success of these groups may often be due to sheer luck or to environmental factors such as resource endowment, matters will not be left there. Those who have been caught by progress will always maintain that they were the ones who did the catching; they will easily convince themselves, and attempt to convince others, that their accomplishments are primarily owed to their superior moral qualities and conduct. It is precisely this self-righteousness that will tend to produce its own evidence: once these groups have spread the word that their success was due to hard work and virtuous living, they must willy-nilly live up to their own story, or at least make their children do so.[4] In other words, there is reason to think that the "Protestant ethic," instead of being the prime mover, is often implanted *ex post facto* as though to sanctify and consolidate whatever accumulation of economic power and wealth has been achieved. To the extent that this happens, a climate particularly favorable to further growth will actually come into existence in the sectors or regions that have pulled ahead, and this will confirm the economic operators in their preference for these regions and make it somewhat less irrational.

The less developed groups and regions also make unwittingly a contribution to the process which we can only sketch here. Faced with the sudden improvement in the fortunes of some of their own compatriots, they will frequently counter the claims of superiority of these *nouveaux riches* by accusing them of crass materialism, sharp practices, and disregard for the country's traditional cultural and spiritual values. While such charges are directed with particular relish at minorities, whose importance in the process of development is well recognized, purely indigenous entrepreneurial groups are by no means exempt from them. In this way these groups are, as it were,

4. Observation would seem to confirm that the behavior of second-generation businessmen is far more compulsively "businesslike" than that of the pioneer generation.

converted into minorities in their own country,[5] often estranged from the rest of their compatriots, and ostracized by the traditional elites. Such a development is particularly likely when the first stages of commercial and industrial progress are localized in a center other than the capital city. In this case, the rift between this center and the capital may well widen cumulatively over a long period of time. The very fact that the leading families of such cities as Barcelona, São Paulo, Medellín, and Guayaquil lived far away from, and often in conflict with, the centers of politics, public administration, and education made for a dogged concentration of succeeding generations on business pursuits rather than for absorption of the most talented by other careers that carry more prestige in a traditional society. This situation may again lead to a clustering of investment around the initial growing point, which is healthy for the consolidation of economic growth at its beginning but may represent irrational prejudice and clannishness at a later stage.

## TRICKLING-DOWN AND POLARIZATION EFFECTS[6]

No matter how strong and exaggerated the space preference of the economic operators, once growth takes a firm hold in one part of the national territory, it obviously sets in motion certain forces that act on the remaining parts. In examining these direct interactions, we shall call "North" the region which has been experiencing growth and "South" the one that has remained behind. This terminology is

5. A good example is supplied by the inhabitants of Antioquia, a province of Colombia. The Antioqueños have been outstandingly enterprising in bringing virgin lands under coffee cultivation and in establishing industries, mostly in their capital of Medellín. Their racial, religous, and cultural characteristics do not differentiate the Antioqueños from the other Colombians, but having taken such a prominent part in the country's development, they are *now* considered practically as a separate group; and even though it is unsupported by any evidence (see J. J. Parsons, *Antioqueño Colonization in Western Colombia* [Berkeley, 1949], p. 62), the conviction is widespread that they are really of Jewish, or at least of Basque, origin!

6. The argument of the following sections was outlined originally in my article "Investment Policies and 'Dualism' in Underdeveloped Countries," *American Economic Review*, XLVII (Sept., 1957), pp. 550-70. I now find that Gunnar Myrdal has addressed himself to similar problems in *Economic Theory and Underdeveloped Regions* (London: Gerald Duckworth & Co., Ltd., 1957), particularly in chapters 3 to 5, and has had recourse to the same conceptual tools that are employed here: his "backwash" and "spread" effects correspond exactly to my "polarization" and "trickling down" effects. Nevertheless, there are considerable differences in emphasis and conclusions. Myrdal's analysis strikes me as excessively dismal. In the first place, he fails to recognize that the emergence of growing points and therefore of differences in development between regions and between nations is inevitable and is a condition of further growth anywhere. Secondly, his preoccupation with the mechanism of cumulative causation hides from him the emergence of the strong forces making for a turning point once the movement toward North-South polarization within a country has proceeded for some

suggested by the fact that a large number of lagging areas, at least in the Northern Hemisphere, appear to be located in the southern parts of the countries to which they belong. The term "South" as used here does not include *undeveloped* — i.e., largely unsettled — areas.

The growth of the North will have a number of direct economic repercussions on the South, some favorable, others adverse. The favorable effects consist of the *trickling down* of Northern progress: by far the most important of these effects is the increase of Northern purchases and investments in the South, an increase that is sure to take place if the economies of the two regions are at all complementary. In addition, the North may absorb some of the disguised unemployed of the South and thereby raise the marginal productivity of labor and per capita consumption levels in the South.

On the other hand, several unfavorable or *polarization* effects are also likely to be at work. Comparatively inefficient, yet income-creating, Southern activities in manufacturing and exports may become depressed as a result of Northern competition. To the extent that the North industrializes along lines in which there is no Southern production, the South is also likely to make a bad bargain because it will now have to buy Northern manufactures, produced behind newly erected tariff walls, instead of similar goods previously imported from abroad at lower prices.

A most serious, and frequently observed, polarization effect consists in the kind of internal migration that may follow upon the economic advances of the North. Instead of absorbing the disguised unemployed, Northern progress may denude the South of its key technicians and managers as well as of the more enterprising young men. This type of migration may actually be undesirable not only from the point of view of the South but also from that of the country as a whole, for the loss to the South due to the departure of these men may be higher than the gain to the North. This possibility is inherent in the contact between the expanding North and the stagnant South: in the North new jobs must be manned and, at least in the skilled grades, the wage and salary scale will reflect relative scarcities and productivities; whereas in the South skilled work and better-than-average performance will often be poorly remunerated either because they are simply not recognized or because they are not

---

time. Finally, the picture he paints of international transmission of growth is also too bleak in my opinion, as he overlooks that the polarization (backwash) effects are much weaker between nations than between regions within the same country. However, I fully agree with Myrdal on the importance of political forces in effecting a North-South rapprochement within a country and on the need for the emergence of such forces on the international level to help narrow the gap between the developed and the underdeveloped countries. I have anticipated here the discussion contained in the remainder of this chapter.

valued very highly[7] or because they carry nonmonetary rewards. Thus actual pay differentials between North and South are likely to overstate considerably the real productivity differentials in the most productive and skilled grades. In addition, of course, mobility is highest in these same lines so that it becomes almost a certainty that the South will lose to the North first and foremost its more highly qualified people. And, along with skill and enterprise, what little capital the South generates is also likely to migrate northward.

In spite of this bleak picture, we would still feel confident that in the end the trickling-down effects would gain the upper hand over the polarization effects if the North had to rely to an important degree on Southern products for its own expansion. For instance, if the North specializes in manufactures and the South in primary production, the expanding demand of the North ought to stimulate Southern growth. But things may go less smoothly. It is likely, in particular, that the short-run supply elasticity is low in the South so that the terms of trade will move against the North.[8]

In this case, three possibilities arise. In the best of worlds, the rise in Southern prices would fairly soon prove effective in raising production. Another possible, though far less satisfactory, outcome would consist in the slowing down of Northern progress resulting from rising labor and material costs. But such a development is unlikely as long as the North is not entirely dependent on the South. The third possibility is therefore for the North to alter its method of procuring needed primary products. Faced with the upward trend in Southern prices and exasperated by the unreliability of Southern production, Northern operators may draw on imports from foreign areas or may replace Southern products by developing their own primary production. In this way, *checks to the trickling-down effects* may well come into play, and as a result the South could be left in a far worse backwater than before. For once the North possesses within itself a large and productive agricultural area or is able to supply its needs in primary products from abroad and through domestic synthetic production, the South will be largely cut off from beneficial contact with Northern development, while remaining exposed to the adverse polarization effects. Under these conditions—which are or were fairly typical of such backward regions as Brazil's Nordeste, Colombia's Oriente, and Italy's Mezzogiorno—the stage would be set for a prolonged split of the country into a progressive and a depressed area.

7. Even societies that actively discourage better-than-average performance are unable to abolish it altogether simply because of innate differences.
8. This situation has been fully analyzed by H. G. Johnson for the case in which a developing industrial country trades with a stagnant agricultural country; see his "Economic Expansion and International Trade," *Manchester School of Economic and Social Studies, XXIII* (May, 1955), pp. 96–101.

Eventually, economic pressures to remedy such a situation are likely to assert themselves again. Industry will become congested in Northern cities and its expansion will be hampered by the insufficient size of the home market resulting from the depressed income levels in the South. Also, economic policy makers will be impelled to take a close look at Southern development potentials whenever balance-of-payments or other supply difficulties make it clear that the country is harming itself by its failure to utilize fully its Southern resources.

In other words, if the market forces that express themselves through the trickling-down and polarization effects result in a temporary victory of the latter, deliberate economic policy will come into play to correct the situation. Actually, of course, economic policy will be an important influence throughout the process. The nature of this influence will be analyzed presently.

## THE REGIONAL DISTRIBUTION OF PUBLIC INVESTMENT

The most obvious manner in which economic policy affects the rates of growth of different parts of a country is through the regional allocation of public investments. Three principal patterns of allocation can be distinguished: dispersal, concentration on growing areas, and attempts to promote the development of backward areas.

In contrast to widespread impressions, the most pervasive tendency of governments of underdeveloped countries in making their investment decisions is not so much the obsession with one showpiece as the dispersal of funds among a large number of small projects scattered widely over the national territory.

While this pattern is *dominant* only in countries where dynamic economic growth has not yet taken hold, it can be said to exert a steady pull in practically all underdeveloped countries. The most obvious reason is that public investment decisions are easily the most political ones among the economic policy decisions taken by governments. Whether to build a road here rather than there, whether to construct a power plant that is to supply towns $A$, $B$, and $C$, rather than $D$, $E$, and $F$ — these are questions that have decisive local political impact.

Thus, as all governments regardless of their democratic character desire and need support from all sections of the country, the temptation is strong to scatter the investment effort far and wide. Disconnected roads are built at many points; small Diesel power plants and aqueducts are installed in many towns; even low-cost housing programs which should obviously concentrate on relieving critical shortages and on slum clearance in the big cities are often similarly dispersed.

More fundamentally, the tendency toward wide dispersal of investment funds may be due to what we have called the group-focused image of change, *i.e.*, to the fact that economic progress is conceived of as a force that ought to affect equally all members and sections of the community. Wherever this idea prevails, governments are unprepared and unwilling to make the choices about priorities and sequences that are the essence of development programs. When the feeling is widespread that something is wrong with even temporarily preferred treatment for some regions, the government may find it politically dangerous not to take this factor into account.

Finally, the dispersal pattern can be explained by certain shortages usually affecting underdeveloped countries. The elaboration of the many small projects into which public investment is typically split up when this pattern is dominant requires comparatively little engineering and planning talent, whereas the larger projects in electric power, transportation, or basic industry require far more such talent than is usually available to the government. This is why entirely too much has been made of the argument that development is held back not by the scarcity of funds, but by a scarcity of "bankable," *i.e.*, well-conceived and engineered, projects. The question which should come first, the project or the funds, is really of the chicken-egg variety. Obviously funds can be spent only on clearly defined projects. But without definite expectations that funds—from domestic or foreign sources—will be forthcoming, the considerable cost of engineering and economic studies and the administrative effort required to gather the necessary staff and to obtain the assistance of foreign consultants will most likely not be undertaken. The promise of foreign funds—provided the studies prove the project feasible and worthwhile—is particularly important if this effort is to be made, as a large project usually results in one region's obtaining for the time being a substantial advantage over all others. This is an investment decision which a national government may find it difficult and imprudent to make unless it has the feeling—and the excuse vis-à-vis the other regions—that international development capital is not to be had at all on other terms.

Moreover, the study and preparation of a large-scale project implies in itself—especially in countries where there is the rhetorical tradition of confusing the word with the deed and the announcement of plans with their realization—a commitment to the region that is going to be principally benefited. Governments are therefore reluctant to start such studies unless they feel reasonably sure that they will be able to "deliver." Unless they have assurances in this regard, they would be politically much better off to let sleeping projects lie.

The International Bank for Reconstruction and Development has often defended itself against charges of insufficient lending by the argument that there were not enough "bankable" projects available.[9] But in fact the Bank has frequently acted in accordance with the point of view just outlined — *i.e.*, it has helped in the preparation of such projects by virtually committing itself in advance to the financing of their foreign exchange costs, including even the cost of the preliminary engineering surveys.

In this way the availability of international development capital may make for a shift from dispersal of public investment toward concentration on a few key projects. The "demonstration effect" of similar projects undertaken in other countries also works in this direction. But the most important force opposing the tendency toward excessive dispersal of public investment is the growth pattern characteristic of rapidly developing countries. Development often begins with the sudden, vigorous, and nearly spontaneous growth of one or a few regions or urban centers, resulting in serious shortages of electric power and water supply, as well as in housing and transportation bottlenecks. Thus, urgent demands for several types of capital-intensive public investment appear and must be given the highest priority whether or not they correspond to the government's sense of distributive justice and to its pattern of regional political preference. The public investment in overhead capital in turn makes possible further growth of industry and trade in the favored areas, and this growth requires further large allocations of public investment to them.

Determined as it is by the volume of private investment and the general rise in income in the developing areas, public investment clearly plays here an "induced" role, and investment choices are often remarkably and unexpectedly obvious. It is not always easy, however, to have these obvious choices adopted, partly because of the continuing desire of governments to revert to the policy of scatter, and partly because a new pressure soon makes itself felt — namely, to accelerate development in the areas that have fallen behind.

A situation in which the bulk of public investment is continuously

9. Statements to this effect can be found in several of the Bank's annual reports; *e.g.*: "Perhaps the most striking single lesson which the Bank has learned in the course of its operations is how limited is the capacity of the underdeveloped countries to absorb capital quickly for really productive purposes .... The Bank's experience to date indicates that the Bank now has or can readily acquire sufficient resources to help finance all the sound productive projects in its member countries that will be ready for financing in the next few years, that can appropriately be financed through repayable foreign loans and that cannot attract private capital." *Fourth Annual Report* (Washington, 1948–49), pp. 8, 13.

being sucked into the comparatively developed portions of the national territory cannot in the long run be considered satisfactory by governments because of compelling considerations of equity and national cohesion. In fact, the attempt to change drastically the distribution of public investment in favor of the country's poorer sections often comes at a point that seems premature to the foreign observer or adviser for the simple reason that the more rapidly advancing sections do not strike *him* as so outstandingly prosperous. It is, however, quite understandable that the attempt should be made long before these sections have come anywhere near fully developing their potential. Moreover, the poorer sections of the country, where careers in industry and trade are not promising, often produce, for this very reason, a majority of the country's successful politicians and thereby require influential spokesmen in the councils of government.

It is possible that the transition from the second pattern — concentration of public investment on spontaneously growing areas — to the third — the attempt to ignite development in the heretofore stagnant areas through "autonomous" public investment — is facilitated by certain peculiar properties of public investment. Usually the second phase results not in a mere shift from scatter to concentration of a given investment total, but in a considerable enlargement of the total amount of funds required for public investment. These funds are secured through the introduction of new and higher taxes or through other *permanent* revenue-raising devices.

On the other hand, it is probably reasonable to assume that the need for the investment of public funds in the country's spontaneously growing areas is particularly great in the initial stages of development, as basic utilities are created and rapidly expanded. After development has proceeded for some time, the need for public investment in relation to private investment tends to decline and in any event an increased portion of public investment can be financed out of earnings of previous investments. This kind of change in the composition of investment is implicit in the term "social *overhead* capital."

As the taxation and other measures that have financed the original spurt in public investment continue to yield revenue, some funds may thus become, if not unemployed, at least less compellingly employed than previously. This is likely to be immediately sensed by the officials responsible for apportioning public investment and provides an excellent opportunity to those among them who want to change its geographic composition in favor of the less developed sections.

Thus, while public investment policy may accentuate at one stage the North-South split, it can be counted upon to stage at least an attempt to heal the split should it turn out to be prolonged. For this reason governmental intervention is particularly prevalent in the development of the backward areas within underdeveloped countries. In fact, the government will, to the best of its ability, attempt to counteract in part the polarization effects that result from the operation of market forces: to counterbalance the northward emigration of capital and talent, an even larger flow in the opposite direction will be organized; to offset the locational advantages of the North, governments may offer special tax advantages or create similar external economies in the South through public investments.

Naturally, the channeling of large-scale expenditures toward the underprivileged areas of a country contains the danger of misguided investment to a much higher degree than where spontaneous growth has already staked out fairly well the areas in which public investments are urgently required. The most obvious and least "risky" course is to endow the South with just as good a system of transportation, electric power stations, and other social overhead capital facilities as are available in the North. But we have already explained that this may not be the most efficient method of inducing growth in the South because of the weakness of its entrepreneurship and the purely "permissive" character of the inducement mechanisms set in motion by these investments. Although some investment in public utilities may be indispensable, the essential task is to endow the South with some ongoing and actively inducing economic activity of its own, in industry, agriculture, or services. For this reason, the building of a steel mill in Colombia's Oriente and the founding of the new Brazilian capital in the long neglected "interior" will probably turn out to be effective governmental development moves in spite of initial mistakes, difficulties, and setbacks.

## INTERREGIONAL AND INTERNATIONAL TRANSMISSION COMPARED

Our discussion has made it clear that the interregional transmission of growth cannot be expected to proceed smoothly. Obstructionist forces have been seen to be at work alongside those that make for integration, in the economic and political fields. It is tempting then to apply an *a fortiori* argument to the *international* transmission of growth: if interregional transmission is beset with obstacles, is it not natural to conclude that international transmission will be even more difficult?

While the disparity in the development levels of different countries would seem to support such a conclusion, it is not at all justified by the arguments we have used in demonstrating the difficulties of interregional transmission of growth. Some of these arguments rather point to the somewhat unsettling thought that the various "Souths" might be better off if they were sovereign political units, *i.e.*, that in some respects growth may be more easily transmitted from one nation to another than from one region to another within the same country. We will first explore these "economic arguments for separatism" and then show in what respects transmission mechanisms are after all more effective between regions than between sovereign countries.

**The case for separatism**   In general it may be expected that because of the closer contact and more intensive interactions that exist among regions of the same country than among sovereign nations, both trickling-down *and* polarization effects will be found to be stronger in interregional than in international economic relations.

The case for separatism will therefore consist largely in showing that the polarization effects will be far less damaging to a country than to a region. This is certainly the case for the mobility of factors of production. We have seen that within a country this mobility can be highly prejudicial for the South, and conceivably even uneconomic from the point of view of the country as a whole. If the South were an independent country, mobility would certainly be far lower and the Southern development potential would be less impaired.

Another polarization effect consisted in the debilitating influence of Northern competition on Southern economic activities satisfying domestic or export demands. Again, this effect would be virtually absent between independent countries. With respect to the latter, countries compete in international markets on the basis of comparative advantage, regions within a country on the basis of absolute advantage. Suppose that North and South, considered independently, both have a comparative advantage in cane sugar, but that production is more efficient in the North. Then, if each were an independent country, they would both specialize in sugar, with real factor returns being lower in the South. But if North and South are united in one country, sugar production would be expanded in the North and might be abandoned in the South even though the maintenance and expansion of sugar exports could represent the valuable beginning of a "growth pole" for the South.

The same reasoning holds for industrialization. It has frequently been pointed out that, if there is any substance to the various arguments for protection, they must apply just as much to a region as to a country; but the region cannot ordinarily protect its industries except through exemption from minor local taxes. Also, within a country (or in relations between a country and its colonies) Northern industrialists may often effectively prevent or delay the development of industry in the South; in relations between sovereign countries, attempts in this direction have sometimes been made, but obviously have far smaller chances of success.

Finally—and related to the previous point—the absence of economic sovereignty with respect to such matters as currency issue and exchange rate determination may be a considerable handicap for the development of a region.

The preceding argument is reminiscent of Viner's celebrated thesis that a customs union between two countries may lead to a less, rather than more, efficient allocation of resources.[10] To prove this proposition, Viner invoked only the "trade-diverting effects," *i.e.*, the possibility that the partners of a customs union will now buy from each other what they could previously obtain more cheaply— and what can be more efficiently produced—in third markets. This argument is also applicable to our problem, but the polarization effects relating to factor mobility and North-South competition in exports and industry are perhaps more important in a developmental situation.

**The case for surrender of sovereignty**   We must now come to the other half of our story. As the polarization effects will be stronger when there are no frontiers to cross, so will the trickling-down effects. The advance of the North is bound to lead to purchases and investments in the South. All complementarities that exist within a country will be readily exploited. Regional specialization patterns will emerge and are not likely to be tampered with even when they are based more on historical accident than on comparative resource endowments. Not so between sovereign countries. Here potential complementarities are likely to be taken advantage of in a far more selective and spotty fashion, not only because of the "friction of space" but because of the many other frictions that are encountered as soon as frontiers are crossed. Protectionist movements and reactions to balance-of-payments difficulties will set up strong obstacles to the emergence of a finely articulated division of labor and will always threaten it if it should arise.

The trickling-down effects will still be powerfully effective in promoting development of countries with resources that are highly prized by the industrial countries. But if a country has nothing particularly essential or attractive to offer, it may remain excluded for a long time from any important participation in world trade when,

10. Viner, *The Customs Union Issue* (New York, 1950), Ch. 4. For a systematic discussion of the issues raised by Viner, see J. E. Meade, *The Theory of Customs Unions* (Amsterdam, 1955).

as a region integrated into a larger country, it might have contributed quite nicely to interregional trade.

In our treatment of interregional transmission of growth we saw the principal danger of an emergence of a North-South problem in the low supply elasticity characteristic of the South and in the consequent loss of interdependence as the North extricated itself from dependence on Southern products in a variety of ways. In international relations these checks to the trickling-down effects are stronger, just as the trickling-down effects themselves are weaker, than in interregional relations. Within a country, the loss by the South of its markets in the North will be resisted: not entirely unselfish efforts will be made by Northern interests to help the South overcome its supply difficulties which, if unresolved, will make it necessary for the North to look elsewhere. And, as has already been pointed out, even if a temporary lapse in North-South trade occurs, such efforts are likely to be resumed whenever balance-of-payments or other supply difficulties press upon the country.

In relations between advanced and underdeveloped nations, one of the major forces making for the growth of the latter is the need of the advanced nations for certain, usually primary, products of the underdeveloped areas. But if the foreign producers for one reason or another are unable to fulfill the rapidly growing requirements of the industrial centers, they cannot expect to be treated with the same patience and periodic consideration that they would receive if they were part of the industrial countries themselves. Domestic or other foreign sources of supply will be tapped or synthetic production will be undertaken largely on the basis of economic calculations, whereas political and social considerations will importantly affect similar decisions in North-South relations and are likely to help the South retain its role as a supplier of the North.

In this fashion we are brought back to the political forces making for the transmission of growth. These forces help definitively to redress the balance of our argument away from separatism. Within a country, as we have seen, there will come a point when a determined effort will be made to pull the underdeveloped regions within that country out of their stagnation. The ultimate reason for the confidence one may have in the emergence of such an effort is the solidarity that binds different parts of a nation together and the ability of each part to make itself heard and to bring pressures to bear on the central government. In spite of much progress in recent years, international solidarity of this kind is unfortunately still in its infancy.

We conclude that, on balance, the forces making for interregional transmission of growth are likely to be more powerful than those making for international transmission.

## OPTIMAL INSTITUTIONAL ARRANGEMENTS

The reader may wonder why we examined in so much detail whether it is better for an underdeveloped area to be a region or a nation. Few areas can choose. Nevertheless, the realization that growth is transmitted more easily between nations than between regions from the point of view of some of the mechanisms we have analyzed, while the opposite holds for others, makes it tempting to think about the possibility of optimal institutional arrangements. If only we could in some respects *treat a region as though it were a country* and in some others *treat a country as though it were a region*, we would indeed get the best of both worlds and be able to create situations particularly favorable to development.[11]

Let us look first at the regions. Their advantage consisted largely in their greater exposure to the trickling-down effects and in their ability to call for help from the larger unit to which they belong. Their disadvantage seemed to lie principally in their exposure to polarization effects, in their inability to develop production for exports along lines of *comparative* advantage, and in the absence of certain potentially development-promoting policy instruments that usually come with sovereignty. A nation attempting to develop its own backward regions should therefore provide certain "equivalents of sovereignty" for these regions. The most important of such equivalents is a reaction against the feelings of despondency and self-denigration so often encountered in the South, and the mobilization of its energies through regional institutions and programs. The need for this approach has been felt in several countries where regional development corporations and banks have been set up. Effective aid to the establishment of industries in the South may call also for national income tax deductions (equivalent to tariff protection) and some autonomy in bank credit policy. To permit production to proceed on the basis of comparative advantage, Southern exports could be—and have at times been—stimulated through preferential exchange rates. Under such conditions, it might be held that imports into the South should be subject to compensating surtaxes, but this complication can be avoided on the ground that the South could satisfy many of its needs more cheaply in world markets if it were not prevented from doing so by the protection of Northern industries.

It is in line with our analysis that a policy of closing the gap between the South and the North requires the use of instruments that

11. We assume that the areas we are talking about have a substantial untapped development potential. There are, of course, many regions and perhaps even some countries whose natural resources are so poor or depleted that their best hope lies in becoming empty spaces—or at least far emptier than they are now.

would ordinarily be thought to be disruptive of the very integration they are designed to achieve. While it is the purpose of these instruments to cut down the strength of the polarization effects, great care must be taken, of course, not to interfere with the efficacy of the trickling-down effects. Thus, the economic policies just outlined are designed to insulate the South sufficiently so that it may undertake certain industrial and export activities in competition with the North; but, at the same time, the complementary relationships that make the South a supplier of the North must be preserved and intensified.

For *international* transmission of growth, the optimal institutional arrangements would be of the opposite kind. The task here is to keep the polarization effects as weak as they normally are among independent nations, but to increase the strength of the trickling-down effects. In other words, the underdeveloped countries ought to retain the developmental advantages of sovereignty: obstacles to the emigration of skills and capital and a measure of independence in tariff, monetary, and foreign exchange policy. At the same time, they must be more closely integrated into the world economy through arrangements that make for more rapid growth and greater stability in their export markets. In addition, their development could of course be greatly accelerated if the community of nations disposed of a political mechanism similar to the one that within a nation makes eventually for a redistribution of public investment funds in favor of the South.

The world is already groping for formulas that would combine in this way the advantages of sovereignty with those of integration.[12] For the time being, these efforts are largely the incidental results of a struggle for power. Yet it is obvious that they would be intensified rather than abandoned if this struggle were to cease tomorrow. It seems a pity, therefore, that we in the United States insist so loudly that the bold and pioneering steps we are taking to help the underdeveloped countries are dictated by military necessity or are "straightforward business transactions."[13] Must we thus pave with apologies the road to what can be one of mankind's highest achievements? But perhaps it is inevitable that progress along this road should be reluctant. For, as Bergson has said, "the moral, original and fundamental structure of man is made for simple and closed societies... man outwits nature when from the solidarity of these societies he steps into human fraternity."[14]

12. Attempts of sovereign countries to assess themselves for costs incurred in joint programs are reviewed in Thomas C. Schelling, *International Cost-Sharing Arrangements*, Essays in International Finance No. 24 (Princeton, 1955).

13. Gunnar Myrdal makes some interesting observations on this point in *An International Economy* (New York, 1956), Ch. 9.

14. *Les deux sources de la morale et de la religion* (Paris, 1934), pp. 53–4.

NILES M. HANSEN

# Development Pole Theory in a
# Regional Context

## I. INTRODUCTION

Economic analysis generally has tended to emphasize how much of a given resource should be allocated to a given end while neglecting the related issue of where the activity in question shall be located. Nevertheless, as Friedmann and Alonso have pointed out, the decision of *where* to locate a new project is as important as the decision to invest in it. The questions of social justice in the distributions of the fruits of economic development are as important and as difficult in terms of regions as in terms of social classes.[1]

One of the principal difficulties in applying economic analysis to spatial aspects of public policy has been the highly simplified and abstract nature of the purely deductive models of classical location theory.[2] For example, the classical framework assumes that all activities are located on a smooth undifferentiated surface; all considerations of geographic terrain are eliminated. It is further assumed that a transport surface exists, such that costs of moving a good are constant for any given distance in any direction. Transport facilities in all directions, distribution of agricultural population, tastes and scales of preferences, industrial raw materials, technical knowledge, and availability of production opportunities are uniform over the surface. Within this framework activities are allocated by means of purely market forces. Unfortunately, most contemporary problems of resource allocation in space necessarily involve complex urban-industrial growth patterns that are not amenable to treatment in terms of a theoretical analysis which makes such assumptions and which also abstracts from external effects. Thus, Rodwin finds that turning to the traditional theorists for guidance in regional resource allocation problems "is a disappointing experience since the assistance

1. John Friedmann and William Alonso, "Introduction," in *Regional Development and Planning*, J. Friedmann and W. Alonso, eds. (Cambridge: The MIT Press, 1964), p. 1.

2. See, for example, Johann H. von Thünen, *Der isolierte Staat in Beziehung auf Landwirtschaft und Nationalökonomie* (Hamburg: Fr. Derthes, 1826); August Lösch, *The Economics of Location*, translated by William Wolgom and W. F. Stolper (New Haven, Conn.: Yale University Press, 1954).

Hansen, Niles M., "Development Pole Theory in a Regional Context," Kyklos, XX (1967), pp. 709–725.

furnished by them on this topic is relatively meager whereas one might have expected them to be the most helpful."[3] Similarly, Bauchet has remarked that the classical approach to location "has remained liberal; it has not proposed guidelines for action."[4]

As a result of inadequacies in the traditional approach to location problems a new body of thought has emerged in recent years which centers on the notion of development poles (pôles de croissance). This concept was first put forth systematically in a well-known article by Perroux, who argued that the fundamental fact of spatial, as well as sectoral, development is that "growth does not appear everywhere and all at once; it appears in points or development poles, with variable intensities; it spreads along diverse channels and with varying terminal effects for the whole of the economy."[5] Following Perroux, Hirschman finds that for any economy to attain higher income levels it "must and will first develop within itself one or several regional centers of economic strength. This need for the emergence of growing points or growth poles in the course of the development process means that international and interregional inequality of growth is an inevitable concomitant and condition of growth itself."[6] This approach likewise is reflected in a recent British study of European regional policies:

> At any one time there will be some industries, firms or regions which, acting as "poles" of growth, are developing rapidly while others are at a standstill or declining. Conditions of decline—in an industry or in a region—may give rise to . . . a demand for state intervention. The question as to whether the state should intervene in such circumstances cannot be resolved in purely economic terms; but economic analysis can evaluate the nature of the choice.[7]

Although the development pole concept has now come into use in many countries, its relevance as an analytic device and a tool for guiding public policy decisions has continued to receive greatest attention in France. This phenomenon is no doubt largely a consequence of France's unique efforts to create a comprehensive and

3. Lloyd Rodwin, "Choosing Regions for Development," in C. J. Friedrich and S. Harris, eds., *Public Policy*, XII (1963), p. 149.

4. Pierre Bauchet, "La comptabilité économique régionale et son usage," *Economie appliquée*, XIV (January, 1961), p. 69.

5. François Perroux, 'La notion de pôle de croissance," *L'économie du XX$^{ème}$ siècle*, 2nd ed. (Paris: Presses Universitaires de France, 1964), p. 143. This article originally appeared in *Economie appliquée*, Nos. 1–2 (1955).

6. Albert O. Hirschman, *The Strategy of Economic Development* (New Haven, Conn.: Yale University Press, 1958), pp. 183–4 [Selection 8 of this volume].

7. Political and Economic Planning, *Regional Development in the European Economic Community* (London: Political and Economic Planning, 1962), p. 13. The development pole concept is also prominent in relevant policy studies of the European Economic Community. See, for example, *La politique régionale dans la Communauté Economique Européenne* (Brussels: Communauté Economique Européenne, 1964), pp. 46, 73.

coherent set of regional planning institutions (including the 21 "program regions" and their respective *préfets* and regional economic development commissions) and to regionalize the annual budget of the central government. In fact, "up to the present France is the only European state which has undertaken to create regional institutions on an economic base."[8] It is now generally accepted in France, as elsewhere, that the central government has the possibility "to create the bases for equilibrium growth throughout the country . . . by means of public intervention," as well as the means to bring about "a balanced division of economic activity among regions."[9] Unfortunately, these very general aims are not in themselves adequate as policy guidelines because one must specify more carefully what is meant by "equilibrium growth" throughout a country and a "balanced distribution of economic activity." Of course, value judgments concerning more specific variables such as regional income, migration, and public investment patterns must to a great extent be taken by the economist as given. Nevertheless, consideration of these issues requires considerable refinement of the highly general notion of a development pole. It is the purpose of this article, therefore, to examine the often ambiguous uses which have been made of this concept, and to evaluate its strengths and weaknesses as a tool of economic analysis.

## II. DEVELOPMENT POLES AND ECONOMIC SPACE

Although the theory of development poles may be useful in examining and comparing differing consequences of alternative choices of location, it is not in itself strictly speaking a theory of location. Thus, a development pole is not equivalent to a key industry, an economic base, an industrial zone, or even some geographically concentrated phenomenon. Rather, it should be interpreted in its essentially economic and functional sense.[10] To fully appreciate this perspective it is necessary to place Perroux's original article on development poles in the context of his somewhat earlier work on economic space.

8. J. F. Gravier, *L'aménagement du territoire et l'avenir des régions françaises* (Paris: Flammarion, 1964), p. 127. Unfortunately, detailed consideration of these institutions is beyond the scope of the present article. In this regard, however, there exist a number of good sources. See, for example, Jacques de Lanversin, *L'aménagement du territoire* (Paris: Librairies Techniques, 1965), and Olivier Guichard, *Aménager la France* (Paris: Laffont-Gonthier, 1965).

9. P. Pottier, "Axes de communication et théorie de développement," *Revue économique,* XIV (January, 1963), p. 128.

10. Jean Paelinck, "La théorie du développement régional polarisé." *Cahiers de l'Institut de Science Economique Appliquée,* Série L, No. 15 (March, 1965), pp. 10–11.

Perroux's concept of economic space should not be confused with simple location as defined by geographical or political divisions. "A banal sense of space location creates the illusion of the coincidence of political space with economic and human space;" but by distinguishing between Euclidean and abstract space "we may distinguish in our discipline as many economic spaces as there are constituent structures of abstract relations which define each object of economic science." For Perroux, there are three types of economic space: economic space as defined by a plan, economic space as a field of forces, and economic space as a homogeneous aggregate. Moreover, in each case it is quite clear that Perroux's analysis centers on complex economic relations rather than on specifically geographical considerations. In particular, the second type, that which is most relevant in the present context, "consists of centers (or poles or foci) from which centrifugal forces emanate and to which centripetal forces are attracted. Each center, being a center of attraction and repulsion, has its proper field, which is set in the field of other centers."[11]

In contrast to Perroux's nongeographical orientation is Boudeville's emphasis on the regional character of economic space. Following Perroux, Boudeville maintains that from an economic viewpoint there are three types of space: homogeneous, polarized, and program, or planning space. Thus, in the first instance a region can be characterized by its degree of uniformity; the notion of a homogeneous region corresponds to a continuous space wherein each of the constituent parts or zones has relevant characteristics as close as possible to those of the others. In the second case a region can be studied in the light of the degree of interdependence of its diverse parts. Polarized space is closely related to the notion of a hierarchy of urban centers ranked according to the functions they perform; a polarized region is a heterogeneous space whose different parts complement and support one another, and where they have more exchange of goods and services with a dominant intraregional urban center, or pole, than with neighboring regions. Finally, a region can be envisaged from the point of view of the aims which it pursues. Thus, the planning, or program, region is a space whose various parts depend upon the same decision; in addition, it is an instrument placed in the hands of an authority, not necessarily localized in the region, to attain a given economic goal.[12] The fact that the twenty-one geographic units that have been created in France for regional

11. François Perroux, "Economic Space: Theory and Applications," *Quarterly Journal of Economics*, LXIV (February, 1950), pp. 90–7.
12. Jacques Boudeville, *Les espaces économiques* (Paris: Presses Universitaires de France, 1961), pp. 8–16.

planning purposes are termed *régions de programme* is no mere co-incidence, since government policy in this regard is generally associated with the corresponding theoretical concept. Boudeville himself has explicitly made this connection.[13] In general, then, although Boudeville (and others) adopts Perroux's terminology, he gives it a more concrete usage by maintaining that the theory of economic space "is the application of a mathematical space on or in a geographic space."[14] However, any evaluation of this approach first requires consideration of another aspect of development pole theory, namely, the concept of dominance.

## III.  ECONOMIC DOMINANCE AND THE PROCESS OF POLARIZATION

The concept of dominance, like the related concept of development poles, marks a key element in Perroux's general effort to provide a dynamic interpretation of economic activity. For Perroux, the effect of domination "consists of an irreversible or partially reversible influence exercised by one unit upon another. An economic unit exercises this effect by reason of its dimension, its negotiating strength, the nature of its activity, or because it belongs to a zone of dominant activity." The effect of domination has both a purely economic dimension, abstracted from considerations of geographic space, and a spatial dimension. At the level of the firm this effect may exist between production and consumption units, or between differing production units. Domination occurs when "a firm controls an abstract economic space, the market for a product or a service or a group of products or services." Moreover, a firm "exercising its control in one economic space exercises its influence on another economic space, either in a permanent and structural manner (a commercial bank), or in an accidental fashion (a firm becomes dominant by the presence of temporary bottlenecks)."[15] In addition, "as soon as any inequality among firms appears, the breach is opened by which the cumulative effect of domination insinuates itself."[16] Given these phenomena, it follows that the dominant, or propulsive, firm generally will be oligopolistic and large, and will exert an important influence on the activities of suppliers and clients. Moreover, in terms of geographic space dominant and propulsive industries

13. *Ibid.*, p. 16.
14. Jacques Boudeville, "Les notions d'espace et d'intégration," Paper given at the International Congress for Town and Regional Planning, Basle, Switzerland, September 22–25, 1965, p. 2.
15. Perroux, *L'économie du XXe siècle, op. cit.*, pp. 85–7.
16. *Ibid.*, p. 40.

make the agglomerations where they are located the poles of their regions.[17]

The concept of dominance does in fact have a corresponding empirical counterpart. Aujac, for example, has developed a model that orders French sectors in input-output form in such a manner that relatively large intermediate demands are situated below the principal diagonal, whereas those that are relatively weak are situated above it. This triangularization of the matrix is carried out by the criterion of the best customer. If $A_{ij}$ represents sales from industry $i$ to industry $j$ and $A_{ji}$ the converse, then $j$ is said to dominate $i$ if $(A_{ij}/P_i) > (A_{ji}/P_j)$, where $P_i$ and $P_j$ are, respectively, the total sales of $i$ and $j$. On the basis of such calculations a hierarchy is established in which each sector dominates the one that follows.[18] However, the difficulties involved in any straightforward application of the national pattern of flows on a regional level would be considerable. Depending on the number and magnitude of interregional linkages, which are certain to be very great for areas such as those of the French program regions, many interindustry linkages will pass to the "rest of the world." Links between local production and local consumption, as well as the effects of investment on employment, would require a great deal of special attention. Moreover, the prospects for effectively utilizing interregional matrices are not bright. As Rodwin has aptly remarked, "the neglect of price effects, the difficulty of getting data for these models, the vastly increased computational problems which regional breakdowns entail coupled with the egregious simplifications of industry categories and the unrealistic linearity assumptions makes one skeptical of the immediate, not to mention the long-term, usefulness of this instrument."[19] In general, then, while the notion of dominance has been given empirical verification for the structure of industry in a nation as a whole, it is not now operationally feasible to regionalize or otherwise give spatial content to the national model.

Nevertheless, the problem of analyzing the role of dominant sectors as localized development poles need not be limited to input-output techniques. Indeed, it can be argued that these would not be sufficient in any event, even if the purely technical difficulties in-

17. *Ibid.*, p. 152.
18. H. Aujac, "La hiérarchie des industries dans un tableau des échanges inter-industriels, et ses conséquences dans la mise en œuvre d'un plan national décentralisé," *Revue économique*, XI (May, 1960), pp. 169–238.
19. Rodwin, *op. cit.*, pp. 150–1. Even on a national level, "the precision of the input-output table in a medium-sized economy like France, more and more open to foreign markets, actually seems questionable." Sylvan Wickham, "French Planning: Retrospect and Prospect," *Review of Economics and Statistics*, XLV (November, 1963), p. 340.

volved in their preparation and utilization could be overcome. Input-output data are incapable in themselves of explaining the process of economic development, though they may aid in giving insights into its manifestations. Therefore, if it may be assumed that the economic development of a region generally is related to its degree of industrialization, it is necessary to examine more carefully the process of change in industrial interdependencies. Systematic study of these linkages and their evolution under different conditions is required if regional policy is to have the means for initiating and reinforcing optimal growth patterns. As Paelinck has stated, it is not enough for the economist working on regional development problems to limit analysis to "the classical interdependencies (of either the Walras or Leontief type) of economic flux, whether in quantity or in value terms. He must be able, in addition, to recognize the *technical origin* of this interdependence, which explains its ever-increasing complexity."[20]

It will be recalled that the concepts of economic space and development poles have been defined in terms of abstraction from concrete spatial location and in terms of geographical areas. The dominance of a propulsive industry has been treated similarly. Perroux's view of the growth process is consistent with this theory of economic space in that the industry remains his point of departure and the essential element in subsequent development. Aydalot has correctly maintained that while Perroux sometimes "seems to study the localization of the growth process, in fact this localization seems secondary to him" since "the primary phenomenon is 'the appearance and disappearance of industries,' 'the diffusion of the growth of an industry.'"[21]

The effects generated by a propulsive industry that qualify it as a development pole have been explored in theory by a number of writers. Some of these effects are internal to the industry itself; that is, its own growth generates increased investment, employment, and distribution of factor payments, including profits that may be retained and reinvested. The internal growth of an industry also generates numerous external effects; vertically and horizontally induced effects of course may be dealt with in the framework of input-output matrices. The effects of polarization may be further examined theoretically by the application of appropriate matrices or vectors to the initial Leontief-type matrix. Among the phenomena which have been explored in this context are the classic Keynesian multiplier based on marginal propensities to consume applied to income

20. Paelinck, *op. cit.*, p. 8.
21. Philippe Aydalot, "Note sur les économies externes et quelques notions connexes," *Revue économique*, XVI (November, 1965), p. 962.

increases, the accelerator principle in connection with change in final demand, and the interplay of prices among related sectors and enterprises.[22]

Despite some differences of emphasis, three basic characteristics of a propulsive industry (or firm) emerge from the relevant literature. First, it must be relatively large in order to assume that it will generate sufficient direct and potentially indirect effects to have a significant impact on the economy; second, it must be a relatively fast-growing sector; and third, the quantity and intensity of its interrelations with other sectors should be important so that a large number of induced effects will in fact be transmitted.

The importance of bigness, first emphasized by Perroux, has been equally stressed in subsequent writings of other scholars. Bauchet, for example, writes that the growth of an underdeveloped region depends upon the actions of large economic units. "Their mass alone is capable of starting the region on the path to economic growth."[23] Similarly, Davin maintains that "the principal poles are found in heavy, highly capitalized industry, and are the domain of large firms; it is essentially a matter of metallurgy involving special types of steel, metal manufacturing industries using the most evolved possible products, chemistry, and activities destined to furnish products for which the demand is in fundamental expansion."[24] Thus, "the multiplicity of small firms of small dimension, working in dispersed fashion, without relying on a few large firms, is not of a nature to set in motion a truly dynamic regional economy."[25] Nevertheless, as will be discussed shortly, the notion of industrial bigness is not without difficulties in this regard. On the other hand, it is reasonable to assume that a propulsive firm or industry should be rapidly growing. However, when it comes to the third criterion, that of interrelations with other sectors, several problems may be raised.

Aydalot has argued that, all things considered, the most simple definition that may be given of a propulsive industry is that it is a producer of external economies.[26] Here again, though, the question

22. See, for example, Jacques Boudeville, "La région plan," *Cahiers de l'Institut des Science Economique Appliquée*, Série L, No. 9 (October, 1961); François Perroux, "La firme motrice dans une région, et la région motrice," *ibid.*, pp. 192–241; Jean Paelinck, *op. cit.;* and Louis Davin, *Economie régionale et croissance* (Paris: Editions Génin, 1964), pp. 54–72.

23. Pierre Bauchet, *Les tableaux économiques, analyse de la région lorraine* (Paris: Editions Génin, 1955), p. 10. Another discussion of development poles maintains that in the initiation of growth in a region the role of large industrial ensembles is capital. L. E. Davin, L. Degeer and J. Paelinck, *Dynamique économique de la région liègoise* (Paris: Presses Universitaires de France, 1959), p. 156.

24. Davin, *op. cit.*, p. 56.

25. *Ibid.*, p. 64.

26. Aydalot, *op. cit.*, p. 963.

must be posed as to what kind of economic space is involved. Aydalot is quite correct in pointing out that *a priori* the concept of polarization does not imply geographic concentration. Polarization "is the process by which the growth of an economic activity termed propulsive sets in motion that of other economic activities by the channel of external economies."[27] But this process takes place in abstract economic space. Thus, although a propulsive industry certainly must have a location in geographic space, the *process* of polarization is not amenable to unambiguous geographic location.

Proceeding from his definition of the polarization process, Aydalot points out that the automobile industry is an example of a propulsive industry, and that the Régie Renault provides an example of a propulsive firm. In view of its worldwide affiliates on both input and output sides, one can say that Renault is a pole whose center is Paris and whose periphery embraces most of the world. However, this denies an autonomous spatial existence to the pole. Thus, although one may understand why Renault is an industrial pole, it is not apparent that this makes Paris a geographic pole.[28] Moreover, contrary to the approach taken by many writers, the propulsive industry is not necessarily the causal agent in the polarization process. To say that a given area constitutes a growth pole because of the agglomerating power of its propulsive industries does not explain why these industries are themselves located in this area; the spatial pole also has a causal role in the location of propulsive industries. In other words, even if propulsive industries do induce other activities, they constitute only one link in the process of industrial-geographic polarization because they too are induced. Therefore any adequate treatment of this phenomenon should take account of the pronounced tendency for industrial growth to be oriented primarily toward already industrialized areas because of the external economies which the latter generate, including a wide range of tertiary services, close proximity to buyers and suppliers, labor with necessary skills and training, and plentiful public overhead capital. Of course, this also implies that insofar as a central government has a regional policy, external economies which it provides directly (public overhead capital) or indirectly (tax and credit policy) can be used to modify economic growth along lines consistent with policy objectives.[29]

27. *Ibid.*, p. 964.
28. *Ibid.*
29. For more detailed evidence and discussion concerning these issues see the following articles by the present author: "Regional Planning in a Mixed Economy," *Southern Economic Journal*, XXXII (October, 1965), pp. 176–90; "The Structure and Determinants of Local Public Investment Expenditures," *Review of Economics and Statistics*, XLVII (May, 1965), pp. 150–62; "Unbalanced Growth and Regional Development," *Western Economic Journal*, IV (Fall, 1965), pp. 3–14; "Some Neglected Factors in

## IV. A CRITIQUE OF DEVELOPMENT POLE THEORY

One of the basic common denominators in the development pole literature is the idea that the process of economic growth has its origin and continuing stimulus as a result of big industrial undertakings, a notion that derives from the theory of dominance. Some of the more naively enthusiastic interpretations of the theory would maintain that to generate economic growth in a region it is merely necessary to establish a large firm or several large firms, preferably in a relatively fast-growing industry. The fact that bigness alone is not sufficient in this regard is well illustrated by the case of the steel industry in Lorraine. The development of this industry was not accompanied by a corresponding development of industries consuming steel. As a result, Lorraine became highly dependent upon exterior sources of supply for machinery and other equipment. Despite the existence of coal mines, energy sources, transportation facilities, and markets in close proximity to the steel complex, it would appear on the basis of input-output data that only a very small part of regional steel output was consumed in the region. Thus, there exists the paradox of relatively weakly developed industry existing side by side with conditions highly favorable to industrial location.[30] As Paelinck has emphasized, "the facts do not indicate that one may consider any isolated industrial implantation as a necessarily efficient development pole, by which effective polarization relations, technical or otherwise, are produced."[31]

The type of development that characterized the Lyon region provides a striking contrast to the experience in Lorraine:

> Parting from an economy based essentially on textiles, the Lyon region progressively developed the construction of machines for the textile industry (a derived pole) and, by induction, specialized mechanical and foundry sectors (lateral pole). At the same time, there developed an industry producing chemical products for the textile industry, which in turn stimulated the chemical sector in general; the latter became a lateral development pole of the greatest importance for the region.[32]

It should be pointed out, however, that even where the complexity of the functional conditions for successful implantation of a potentially propulsive industry are fully appreciated, there may still be a tendency to be overoptimistic about the chances for success. For example, Hirschman's growth theory is quite similar to development

---

American Regional Development Policy: The Case of Appalachia," *Land Economics*, LXII (February, 1966), pp. 1–9.

30. Paelinck, *op. cit.*, pp. 12–13; Bauchet, *Les tableaux économiques, op. cit.*, pp. 58–9.

31. Paelinck, *op. cit.*, p. 13.

32. *Ibid.*

pole theory as it has been elaborated in France and Belgium, especially in its emphasis on unbalanced growth in relation to the polarization process. Hirschman remarks that public investment policies
"can be counted upon to stage at least an attempt to heal the split"
between regional economic levels. One approach would be to give
poorer regions as good an infrastructure system as exists in more
advanced areas; however, according to Hirschman, this may not be
the most efficient way of inducing growth because lack of sufficient
entrepreneurship may well mean that the purely permissive nature
of this approach will not be exploited. Therefore, although some
infrastructure investment may be required, the "essential task" is to
endow poorer regions "with some ongoing and actively inducing
economic activity" of their own. Among the government development moves which he believes may be effective in this respect are the
building of a steel mill in Columbia's Oriente and the founding of
Brazil's new capital in that nation's interior.[33] Nevertheless, although
such activities have considerable potential as development poles,
their induced effects will become active only in the presence of
already existing external economies. Of course, Hirschman would
maintain that a pronounced need for the latter, made evident by the
introduction of a propulsive activity, is in fact just what is needed to
generate their appearance. However, the evidence thus far in this
regard is not impressive. Aydalot has pointed out correctly that
"development theory has tried to integrate the theory of development poles, but without great success. Indeed, the great complexes
of 'propulsive industries' which have been set up in certain African
countries have not, in most cases, fulfilled this role."[34] The difficulties
confronting newly developing countries in this regard also apply to
problems of regional development in more developed countries,
even though the latter have external economies not found to the same
degree in the former. The case of Lorraine has already been cited.
An even better illustration of this point is provided by the case of
Lacq, in southwestern France.

The discovery of large natural gas deposits at Lacq aroused great
hopes that industrialization of the relatively undeveloped Southwest
would be assured by the presence of this energy source. In fact, "the
Lacq complex corresponds perfectly well to the definition that F.
Perroux has given of propulsive industries (asymmetric effects, rate
of growth superior to the national average)."[35] A British study

33. Hirschman, *op. cit.*, pp. 194–5. [Selection 8 of this volume].
34. Aydalot, *op. cit.*, pp. 967–8.
35. Aydalot, "Etude sur le processus de polarisation et sur les réactions des
industries anciennes à la lumière de l'expérience de Lacq," *Cahiers de l'Institut de
Science Economique Appliqué*, Série L, No. 15 (March, 1965), p. 111.

stressed not only the potential opportunities presented by the Lacq discovery, but also treated its regional significance as a development pole as an accomplished fact.[36] In reality, however, the Lacq complex has been essentially a local phenomenon which has done little to modify the general economic situation of the Southwest. Because of the presence of vastly greater external economies in other regions, it generally has been more economical to transport the gas to already industrialized areas than to create new industry around Lacq. Thus, Guglielmo is correct in remarking:

> It remains to be seen if the indicative planning of liberal economies is capable of resolving the problem of the industrialization of depressed rural regions. The "Cassa di Mezzogiorno" has not succeeded in creating the basis for regional industrial development in southern Italy. Indeed, the only new industries which have located in these regions are extractive industries or highly automated basic industries (petroleum refineries, chemical plants) which employ few persons and are scarcely capable of producing the multiplier effect which people sometimes expect, as is illustrated by the example of Lacq, whose complex remains isolated in the countryside.[37]

If the stimulating effects on general regional growth resulting from the location of "propulsive" industries often have been over-estimated, so have the importance of both bigness and industry. Boudeville, for example, considers that on a European scale Denmark just fulfills the minimum requirements with respect to area, population, and income in order to qualify as an "independent" region.[38] Yet the prosperity of this region was not initiated and has not been sustained by a big, propulsive industry, but rather by scattered (though cooperating) and relatively small agricultural units.

Moreover, even if a propulsive industry is considered as being as much an effect of the polarization process as a cause of it, it is clear that development pole theory has not given a satisfactory general explanation of the agglomerating process. As Vernon has shown, the industries which are most attracted by the external economies generated by large urban areas are not characterized by a highly oligo-polistic structure but rather are industries with numerous small and medium-sized firms, which are highly dependent upon auxiliary business services and need frequent direct personal contacts with buyers and sellers.[39]

36. Political and Economic Planning, *op. cit.*, p. 51.

37. Raymond Guglielmo, "Géographie active de l'industrie," in *La géographie active* (Paris: Presses Universitaires de France, 1964), pp. 223–4.

38. Jacques Boudeville, *Les programmes économiques* (Paris: Presses Universitaires de France, 1963), pp. 80–2.

39. Raymond Vernon, *The Changing Economic Function of the Central City* (New York: Committee for Economic Development, 1959), pp. 28–37.

Another difficulty with development pole theory is that its regional policy criteria have not been explicitly related to the goals that are often sought in practice. For example, Davin poses the following question: From the viewpoint of political economy, what is the nature of the principal polarizing activities (active or potential), and how can the flux among these poles be created or increased? In response, he maintains that the industries or industrial sectors that are most favorable to regional growth (defined as a significant increase in the flux of products and of revenues) are those where: (1) the value added per worker is the highest or most likely to increase; (2) the foreseeable increase in production indicates an accelerated rate of expansion, and where technological progress is the most rapid and the most probable; (3) the process of automation or semi-automation can be most easily applied; (4) the flux of products and of services with the development poles are most intense; and (5) the constitution of large production units is achieved most easily, as these units are capable of releasing a maximum of induced reactions and of realizing a maximum of technical and commercial productivity.[40]

However, these criteria are not related to specific policy objectives. Is the "increase in flux of products and of revenues" supposed to increase hourly earnings of workers, annual income per employed inhabitant, the number of persons employed, or some other possible regional variables? The emphasis put upon automation and high worker productivity would conflict with what is perhaps the most generally sought-after goal of regional policies, namely, increased employment opportunities. Even if one adds, for example, the goal of increased earning power per employed inhabitant, it is not clear that these criteria would guarantee success. The outcome in this regard would depend in large measure upon the extent to which induced effects actually are localized in the region in question. If regional policy is to aim for increased flux in economic activity, then opportunity cost considerations would lead to implanting firms or industries characterized by Davin's criteria in already advanced regions, where they could benefit from relatively large external economies. On the other hand, if these firms or industries are established in lagging regions the flux may be dissipated as a result of linkages with other regions. A particular difficulty in this case would be income flows to owners of capital who reside outside the region; lagging regions generally would not be the type to furnish the savings required for investment in the big, capital-intensive undertakings described by Davin.

40. Davin, *op. cit.*, p. 57.

Finally, it should be emphasized that development pole theory is badly in need of a thorough semantic reworking; the concepts and the language that characterize it need more precise definition and more consistent usage. The very notion of a development pole is still used in contradictory ways. Thus, Davin states that "the idea of a development pole is made more precise by that of a propulsive industry (*industrie motrice*) and a key industry (*industrie clef*). The first engenders activities in other industries, either suppliers or clients for merchandise or services; the second determines the increase of maximum activity."[41] Paelinck, on the other hand, states that:

> The development pole concept often has been misunderstood. It has been confused with the notions of key industry, basic industry, and industrial ensemble; from this follows the erroneous conception according to which the development pole would be an industrial monument raised to the glory of future regional industrialization, a guarantee of certain economic growth. Or again . . . some would have as a development pole any important establishment of firms, preferably industrial, that would exercise beneficial effects on the geographic area where it is located.[42]

A great deal of semantic confusion arises because the same nominal concepts are employed sometimes in the context of abstract, nongeographic space, at other times in the context of certain well-defined geographic areas, and at yet other times in a fashion that indiscriminately mingles abstract and geographic space in the same context. Of course, a scholar should be free to define his terms of discourse, provided that he then proceeds to employ them in a systematic and consistent manner. Too often, however, articles in the development pole literature define (no matter how vaguely) essential concepts and then bring in references to nominally identical concepts from other articles that, unfortunately, have been defined or used in a different manner. Even this would not be objectionable if the various definitions or usages were contrasted critically or otherwise differentiated, but this is rarely the case. In general, then, greater emphasis on conceptual clarity is needed if development pole theory is to provide tools for regional development models that are more operationally feasible.

On the positive side, it may be said that development pole theory still represents a potentially promising effort to come to grips with the complexity of the process by which economic growth is initiated and sustained, a process that has been treated too frequently in oversimplified terms. In particular, the theory's main concepts — development poles, propulsive firms and industries, dominance, etc. — are correctly posited on the assumption that economic growth is

41. *Ibid.*, p. 56.
42. Paelinck, *op. cit.*, pp. 10–11.

basically unbalanced. Moreover, even if the emphasis that has been given to heavy industry and to bigness has been overdrawn, these factors undoubtedly are relevant to many situations involving the stimulation of economic growth.

Perhaps the best approach to development pole theory as applied to regional problems is that given by Paelinck, who proposes that it be regarded as "a *conditional* theory of regional growth; it is valuable chiefly to the extent that it clearly indicates the conditions under which accelerated regional development can occur."[43] Of course, this conditional approach implies that the relevance of the theory to concrete regional cases must be judged on the basis of the nature and prospects of the particular regions, or types of regions, in question. Thus, the policy implications of the disequilibria involved in the growth process, and the various and complex ways in which growth may be transmitted (or inhibited) may vary from place to place and over time for any given place. Further progress in relevant theoretical refinements and classifications therefore will probably depend upon the extent to which they are associated with systematic empirical studies of growth at the regional level. France's new system of regional planning institutions and the regionalization of the government's budget should provide unique opportunities in this regard. For example, French regional policy is now giving priority to eight "*métropoles d'équilibre*," primarily in the form of increased promotion of infrastructure and tertiary activities, in order to balance the growth of the Paris region and to create provincial development poles. This means, of course, that the polarization process is being treated increasingly in terms of external economies rather than as a more direct means of attracting industry, *e.g.*, investment subsidies, and that industrial growth is being regarded increasingly as an effect, as well as a cause, of economic development. Thus, French regional planning experience should provide valuable data in the near future for refining the theory of rational spatial resource allocation to which French economists have so largely contributed.

43. *Ibid.*, p. 47. The emphasis is Paelinck's.

# PART IV

# TOWARD A REGIONAL EQUILIBRIUM ANALYSIS

WALTER ISARD AND DAVID J. OSTROFF

# 10

# *General Interregional Equilibrium**

## 1. INTRODUCTION

In this brief paper we reformulate and further develop certain materials on a general equilibrium model of the Walrasian type for an interregional economy.[1] The notation follows that of existence theorems in Arrow and Debreu and in Isard and Ostroff.[2]

1.0. Let there be $U$ one-point regions $(L = 1, \ldots, U)$ and $l$ commodities $(h = 1, \ldots, l)$. For notational convenience alone, posit in each region: (1) $n$ producers $(j = 1, \ldots, n)$; and (2) $m$ consumers $(i = 1, \ldots, m)$, each of whom possesses initial holdings of commodities as given by the vector $\zeta_i^L$ ($\zeta_i^L \in R^l$ where $R^l$ is the Euclidean space of $l$ dimensions), any component $\zeta_{h,i}$ representing the initial stock of commodity $h$ held by consumer $i$ in region $L$.[3] Let there also be one world trader, free to ship any non-negative amount of commodity $h$, $(h = 1, \ldots, l)$ between any two regions $J$ and $L$ ($J, L = 1, \ldots, U; J \neq L$).

## 2. VARIABLES IN THE SYSTEM

The variables of the system are as follows:

1. For each producer the inputs and outputs of all commodities as given by the vector $y_j^L \in R^l$ ($J = 1, \ldots, n; L = 1, \ldots, U$), any

*The authors wish to acknowledge support of their research by a grant from Resources for the Future, Inc. They are also indebted to Benjamin H. Stevens for fruitful comments and suggestions, though they alone are responsible for any shortcomings of the analysis.

1. Particularly those contained in W. Isard, "General Interregional Equilibrium," *Papers and Proceedings of the Regional Science Association*, III (1957), pp. 35–60.

2. K. J. Arrow and G. Debreu, "Existence of an Equilibrium for a Competitive Economy," *Econometrica*, XXII (July, 1954), pp. 265–290; and W. Isard and D. J. Ostroff, "*Existence of a Competitive Interregional Equilibrium*," *Papers and Proceedings of the Regional Science Association*, IV (1958), pp. 49–76.

3. An alternative is to treat the components of $\zeta_i^L$ as variables, and to introduce below supply functions, $\zeta_{h,i}^L(p_1^L, \ldots, p_l^L)$ where $h = 1, \ldots, l$; $i = 1, \ldots, m$; and $L = 1, \ldots, U$, which govern the amounts of commodity (resource) $h$, (i.e. $\zeta_{h,i}^L$), supplied by consumers. By so doing, we would increase the number of both variables and equilibrium conditions, as described below, by $Uml$. For further discussion, see Isard, *op. cit.*, pp. 27–44.

*Isard, Walter and Ostroff, David J., "General Interregional Equilibrium," Journal of Regional Science, II, No. 1 (1960), pp. 67–74.*

component $y_{h,j}^l$ being negative when the commodity $h$ is an input and positive when $h$ is an output. Over all producers, these variables are $Unl$ in number.

2. For each consumer, the final demand for all commodities as given by the vector $x_i^l \in Rl$ $(i = 1, \ldots, m; L = 1, \ldots, U)$ any component of which $x_{h,i}^l$ represents final demand for the commodity $h$ $(h = 1, \ldots, l)$. Over all consumers these variables are $Uml$ in number.

3. For the world trader, the shipment of all commodities between any combination of originating region $L$ $(L = 1, \ldots, U)$ and terminating region $J$ $(J = 1, \ldots, U; J \neq L)$, as given by the non-negative vector $\$^{L \to J} \in R$ where the component $\$_h^{L \to J}$ refers to the shipment of commodity $h$. There are $U(U-1)$ combinations of such regions, and therefore $U(U-1)$ such vectors. The number of variables—i.e., components of such vectors—is $U(U-1)l$.

4. For each region, the set of internal (market) prices which can be represented by the non-negative price vector $p^L \in R^l$ where the component $p_h^l$ represents the price of commodity $h$. Over all regions, there are $(Ul-1)$ variable price ratios to be determined since the system is homogeneous in prices.

5. For each region, an asset transfer $Q^L$ (which can be either positive or negative), necessary to effect a balance of payments. Since $\sum_L Q^L = 0$ there are only $(U-1)$ of such variables that are independent.

## 3. EQUILIBRIUM CONDITIONS

We have the following *equilibrium conditions:*

(1a) For each producer, his production vector must be contained within the space defined by a production function (representing technical conditions):

$$\phi_j^L(y_{1,j}^L, y_{2,j}^L, \ldots, y_{l,j}^L) = 0.$$
$$\begin{array}{c} j = 1, \ldots, n \\ L = 1, \ldots, U \end{array} \qquad (1a)$$

having continuous partial derivatives. Over all producers in all regions, there are $Un$ such conditions.

(1b) His production plan must meet the following efficiency conditions:

$$\frac{\phi_{h,j}^L}{\phi_{h',j}^L} = \frac{p_h^L}{p_{h'}^L} \qquad \begin{array}{l} h = 1, \ldots, l; \quad h \neq h' \\ j = 1, \ldots, n \\ L = 1, \ldots, U \end{array} \qquad (1b)$$

where $\phi_{h,j}^L$ and $\phi_{h',j}^L$ are the partials of the function $\phi_j^L$ with respect to $y_{h,j}$ and $y_{h',j}$ respectively. When outputs are specified in *net* terms, there are $Un(l-1)$ of such independent conditions for the inter-regional economy.

It should be noted here that for ease of presentation, it is assumed that none of the components of a producers' equilibrium production plan is zero, *i.e.*, that some of each commodity is either produced or used as an input. A more realistic assumption can be made, namely, that any producer is concerned with the selection of nonzero amounts of only a limited number of commodities, which commodities are specified beforehand. For any pair of such commodities, relations (1b) must hold. If neither of these assumptions is made, inequalities and "do not exist" conditions must be considered.

(2) For each consumer, there is assumed an ordinal utility function:

$$u_i^L = u_i^L(x_{1,i}^L, x_{2,i}^L, \ldots, x_{l,i}^L) \qquad \begin{aligned} i &= 1, \ldots, m; \\ L &= 1, \ldots, U. \end{aligned}$$

with continuous partial derivatives

$$u_{h,i}^L = \frac{\partial u_i^L}{\partial x_{h,i}^L} \qquad h = 1, \ldots, l$$

The equilibrium condition that $u_i^L$ $(i = 1, \ldots, m; \ L = 1, \ldots, U)$ be a maximum subject to budget balance:[4]

$$p^L \cdot (x_i^L - \zeta_i^L) = 0 \tag{2a}$$

is:

$$\frac{u_{h,i}^L}{u_{h',i}^L} = \frac{p_h^L}{p_{h'}^L} \qquad h = 1, \ldots l; \quad h \neq h' \tag{2b}$$

Over all consumers over all regions, there are $Um$ equations (2a) and $Um(l-1)$ independent equations (2b), on the assumption that at equilibrium $x_i^L > 0$. If for commodity $h$, we allow $x_{h,i}^L = 0$ at equilibrium, inequalities and "do not exist" conditions must be considered.

4. To avoid additional notation, we posit that entrepreneurial (risk-taking, management, etc.) services represent a commodity of which each individual may hold a stock. The price of this commodity is taken to be correlated with a "normal" profit or return. Thus, profits resulting from production and export activities are payment for entrepreneurial service, which payments are included in the lefthand side of equation (2a). The reader, however, may wish to treat profits explicitly as is done in Isard and Ostroff, *op. cit.*

(3) For the world trader, there is defined a "gains from trade" function:

$$G = \sum_{L} \sum_{J} \tau^{L \to J} \, s^{L \to J} \qquad (3a)$$
$$L \neq J$$

where $\tau^{L \to J} \epsilon R^l$ and for any $h$th component $(h = 1, \ldots, l)$

$$\tau_h^{L \to J} = p_h^J - p_h^L - p_{h'}^L d^{L \to J} w_h \qquad (3b)$$

In (3b), $h'$ refers to the commodity transportation service (transport inputs), its price $p_{h'}^L$ being the transport rate at $L$; $d^{L \to J}$ is a predetermined number indicating distance from region $L$ to region $J$, and $w_h$ is another predetermined number indicating the ideal weight (*à la* Weber) of commodity $h$. The last term on the righthand side of equation (3b) represents the cost of transporting a unit of commodity $h$ from region $L$ to region $J$.[5]

Assuming that the world has no control over prices and any $\tau_h^{L \to J} (h = 1, \ldots, l; L, J = 1, \ldots, U; L \neq J)$, and *thus views these as constants*,[6] the equilibrium condition that $G$, a linear function in $s_h^{L \to J}$, be a maximum, is:

$$\tau_h^{L \to J} \cdot s_h^{L \to J} = 0. \qquad\qquad h = 1, \ldots, l$$
$$L, J = 1, \ldots, U; L \neq J \qquad (3c)$$

It is clear that for any $\tau_h^{L \to J} > 0$, an equilibrium cannot exist. At an equilibrium point, whenever $s_h^{L \to J} > 0$, $\tau_h^{L \to J} = 0$, i.e., whenever there are positive shipments, the price spread for any commodity $h$ between any two regions $J$ and $L$ must equal the cost of transporting a unit of commodity $h$ from $L$ to $J$; and whenever $\tau_h^{L \to J} < 0$, $s_h^{L \to J} = 0$, i.e., whenever the price spread is less than this cost of transportation, shipments of commodity $h$ are zero, although shipments may be zero when the price spread is just equal to this transportation cost.

The number of relations (3c) is $U(U-1)l$.

5. Note that we adopt the convention that the world trader purchases the necessary transportation service to effect any export from the local market of the region of export. The region of export, however, may receive (via import) supplies of transportation services produced by units in other regions. Other conventions are obviously possible; they would not require any basic changes in our statement. Observe, too, that the world trader requires as inputs only transport services and the commodities to be shipped; his outputs are the commodities delivered to the regions of import.

6. Our fiction of a world trader is analogous to the fiction of a *market participant* in Arrow and Debreu, *op. cit.*. The market participant, who sets price but views $z^L$ (to be defined below) as a set of constants, reflects the operation of the competitive mechanism on the local market. Our world trader reflects the competitive mechanism as it governs trade among regions.

(4) Following the traditional procedure of excluding from our framework zero-price commodities, we have for each region the following supply equals demand relationships:

$$\sum_i x_i^L + \sum_{\substack{J \\ J \neq L}} s^{L \to J} = \sum_i \zeta_i^L + \sum_j y_j^L + \sum_{\substack{j \\ J \neq L}} s^{J \to L} \tag{4a}$$

In (4a) $s^{L \to J}$ is equivalent to $s^{L \to J}$ except for the $h'$ (transportation service) component. We define

$$s_{h'}^{L \to J} = s_{h'}^{L \to J} + d^{L \to J}(s^{L \to J} \quad w) \tag{4b}$$

where the vector $w \in R^l$ with components $w_h(h = 1, \ldots, l)$. For all regions, we have $Ul$ supply-demand conditions.

(4′) As an alternative to 4, let there be in each region a fictitious market participant (à la Arrow and Debreu) who desires to maximize $p^L \cdot x^L$ where

$$z^L = \sum_i x_i^L - \sum_i \zeta_i^L - \sum_j y_j^L + \sum_{\substack{J \\ J \neq L}} s^{L \to J} - \sum_{\substack{J \\ J \neq L}} s^{J \to L} \tag{4a′}$$

Since the market participant has no control over any $z_h$ ($h = 1, \ldots, l$) and *thus views these as constants*, but is free to select $p^L(p^L \in R^l, p_h^L \geq 0)$, the condition that $p^L \cdot z^L$ be a maximum is:

$$p_h^L \cdot z_h^L = 0 \qquad (h = 1, \ldots, l) \tag{4b′}$$

It is clear that for any $z_h^L > 0$, an equilibrium cannot exist. At an equilibrium point, (1) whenever $p_h^L > 0$, $z_h^L = 0$, i.e., supply equals demand for all commodities with positive price; and (2) whenever $z_h^L < 0$, $p_h^L = 0$, i.e., whenever the demand for a commodity falls short of available supply, the price is zero, although price may be zero for a condition of equality between demand and supply. In this manner free goods may be incorporated into the framework of our interregional economy, although to do so would require reformulation of conditions (1b) and (2b).

All told there are $Ul$ conditions of the type (4b)′.

(5) Finally, for each region we have a balance of trade condition:

$$p^J \cdot \sum_{\substack{J \\ J \neq L}} s^{L \to J} - p^L \sum_{\substack{J \\ J \neq L}} s^{J \to L} \quad Q^L = 0. \tag{5}$$

Over all regions, there are $U$ such conditions of which only $U - 1$ are independent.

All told there are $Ul[n+m+U]+U-2$ variables whose values are to be determined and that many plus one conditions for their determination. However, one of the latter can be shown to be redundant.[7] Hence, the count of unknowns and conditions is the same.

## 4   TRANSPORTATION AND ASSET TRANSFERS

It is to be noted that the shipment variable $s_h^{l\to J}$ and the asset transfer variable $Q^L$ cannot directly be determined as can the other variables of the system once an equilibrium set of prices is given. For example, for such prices, we determine directly an equilibrium input-output schedule for each firm from (1a) and (1b). But we only know directly that when a $\tau_h^{l\to J}=0$, the corresponding shipment is non-negative (although when a $\tau_h^{l\to J}<0$, the corresponding shipment is zero). However, an equilibrium set of shipments and asset transfers can be determined indirectly via a computation somewhat related to linear programming.

For an equilibrium set of prices (zero price commodities excluded from the model),[8] $z_h^L=0$, and $\sum_i x_{h,i}^L$ and $\sum_j y_{h,j}^L$ can be determined from relations (1a), (1b), (2a), and (2b). From (4a) the net export (or import) of $h$ is then obtained for each region. (Note that cross-hauling is inconsistent with a maximum value for $G$, as will be evident later, and that shipments from one region to a second which happen to pass through a third are by definition not recorded in the export and import data of the third.) Further, from (3b) we have:

$$\tau^{L\to J}=p^J-p^L-p_h^L\cdot d^{l\to J}w$$

By substitution into (3a):

$$G=\sum_L\sum_J p^J\cdot s^{l\to J}-\sum_L\sum_J p^L\cdot s^{l\to J}-\sum_L\sum_J p_h^L d^{L\to J}(s^{l\to J}\cdot w)\qquad(6)$$
$$\phantom{G=\sum}{}_{L\neq J}\phantom{\sum_J p^J}{}_{L\neq J}\phantom{\sum_J p^L}{}_{L\neq J}$$

Let

$$\sigma^J=\sum_L s^{l\to J}\text{ and } s^L=\sum_J s^{l\to J}\qquad(7)$$

7. For example, see Isard, *op. cit.*, pp. 45–46; R. G. D. Allen, *Mathematical Economics* (New York, 1956), pp. 321–322; and R. Dorfman, P. A. Samuelson, and R. M. Solow, *Linear Programming and Economic Analysis* (New York, 1958), p. 354.

8. It is appreciated that one cannot adequately specify beforehand which commodities will be zero price and can be excluded from the framework of a model. And it may well be that at one "low-level" equilibrium point a good such as water may be a "free" good while at a second "high-level" equilibrium point water may have a positive price. Similar difficulties are encountered when one attempts to specify beforehand those commodities for which $x_i^L>0$, or for which $y_{ij}^J\neq 0$ so that equalities (2b) and (1b), respectively, obtain at equilibrium. In this sense our model is not truly general.

Then (6) becomes:

$$G = \sum_J p^J \cdot \sigma^J - \sum_L p^L \cdot s^L - \sum_L \sum_J p^L_{h'} d^{L \to J}(s^{L \to J} \cdot w) \quad (8)$$
$$\scriptstyle L \neq J$$

But for a given set of equilibrium prices, the equilibrium $\sigma^J$ (the total import vector of $J$, $J = 1, \ldots, U$) and $s^L$ (the total export vector of $L$, $L = 1, \ldots, U$) are determined as above. Hence, a maximum $G$ must correspond to a minimum

$$\sum_L \sum_J p^L_{h'} d^{L \to J}(s^{L \to J} \cdot w),$$
$$\scriptstyle L \neq J$$

*i.e.*, to the minimum for total transportation costs when the equilibrium levels of *total* imports and exports by regions are specified. But this is a problem related to the typical Koopmans-Hitchcock transportation problem. Since for any given set of equilibrium prices we know in our problem those shipments which are unprofitable ($\tau^{L \to J}_h < 0$), and hence those shipment variables which can be definitely excluded from a "basic" solution, a simplified version of a linear programming computation will suffice to yield an optimal (equilibrium) pattern of shipments.[9]

Once a pattern of equilibrium $s^{L \to J}$ is found, the determination of the asset transfer variable $Q^L$ can be direct.

It should also be observed that since at equilibrium $\sum_L z^L_{h'} = 0$ for an interregional economy where the transport rate is positive,[10] from (4a)′

$$\sum_L \zeta^L_{h'} + \sum_L y^L_{h'} - \sum_L x^L_{h'} = \sum_L s^L_{h'} - \sum_L \sigma^L_{h'} \quad (9)$$

But, from (4b) and (7)

$$\sum_L s^L_{h'} - \sum_L \sigma^L_{h'} = \sum_L \sum_J d^{L \to J}(s^{L \to J} \cdot w) \quad (10)$$
$$\scriptstyle L \neq J$$

Therefore

$$\sum_L \zeta^L_{h'} + \sum_L y^L_{h'} - \sum_L x^L_{h'} = \sum_L \sum_J d^{L \to J}(s^{L \to J} \cdot w) \quad (11)$$
$$\scriptstyle L \neq J$$

*i.e.*, at an interregional equilibrium, the available world supply of transport services after all consumers and producers have been

9. See P. A. Samuelson, "Spatial Price Equilibrium and Linear Programming," *American Economic Review*, XLII (June, 1952), pp. 283–303.

10. Note that if at equilibrium the transport rate is positive in any one region, it must be positive in all regions.

furnished with their internal (intraregional) requirements of transport services must be exactly equal to the transport requirements to effect a minimum cost interregional shipment program which corresponds to a maximum value for $G$.

# 11

## The Equalization of Returns and Regional Economic Growth

The possibility of interaction between resource earnings and regional growth patterns has been pointed out by many writers.[1] From one point of view, regional growth may be regarded as the outcome of resource movements generated by earnings differentials. In turn, these are caused by initial differences in regional endowments of capital and labor. The resulting pattern of regional growth represents an equilibrating process which will tend to eliminate geographic differences in the returns to resources.

From another point of view, the differentials in resource movements and regional growth patterns are not explainable in terms of initial differences either in the prices of resources or in resource endowments; instead, they are to be explained by a difference in production functions or in the demand for a region's exports.

In this paper I shall examine the empirical implications of these two approaches and try to identify the forces operating through regional growth patterns in the United States in the last four decades. In a sense neither framework offers a complete growth model. Each provides an explanation of the economy's adjustments to changes in tastes, technology, and the stocks of labor and capital. Nor are the two explanations inconsistent. It is conceivable that in some areas, investment is attracted by low real wages and a high marginal product of capital, while in other areas investment is explained by other considerations. It is the purpose of this inquiry to determine which of these relationships has been responsible for the observable growth differentials of the recent past.

The hypotheses to be examined are consistent with the assumptions of a competitive economy, with capital and labor mobile between regions. It is assumed that the total stocks of capital and labor are

The author wishes to thank M. P. Stoltz, J. L. Stein, and M. J. Brennan for kind assistance. This work was supported by a grant from the Ford Foundation for the investigation of regional economic maturity.

1. Statements of this problem may be found in articles by Hoover and Ratchford[5], North[10], [11], and Tiebout[11], [15].

Borts, George H., "The Equalization of Returns and Regional Growth," The American Economic Review, L (June, 1960), pp. 319–347.

fixed in the short run, and expansible in the long run through accumulation and reproduction. It is not intended to explain growth in the country at large. National growth patterns will be taken for granted, and only regional differences will be examined.

# I.  RELATIONS BETWEEN GROWTH AND RETURNS TO RESOURCES

## A.  The Equalization of Returns to Resources

A simple model of regional growth is first constructed wherein observable growth patterns are generated by initial disparities in resource endowment.

If we assume that each region produces the same single output with the same production function, those regions with the highest proportion of capital to labor will evidence the highest real wage and the lowest marginal product of capital. In a free market we would observe capital moving from high-wage to low-wage areas, with the consequence that the low-wage areas experience higher rates of growth of capital and of the return to labor. If the regional wage differentials were large enough initially, we might also observe labor migrating from the low-wage to the high-wage areas. This would yield the same equilibrating effect on the return to capital and labor, although the effects on the growth of output in each region would be somewhat different. Whether or not labor migrates, capital movements would produce an eventual elimination of regional differences in resource endowment, in the real wage, and in the marginal product of capital. The adjustments which this model describes are movements along the production function of each region.

The assumptions underlying the model are: (1) The total supply of labor to all regions taken together is fixed. The only way in which one region may employ more labor is through migration from other regions. (2) A single homogeneous output is produced in each region. (3) There are zero transport costs between regions so that the price of output is regionally uniform. (4) The same production function exists in each region, being homogeneous of degree one in the inputs labor and capital. (5) There are zero costs of converting output into capital goods.

Let $X = f(C, L)$ be the single, regionally uniform production function for output in general. $L$ is the quantity of labor employed, $C$ the physical quantity of capital employed, where $C$ is the accumulated stock of past unconsumed outputs. The assumption of a production function homogeneous of degree one means that the marginal physical product of labor $f_L$ and the marginal physical product of capital $f_C$ are both functions of the capital-labor ratio:

$$f_L = g(C/L); \qquad f_C = h(C/L).$$

Under these assumptions, if $C/L$ is greater in region A than in region B, the real wage is higher in region A; *i. e.*,

$$g(C/L)_A > g(C/L)_B.$$

Further, the marginal physical product of capital is higher in region B,

$$h(C/L)_B > h(C/L)_A.$$

Under the assumption that output is homogeneous, and that there are zero costs of converting output into capital goods, the marginal efficiency of investment is $h^2$. Therefore, capital will flow from region A to region B, and labor may flow from region B to region A.

This model abstracts from differences in production techniques due to the varying fertility and location of natural resources. Nevertheless, it provides a movement towards equilibrium and suggests two testable hypotheses. They are: (1) Low-wage regions will experience the highest rates of growth of capital, and of the ratio of capital to labor. (2) Low-wage regions will experience the highest rates of increase of wages.

The implications of the model will be contradicted if certain of the assumptions are contradicted. For example, in the long run the growth of the labor supply will differ among regions. If the supply of labor grows faster in low-wage regions and if labor is insensitive to regional wage differentials, different conclusions are suggested. Low-wage regions will still experience the highest rates of growth of capital, but they may not experience the highest rate of increase of wages; for the growth of the labor supply would prevent a rise in the ratio of capital to labor.

This problem also arises if we examine separate sectors of a region's economy. The supply of labor in the nonagricultural sector of a low-wage region may be increased through transfer of some of the

---

2. In this simple model, the marginal efficiency of investment and the marginal physical product of capital are identical. This is due to the use of one output which can be consumed or accumulated, and a zero marginal cost of transforming output into capital goods. In the more complex models considered here, the two concepts are not identical. The marginal physical product of capital is $f_C$. Assuming capital to be permanent and to yield a constant annual future income stream, the marginal efficiency of investment is a schedule showing for different levels of investment an ordinate whose value is $(f_C \cdot P_x)/P_C$ where $P_x/P_C$ is the ratio of the price of output to the price of capital goods.

region's labor force from agriculture. At the same time this sector may experience a very high rate of capital accumulation. However, the attraction of labor to the sector would prevent a rise in the ratio of capital to labor and in the real wage in the sector.

## B.  Regional Growth and the Allocation of Resources

The conclusions of the first model depend upon the assumption that a single uniform good is produced by each region. If we consider two output sectors in a region, different conclusions are possible. As will be shown, a high-wage region may then grow faster than a low-wage region. In addition, an increase in physical capital in one region may not yield a change in factor combinations and in factor payments, but instead a reallocation of the region's output in favor of the commodity produced by the capital-intensive sector.

These possibilities have been recognized by Samuelson in his work on factor price equalization [14]. He specifies sufficient conditions for interregional trade in two or more commodities to result in the equalization of factor prices. The conditions imply that a reshuffling of resources within each region is sufficient to eliminate the inducements for interregional factor movements. Though regional growth differences might occur, they would not generate a pattern of differences in returns to resources. Nor would they be generated by such differences.

In the second model, I shall therefore assume empirical restrictions on the data which prevent factor price equalization from occurring through internal reallocation. These restrictions take the form of either: (a) regional differences in production functions, or (b) transport costs that prevent commodities from having the same relative prices in each region.

The model now to be presented is one in which growing regions may have higher real and money wages than declining regions. Let us assume that each region produces a positive quantity of commodities in each of two industrial sectors X and Y; and that the output of sector Y is transportable among regions while the output of sector X is not. Further, sector Y need not be identical among regions.

The money wage level in each region depends upon the marginal physical products of labor and the prices of output in the two sectors of the region; the marginal physical products of labor in turn depend on the ratio of physical capital to labor in the region and the composition of output. The same set of variables determines the marginal efficiency of investment in the region.

A region with low money wages may not grow faster than a

region with high money wages because it may have a lower schedule of the marginal efficiency of investment.[3] It may have a lower schedule if its low wage level is due to a relatively low price of the commodity produced in its transportable sector, or is due to production functions that yield relatively low values of the marginal products of capital and of labor.[4]

We can now specify the conditions under which a region with high money wages will grow faster than a region with low money wages:

(a) A higher marginal efficiency of investment in the high-wage region than in other regions. This could be due to either of two causes: (i) production functions in the high-wage region which yield higher marginal physical product schedules for both labor and capital;[5] (ii) a rise in the price of the region's export commodity relative to the export commodity of other regions.

(b) For noneconomic reasons, population migrates to this region, and the migrants transfer capital with them; or the migrants demand capital once they have completed the move.

(c) Residents of the region save a higher proportion of income than residents of other regions, and this is invested, for noneconomic reasons, in enterprises within the region. Any one of the above causes will lead to a rise in the region's income through the familiar investment income-generating process. The income boom will also lead to a passive current balance and a real transfer of capital from other regions.

This is likely to be true even if the income boom is caused initially by a rise in export prices. The export surplus will be short-lived, because it coincides with a rise in the region's marginal efficiency of investment. That is, the price of export goods rises relative to the price of capital goods which are either produced in the domestic sector or are imported. Unlike the traditional balance-of-payments multiplier, a secondary investment boom generates new income and

3. Define the marginal efficiency of investment schedule for each region as a set of points showing values of $(f_c \cdot P_x)/P_c$ on the ordinate, while the abscissa shows the ratio of investment to the existing stock of capital. If the actual rate of return on investment is the same in all regions, then the region with the lowest schedule will have the lowest rate of growth.

4. Because each region need not produce the same transportable commodity, any particular region may suffer a decline in money wages if, for example, there is a decline in the demand for its product. In addition, a low-wage region might have a low marginal physical product of capital because the ratio of capital to labor is higher in each of its industries than in the high-wage region. This would imply a high marginal physical product of labor, but not necessarily a high money wage.

5. In an analysis that deals with only two resources, labor and capital, it is reasonable to think of differences in production functions among regions, even though the "state of the arts" is widely disseminated.

a new demand for imports. Though the initial impact of the exports boom is a favorable balance of payments with other regions, its eventual effect must be destabilizing with respect to the balance of payments if the region is to import capital.[6]

**1. Accumulation and the increase in wages**  There are two reasons why a growing region will enjoy a rise in the money wage per worker.

(a) The investment income-generating process leads to higher prices of goods in the two sectors X and Y and therefore to a higher marginal value product of labor. This will also represent a rise in the real wage, if the prices of goods imported in the region are now lower relative to the region's money wage.

(b) The accumulation of capital may raise the marginal physical product of labor. To accomplish this, accumulation must raise the ratio of capital to labor in both output sectors. This requires that accumulation be accompanied by an increase in the price of output in the sector which is labor-intensive relative to the price in the sector which is capital-intensive.

With the aid of simplifying assumptions, it is possible to specify the conditions under which this will occur. Let us assume that: (1) production functions for the two outputs are homogeneous of degree one; (2) with given resources, there is a unique ratio of capital to labor for each production function which will yield a given marginal rate of substitution between the two products.

These conditions guarantee that factor proportions in the two sectors are unique functions of the relative prices of their outputs. A rise in the proportion of capital to labor in both sectors requires that there be an increase in the relative price of output in the labor-intensive sector. If during accumulation the relative prices of outputs remained unchanged, the factor proportions would not change. All that would happen would be a simultaneous reallocation of output in favor of the sector which is capital-intensive with no change in marginal physical products.

We must therefore restrict the demand conditions for the outputs of the two sectors. If accumulation is to raise the marginal physical product of labor, the demands for the two commodities must be such that the relative price of the labor-intensive commodity rises as the new capital is associated to the two sectors. A graphic demonstration of these propositions is to be found in the Appendix.

6. It is conceivable that one region may grow faster than other regions in a free-trade economy without importing capital. However, it is difficult to see why this should occur unless the residents of the growing region have an irrational demand for externally generated securities. The forces generating growth in the region should also generate a demand for the region's securities.

**2. Accumulation and the real wage**  With the aid of a number of realistic assumptions, we may specify the effect of growth on the real wage. Let us assume that the products of the transportable sector (Y) of the region are capital-intensive while those of the nontransportable, domestic sector (X) are labor-intensive. For example, the capital-intensive sector may be thought of as manufacturing and mining, while the labor-intensive sector is services.[7] Further assume that the region is experiencing rapid growth because of upward shifts in the demand for the output of its export sector. The major cause of an increase in the real wage is the rise of money wages relative to the prices of commodities imported in the region. It is less certain that the real wage will be improved through an increase in the marginal physical product of labor. As we have seen, it requires an increase in the ratio of capital to labor in each industry. It is brought about by a rise in the price of the product of sector X relative to that in the Y sector. This might be due to the high income elasticity of demand for the product of the labor-intensive sector and to the re-spending of new income generated in the region. However, if this rise went far enough, it would offset any initial increase in the export price and would wipe out the higher marginal efficiency of investment generated by the export boom.[8] For if the growth process is to continue, there can be no rise in the marginal physical product of labor, as this would imply a fall in the marginal physical product of capital. If the marginal physical product of labor does rise, it will impede the growth process by leading to a lower marginal efficiency of investment.

The only exception to this would occur if capital goods were exclusively imported. For then we could have: a rise in the prices of both sectors of the region relative to the price of capital goods; a rise in the price of the labor-intensive domestic sector relative to the

---

7. If we ignore transportation and communications, it appears reasonable to regard as relatively labor-intensive such activities as: wholesale and retail trade; finance, insurance, and real estate; services; and construction.

8. In a two-community framework, the marginal efficiency of investment can be written as $(P_y/P_x) \cdot MP_x{}^y$, where $P_y$ is the price of output, $P_x$ the price of capital and $MP_x{}^y$ the marginal physical product of capital in the Y industry. Let us assume that X, the labor-intensive domestic sector, produces capital goods. If resources are efficiently allocated between the two industries, the following condition holds:

$$\frac{P_y}{P_x} \cdot MP_x{}^y = MP_x{}^x.$$

By assumption, $MP_x{}^x$ is a function of the capital-labor ratio in X. Therefore, a reduction in $P_y/P_x$ (an increase in the relative price of the labor-intensive sector) raises the capital-labor ratio in X and Y, lowers the value of $MP_x{}^x$ and $MP_x{}^y$ and lowers the marginal efficiency of investment in the region. For a graphic demonstration, see the Appendix.

**153**

capital-intensive export sector; a rise in the marginal efficiency of investment, a rise in the marginal physical product of labor, and a fall in the marginal physical product of capital.[9]

This analysis permits us to understand how the real wage and the marginal efficiency of investment may simultaneously be higher than the national average in a growing region and simultaneously lower than the national average in a declining region. It has been shown that the real wage in the region depends upon the marginal physical products of labor and the prices of the region's outputs relative to the prices of its imports. The marginal efficiency of investment depends on the marginal physical product of capital in the region and the prices of the region's exports relative to the prices of domestically produced and imported capital goods. Even though the marginal physical product of labor is inversely related to the marginal physical product of capital through factor proportions, favorable movements of the relevant price ratios may raise both the real wage and the marginal efficiency of investment. The crucial assumptions underlying the analysis are either regional differences in production functions, or regional differences in the ratio of the prices of export goods to the prices of goods produced in the domestic sector.

From this analysis, it becomes clear that a region's growth depends strongly upon the behavior of the prices of its export sector. A high-wage region may grow more rapidly than a low-wage region if the demand for its export goods is growing. Because a high-wage region can produce a different export commodity than a low-wage region, the export boom of one region will not be shared by the other. A high-wage region may, therefore, have a greater growth of capital and a greater increase in money wages than a low-wage region. It may also have an increase in the marginal physical product of labor and in the real wage under the conditions specified above.

This model, therefore, allows conclusions that contradict the one-commodity model. For the one-commodity model implies that capital will grow faster in low-wage regions. Here we see that the opposite is possible. Capital may grow faster in a high-wage region. Further, if the elasticity of labor supply does not differ among regions, the money wage rate will increase fastest where capital is growing the

9. Let $Z$ denote the imported capital goods. Then the marginal efficiency of investment (MEI) is:

$$\frac{P_y}{P_Z} \cdot MP_Z{}^y = \frac{P_x}{P_Z} MP_Z{}^x$$

The values of these terms could rise due to an increase in the price ratios $P_y/P_Z$, $P_x/P_Z$. At the same time, $P_y/P_x$ could be falling with the consequence that $MP_Z{}^y$ and $MP_Z{}^x$ would fall, although not so much that the MEI would decline.

fastest. If the money wage rate does not increase rapidly where capital is growing rapidly, then we may look to a high growth of employment as the explanation.

In the following sections these alternative frameworks will be tested against the experience among United States regions in the last four decades.

## II.  STATISTICAL TESTS

In order to subject the above hypotheses to test, it is necessary to measure the changes in capital, labor, and wages among regions. In all cases, the regions examined are the forty-eight states. The time period runs from 1919 to 1953. This period is broken into shorter intervals marked by business-cycle peaks as the initial and terminal dates. The purpose is to measure growth as the change during each interval. Such changes are independent of cyclical movements in the sense that intervening cyclical troughs do not influence the statistical measurement of growth from one peak date to the next. The intervals chosen are 1919 to 1929, 1929 to 1948, and 1948 to 1953.

The growth of capital in each state is measured by the growth of the income to capital.[10] We can think of the total income produced in the state as the sum of payments to wage and salary earners and to property owners. The percentage change in the income to property owners in the nonagricultural sector of each state is used to measure the change in the total return to capital in that sector in each state.[11]

10. The total return to capital is the product of three elements: the number of physical units of capital, the marginal physical product of capital, and the price of the output produced by capital. In the two models presented above, capital is treated as a homogeneous physical commodity. In the first model, there is one good which can either be consumed or accumulated. In the second model, the capital good is either produced by the domestic sector of the region or imported. In the first model, increases in the quantity of capital employed would in all likelihood be accompanied by increases in the total return to capital. The exception would occur if the schedule of the marginal physical product of capital were inelastic in the range in which accumulation was taking place. In the second model, increases in the quantity of capital employed will be accompanied by increases in the total return to capital. There are two reasons for this: (a) The money return to capital will be increased by an increase in the prices of goods produced by capital. In a growing region experiencing an investment income-generating process, all prices are likely to be rising. In particular, the prices in the capital-intensive sector will rise due to an export boom. (b) The marginal physical product of capital will not fall rapidly, if it falls at all, because of the expansion of the scale of both the capital-intensive and labor-intensive sectors. Thus, increases in physical capital will be accompanied by slight, if any, declines in the marginal physical product of capital.

11. For 1929, 1948, 1953, the payments to wage and salary earners and to property owners are derived from [22]; for 1919, from [7]. This measure of capital accumulation was checked for consistency against three other methods of estimation: (a) growth of corporate income after taxes generated by firms resident in each state; (b) growth of

Percentage changes in nonagricultural employment in each state are computed for the intervals 1919–1929, 1929–1948, and 1948–1953. For 1919 and 1929, the employment estimates are derived from the Census of Population[17, 19]. The employment data for 1948 and 1953 are estimates of the Bureau of Labor Statistics[23].

These sources are also used to derive estimates of employment by states in two nonagricultural sectors, (1) mining and manufacturing, and (2) a composite sector which I have called services. The services sector includes the following employment categories: wholesale and retail trade; finance, insurance, and real estate; service and miscellaneous. This dichotomy excludes employees in construction, transportation, communication, public utilities, and government. In 1950, these excluded sectors made up approximately 30 per cent of employed nonagricultural workers.

The wage per employee in the two nonagricultural sectors is computed from the income and employment data previously mentioned. The wage change used is the percentage change in the wage income per employee between 1919 and 1929, 1929 and 1948, 1948 and 1953.

## A.   The Growth of Wages, Capital, and Employment

We may use the statistical data to test the hypotheses presented earlier: (a) Capital grows fastest in low-wage areas. (b) Wages grow fastest in low-wage areas unless growth of employment prevents a rise in the ratio of physical capital to labor.

Table 1 indicates for each time interval the average wage level and average percentage change in wages for groups of states classified by their position with regard to the median growth of employment and median growth of capital. This is shown for the nonagricultural sector of each state. For each interval the table shows $n$, the number of states; $w$, the average wage income per nonagricultural employee at the initial date; and $\overset{\cdot}{w}$, the percentage change in $w$. Also shown are the average values of $w$ and $\overset{\cdot}{w}$ for all 48 states. If the data are consistent with the hypotheses, we should observe low values of $w$ and high values of $\overset{\cdot}{w}$ in states with a high rate of capital growth. Also, in each interval the value of $\overset{\cdot}{w}$ in the lower left box should be higher than in the upper left box; further, the value of $\overset{\cdot}{w}$ in the upper right box should be lower than in the lower right box.

total assessed value of property by state; (c) growth of cumulative value of construction by state. For the periods under review, the estimates are close enough to permit reliance on the measure described above. An analysis of methods of estimating returns to capital was presented by the author to the 1961 Conference on Research in Income and Wealth, in a paper entitled, "Problems on the Distribution of National Income by Regions."

TABLE 1   Level and Percentage Growth of Wages in 48 States Classified by Growth of Capital and of Employment, 1919–1929, 1929–1948, 1948–1953*

*TIME INTERVAL*

| | | 1919–1929 | | 1929–1948 | | 1948–1953 | |
|---|---|---|---|---|---|---|---|
| | | HIGH CAPITAL GROWTH | LOW CAPITAL GROWTH | HIGH CAPITAL GROWTH | LOW CAPITAL GROWTH | HIGH CAPITAL GROWTH | LOW CAPITAL GROWTH |
| High | $n$ | 13 | 11 | 16 | 8 | 20 | 4 |
| employment | $w$ | $986 | $970 | $1051 | $1355 | $2799 | $2320 |
| growth | $\dot{w}$ | 16.24% | 3.83% | 161.73% | 128.41% | 30.99% | 25.51% |
| Low | $n$ | 11 | 13 | 8 | 16 | 4 | 20 |
| employment | $w$ | $1074 | $1017 | $940 | $1203 | $2912 | $2665 |
| growth | $\dot{w}$ | 16.26% | 11.75% | 158.81% | 127.93% | 30.39% | 26.80% |
| U.S. | $w$ | $1011 | | $1134 | | $2713 | |
| average | $\dot{w}$ | 12.19% | | 144.42% | | 28.75% | |

*$n$: the number of states; $w$: the average wage income per nonagricultural employee at the initial date; $\dot{w}$: the percentage change in $w$.

As the table indicates, we frequently observe the contrary of these events. In two of the three periods, the states with a high rate of capital growth have high values of $w$. In the 1919–1929 interval, the state groups where capital grew fastest had on the average a wage 2 to 5 per cent greater than in the other states. In the 1948–1953 period, the state groups where capital grew fastest had a wage 10 to 20 per cent greater than the other states. In these same two periods, the fastest wage increase occurred among state groups with relatively high wages. Only in the 1929–1948 period do rate of capital growth and rate of wage increase appear greatest in low-wage states. Finally, the value of $w$ does not appear to be influenced by the rate of employment growth. Only in the 1919–1929 interval does high employment growth appear to slow the increase in the wage.

This evidence casts considerable doubt on the hypothesis that low wages are a major influence on capital movements. Or, to put it another way, there is doubt that wage differentials are a prime influence on the marginal efficiency of investment. While it has been true over a long period that wages have tended toward equality among states, the strength of this movement appears markedly weaker in the past four decades.[12]

12. Hanna's data[4] show that the coefficient of variation of wage and salary income per capita declines from 1929 to 1948, and then remains roughly constant to 1951. He does not give any evidence on this coefficient in 1919, presumably because of a different source of data and slightly different definitions. Easterlin's findings[2] indicate that convergence did not occur between 1919–1921 and 1949–1951. Muth's findings[9, pp. 854–77] confirm the failure of state differences in income per worker to narrow in the period between 1920 and 1929, and again after the Second World War.

**157**

The strength of these convergence and divergence patterns may be seen in the following contingency table which covers the three periods examined. Table 2 classifies the states according to wage

TABLE 2   Classification of 48 States by Wage Level and Rate of Wage Increase, 1919–1929, 1929–1948, 1948–1953

| WAGE LEVEL | RATE OF WAGE INCREASE | | | | | |
|---|---|---|---|---|---|---|
| | 1919–1929 | | 1929–1948 | | 1948–1953 | |
| | ABOVE AVERAGE | BELOW AVERAGE | ABOVE AVERAGE | BELOW AVERAGE | ABOVE AVERAGE | BELOW AVERAGE |
| Above average | 14 | 9 | 5 | 21 | 11 | 9 |
| Below average | 6 | 19 | 20 | 2 | 15 | 13 |
| Value of $\chi^2$ | 6.71 | | 24.52 | | 0.01 | |

level and rate of wage increase. Shown at the bottom is the value of chi-square ($\chi^2$) which has been computed for each time-interval as a measure of association.[13] There is a strong divergence pattern among states in the first period, a strong convergence pattern in the second period and no pattern in the third. The association in the last period between high average wages and rate of wage increase alluded to previously results from the classification of states by capital and employment growth. There is nevertheless no pattern of wage divergence in this last period.

Table 1 also supports quite strongly the view that an increase in the total income to capital relative to the amount of labor employed will yield an increase in the wage. Reading across the table, we see that without an exception in each time interval an increase in capital growth relative to employment growth is accompanied by a greater increase in the wage. This conclusion is also supported by evidence on correlation between the change in the total return to capital, the change in employment, and the change in wages. Let us measure the change in the ratio of capital to labor as the difference between the percentage change in capital and the percentage change in labor.[14] Denote this variable as $x$, and denote the percentage change in wages per employee as $y$. Then, we have the following correlation coefficients for each time interval:

$$1919{-}1929 \qquad r_{xy} = +0.508$$
$$1929{-}1948 \qquad r_{xy} = +0.727$$
$$1948{-}1953 \qquad r_{xy} = +0.236$$

13. $\chi^2$ is defined as $\Sigma \, [f_{ij} - Q_{ij}]^2 / Q_{ij}$ where $Q_{ij} = \Sigma f_{ij} \cdot \sum_{ij} f_{ij} / \Sigma f_{ij}$; $f_{ij}$ is the number of observations in the $i$th column, $j$th row.

14. For incremental changes, $\dfrac{\Delta(C/L)}{C/L} = \dfrac{\Delta C}{C} - \dfrac{\Delta L}{L}$.

The first two coefficients are significant in the probability sense at the 5 per cent level, the third is not. However, for the 1948–1953 period, the partial correlation between the change in capital and the change in wages, holding the change in employment constant, is much larger, yielding a significant coefficient of +0.688.[15] The partial correlation results do indicate that wages respond to increases of capital. However, the observed relation for the 1948–1953 period cannot be stated in terms of the ratio of capital to labor.

## B.    The Influence of Agriculture

It is conceivable but unlikely that the widespread decline in agricultural income in the 1919–1929 and 1948–1953 intervals is responsible for the absence of wage equalization in those periods. An examination of the data indicates that it would be a mistake to attribute the different behavior of wages and capital in the three periods to the varying fortunes of agriculture.

The states that suffered declines in agricultural income were in fact largely low-wage states. It is reasonable to expect that the demand for nonagricultural services would also suffer in these states; hence, low-wage states would experience a low rate of increase of nonagricultural wages as a consequence of the depression in the agricultural sector. To carry the argument further, the low-wage states would experience the strongest wage increase in the 1929–1948 period as a consequence of the sharp expansion of agricultural income at that time.

The explanation requires that the wage convergence of 1929–1948, and the wage divergence of the other two periods, be observable mainly in the agricultural states. It is contradicted by the data. The behavior of wages in the agricultural states frequently departs from this historical pattern. Therefore we can reject the presumption that the wage behavior in all states in the three periods is due to the influence of national agricultural patterns acting on the states most heavily dependent on this industry.[16]

15. The discrepancy between the two coefficients occurs because of the nature of the simple correlations between the variates. The correlation of two ratios, $X/Z$ and $Y/Z$, will yield the same results as the partial of $X$ on $Y$, given $Z$, when the regressions of $X$ on $Z$ and $Y$ on $Z$ are homogeneous. This condition is not fulfilled in the 1948–1953 period. For a proof of the proposition, see Meyer and Kuh [8, App. C].

16. These conclusions are based upon an examination of the behavior of wage levels and wage growth in agricultural and nonagricultural states. The states in Table 1 were classified by the importance of agriculture. It was observed that the wage behavior observed in the three periods held as well for the states least dependent upon agriculture.

## C.   The Interaction Between Increase in Wages and Reallocation

In Section I, it was argued that an increase in the relative price of output in labor-intensive industries would raise the real wage. This proposition is demonstrated graphically in the Appendix. It is there also shown that the elimination of excessive employment in labor intensive industries might raise the real wage in states with a high proportion of such industries. The possible existence of these two influences has been investigated for the 1929–1948 period. This period was chosen out of the three because it was long enough to permit the adjustments which the analysis presumes. Further, it encompasses the strongest equalization movement of the three periods. The data indicate that it is the one period out of the three in which the sharpest reallocation of employment occurred between the labor-intensive and capital-intensive sectors of each state. Any effect that the elimination of misallocation might have on the real wage should show up in this period.

If these two influences are to be detected, they will show up as a change in wages over and above that already explained by the change in the return to capital relative to the number employed.[17]

17. The wage per worker in one sector of a region's economy may be written as:

$$W = f_L \cdot P_x$$

where $f_L$ is the marginal physical product of labor, and $P_X$ the price of output. Similarly, the money return per unit of capital may be written as:

$$R = f_C \cdot P_x$$

where $f_C$ is the marginal physical product of capital. $f_L$ and $f_C$ are functions of $C/L$, the ratio of physical capital to labor. Ignoring second-order terms,

$$dW = f_L \cdot dP_x + P_x f'_L d\left(\frac{C}{L}\right)$$

$$\frac{dW}{W} = \frac{dP_x}{P_x} + \frac{f'_L}{f_L} d\left(\frac{C}{L}\right)$$

and

$$dR = f_C \cdot dP_x + P_x f'_C d\left(\frac{C}{L}\right)$$

$$\frac{dR}{R} = \frac{dP_x}{P_x} + \frac{f'_C}{f_C} d\left(\frac{C}{L}\right)$$

Substituting, we have

$$\frac{dW}{W} = \frac{dR}{R} + \left(\frac{f'_L}{f_L} - \frac{f'_C}{f_C}\right) d\left(\frac{C}{L}\right)$$

The wage per worker will rise: (a) if there is a rise in the money return per unit of capital, (b) if there is a rise in the proportion of physical capital per worker, (c) if there is a rise in the marginal product of labor and therefore a fall in the marginal product of

It is not possible to measure directly the change in relative prices of the labor-intensive and capital-intensive sectors of each state. An approximation is made on the basis of empirical specification of the content of the two sectors.[18] I shall approximate the relative increase of prices in each state sector by the difference between the relative increase in wage earnings per employee in the two sectors. This measure is useful only when wages in the two sectors are initially and finally unequal. If they were always equal, the index would have a value of zero. Because wage equality does not exist initially or finally, the index should provide a useful measure of the extent to which the prices of the products of the labor intensive sector have risen relative to the prices of the products of the capital-intensive sector.[19]

The actual measure employed is the percentage rise of service wages less the percentage rise of manufacturing wages. This measure will be used to classify the residuals from the regression of wage growth on the growth of the capital-labor ratio. The relation is summarized in Table 3. There is a strong significant association between the residuals from the regression and the relative increase of wages in the two sectors.[20] In those states where the average wages grew by a greater percentage than predicted by capital accumulation the service wage grew far more rapidly than the manufacturing wage.

TABLE 3    Classification of Residuals from Regression Between Wage Increase and Increase in the Capital-Labor Ratio, 48 States, 1929–1948

| INCREASE IN WAGES IN SERVICES SECTOR LESS INCREASE IN WAGES IN MANUFACTURING SECTOR | WAGE INCREASE GREATER THAN PREDICTED BY REGRESSION | WAGE INCREASE LESS THAN PREDICTED BY REGRESSION |
|---|---|---|
| | STATES | STATES |
| Greater than average | 15 | 9 |
| Less than average | 5 | 19 |

capital. The effects of (a) and (b) on $dW/W$ have been taken into account by correlating the change in wages with the change in the return to capital relative to the number of workers. The effect of (c) is to be taken into account by determining the extent to which unexplained changes in $dW/W$ are related to changes in the relative price of labor- and capital-intensive sectors.

18. The two sectors are defined in footnote 7.

19. The use of this measure requires that technological change either be absent or have little effect on the ratio of prices to wages in each sector.

20. A significance test on the contingency table yields a value of $\chi^2 = 8.58$ which is significant at the 1 per cent level. A test on the average value of the residuals from the regression yields a significant value of $F = 7.758$, with 13 per cent of the variance of the growth of wages explained by this classification.

The interpretation of this relation must be clarified. It may exist because of the elimination of wage differentials in the two sectors or because of the alteration of service prices relative to manufacturing prices.[21] The index of wage changes may be written as follows:

$$\frac{\Delta W_s}{W_s} - \frac{\Delta W_m}{W_m} = \frac{W_s^1 - W_s^0}{W_s^0} - \frac{W_m^1 - W_m^0}{W_m^0}$$

where $W_s$ denotes service wages, $W_m$ denotes manufacturing wages; the superscript 1 denotes the later time period, the superscript 0 denotes the initial time period. If we assume that wages in the two sectors are equalized in the final period, the index becomes:

$$\frac{W_s^1 - W_s^0}{W_s^0} - \frac{W_s^1 - W_m^0}{W_m^0} = \frac{W_s^1(W_m^0 - W_s^0)}{W_s^0 W_m^0}.$$

The index then depends upon the initial discrepancy between wages in the two sectors and the final level of wages. This form of the index was computed to determine its relation to the regression residuals. In a sense this provides a test of the hypothesis that the observed association is explainable in terms of the equalization of wages that took place in the two sectors. For it removes from the index any influence of sectoral wage differences in the final period. The index was computed for each state in the form shown above. When the index is compared with the residuals from the regression, the contingency table that results is not significant. That is, classification by the index in the above form does not classify the regression residuals in a significant fashion.[22] The index was also computed under the assumption that wage equality results among states as well as within states. That is, the index computed was

$$\frac{W_m^0 - W_s^0}{W_m^0 \cdot W_s^0}.$$

21. The elimination of sectoral differentials would yield an increase in the average wage if the sector with growing wages strongly outweighed the other sector in importance.
22. The resulting contingency table is the following:

| INCREASE IN SERVICE WAGES LESS INCREASE IN MANUFACTURING WAGES | WAGE INCREASE GREATER THAN PREDICTED | WAGE INCREASE LESS THAN PREDICTED |
|---|---|---|
| Greater than average | 10 | 14 |
| Less than average | 10 | 14 |

Again, there is no relation between this classification and the residuals from the regression.[23]

From this we conclude that elimination of the initial discrepancy in wages between sectors in each state does not by itself explain any of the wage increase in the period. The residual wage increase is, however, explained by the increase of service wages relative to manufacturing wages. This indicates that those states that enjoyed the greatest increase of service prices relative to manufacturing prices appear to have undergone a reallocation of resources yielding an increase in the capital-labor ratio, and an increase in the marginal product of labor.

The results of these tests indicate that the second model plays a powerful role in explaining the increase of wages and capital among states. In the next section, certain aspects of this model are examined in greater detail.

## D.   The Convergence of Wages

We have seen that nonagricultural wage differences failed to narrow in two of the three time intervals examined. They diverged considerably from 1919 to 1929; and only in the 1929–1948 period was there a continuation of the convergence pattern which investigators found prior to 1920. It is useful to inquire why these different patterns occurred, and what light they shed on the possibility for future narrowing of wage differences. Possible answers can be phrased in terms of the general framework presented at the beginning of this paper.

1. The failure of wages to converge is rather surprising in view of the available evidence that these periods witnessed considerable interstate migration from low- to high-wage states.[24]

While migration was going on in the right direction it is conceivable that varying rates of migration might be responsible for the failure of wages to converge. If interstate migration from low- to high-wage areas slowed down, then the rate of wage convergence

---

23. The resulting contingency table is:

| INCREASE IN SERVICE WAGES LESS INCREASE IN MANUFACTURING WAGES | WAGE INCREASE GREATER THAN PREDICTED | WAGE INCREASE LESS THAN PREDICTED |
|---|---|---|
| Greater than average | 10 | 14 |
| Less than average | 10 | 14 |

24. Migration data have been collected on a uniform basis in [6]. The states have been classified by their average wage and by the degree of in-migration or out-migration (measured in migrants as a percentage of population). The results for the two time-intervals for which migration data are available are shown below. They indicate a

might stop. Further, if the rate of migration failed to empty an area as fast as the birth rate was filling it, the pressure of labor supply on wages in a low-wage area might prevent convergence. What evidence exists seems to contradict this explanation.[25] However, even if the migration data supported this explanation, it would still not deal with the evidence on capital accumulation. Capital was growing more rapidly in high-wage states in two of the three periods examined. Migration in response to wage differentials cannot explain this movement of capital.

Migration might be used to explain capital formation through the influence of new in-migrants on capital requirements. It might be argued that when a large population influx hits an urban area, there is a demand for capital to provide housing and public and private services. This was suggested earlier as one of the causes of growth of high-wage areas. Both the 1919–1929 and 1948–1953 intervals follow periods in which there was strong migration from low- to high-wage states. Prior to each of these periods there were restrictions on the volume of urban construction because of wartime use of materials and of capital funds. It is possible that the higher growth of capital in high-wage areas in these two periods represents a catching up in the stock of urban capital required by prior increases of population.

---

strong positive association between migration and wage level. That is, low-wage states experienced greater out-migration, and high-wage states experienced in-migration.

| | HIGH-WAGE STATES | | LOW-WAGE STATES | |
| --- | --- | --- | --- | --- |
| | 1919–29 | 1929–48 | 1919–29 | 1929–48 |
| States showing net in-migration: | | | | |
| 1920–1930 | 14 | — | 2 | — |
| 1930–1950 | — | 15 | — | 5 |
| States showing net out-migration: | | | | |
| 1920–1930 | 9 | — | 23 | — |
| 1930–1950 | — | 11 | — | 17 |

In both time intervals, the strong association is due primarily to the high out-migration from low-wage areas. The degree of association is stronger in the earlier period.

25. We have already seen in the previous footnote that the relation between migration and wages is stronger in the 1919–1929 period, when wages diverged. In this period, there is also a strong association between wage increase and population growth. That is, migration was strong enough to slow the rate of population growth of low-wage regions. This is seen in the following table which classifies the 48 states by the wage level in 1919 and the rate of population growth between 1919 and 1929.

| | ABOVE AVERAGE WAGES | BELOW AVERAGE WAGES |
| --- | --- | --- |
| Above average population growth 1919–1929 | 14 | 4 |
| Below average population growth | 9 | 21 |

Thus in the period 1919–1929 migration was sufficient to produce an emptying of low-wage areas and yet insufficient to produce wage equalization.

The same capital formation pattern would not be observed in the 1929–1948 period because of the depression followed by the war.

The evidence on migration and on population growth does not give uniform support to this explanation. In Table 4, for 1919–1929 and for 1948–1953, the states are classified by capital growth and employment increase. For each case the average rate of population growth and rate of migration for the period prior to the one examined is shown. If the above explanation be valid, then states with higher rates of capital formation should have had higher rates of in-migration (shown as positive) and higher rates of population growth in the earlier period.

TABLE 4   Average Rate of Population Growth and Average Rate of In-migration (+) in 48 States, Classified by Employment Growth and by Capital Growth, 1919–1929, 1948–1953

*1919–1929*

|  |  | HIGH CAPITAL GROWTH | LOW CAPITAL GROWTH |
|---|---|---|---|
| High employment increase | 1. Average Rate of Population Growth 1910–1920 | 17.84% | 18.64% |
|  | 2. Average Rate of Migration Per Capita 1910–1920 | +0.019 | +0.002 |
| Low employment increase | 1. Average Rate of Population Growth 1910–1920 | 10.60% | 15.63% |
|  | 2. Average Rate of Migration Per Capita 1910–1920 | −0.010 | +0.013 |

*1948–1953*

|  |  | HIGH CAPITAL GROWTH | LOW CAPITAL GROWTH |
|---|---|---|---|
| High employment increase | 1. Average Rate of Population Growth 1930–1950 | 38.86% | 12.05% |
|  | 2. Average Rate of Migration Per Capita 1930–1950 | +0.107 | −0.205 |
| Low employment increase | 1. Average Rate of Population Growth 1930–1950 | 14.54% | 19.66% |
|  | 2. Average Rate of Migration Per Capita 1930–1950 | −0.067 | −0.070 |

The implication of the hypothesis with regard to population growth is contradicted by the data. In 3 out of 4 cases, holding employment increase constant, the states with higher capital growth had smaller rates of population growth. The data on migration agree with the hypothesis in three out of four cases, showing higher in-migration or lower out-migration in states with higher rates of

**165**

capital formation. However, in one case, the agreement is by the very small margin of three migrants per 1,000 of state population. In the cases where agreement is strong, the difference is as large as 310 migrants per 1,000 of state population. The hypothesis receives its strongest support in the 1948–1953 period. It receives no confirmation in the 1919–1929 period. For these reasons I would not attribute a great deal of importance to the role of migration as a general explanation of differences in capital formation.

2. There is a second possible explanation of the failure of wages to converge in two periods. If the marginal efficiency of investment was influenced primarily by the demand for commodities produced by the export sector of each region, there might be an export boom in high-wage states. This explanation requires that in the 1919–1929 and 1948–1953 periods demand for the products of high-wage industries increased relative to the demand for the products of low-wage industries. In the 1929–1948 period the reverse would have to occur.

Investigators have discovered a high correlation between the industrial composition of a state and the average wage level.[26] A state with a large proportion of nationally high-wage industries tends to have a higher average wage than a state with a large proportion of nationally low-wage industries. Therefore, a relative increase nationally in the demand for the products of high-wage industries would primarily affect the states containing such industries.

The influence of demand conditions can be perceived partly through the changes of prices. If demand for a certain class of goods rises more than for another class, we can expect the prices of the former class to rise by a greater proportion, other things being equal. The factors remaining equal would be technology and the other influences on the elasticity of supply. We would also expect the output of this sector to rise more rapidly than in other sectors. Using this as a background, we can inquire how the high-wage and low-wage industries of the country behaved in these periods.

Is there evidence that from 1929 to 1948 demand for the products of low-wage industries rose more rapidly than demand for products of high-wage industries? The price data do not support such an expectation. The wholesale prices of 34 manufactured products were examined between 1929 and 1948. The wage levels and wage increases in the industries producing these commodities were also examined.[27]

26. See Muth[9, pp. 878–939], Hanna[4], and Perloff[12].

27. The rank correlation among industries between the wage level in 1929 and relative price increase from 1929 to 1948 is not significantly different from zero. Price data for 1919, 1929, 1948, and 1953 were taken from [24] [25] [26] [27] [28]. Also, data for 1953 were taken from [29]. Data on wages and wage increases by industry for 1919, 1929, 1948 and 1953 were taken from the relevant Censuses of Manufactures for the years 1919, 1929, and 1947 [18] [20] [21]; data for 1948 and 1953 were taken from [30].

There is no indication that products of low-wage industries rose more in price than products of high-wage industries. At the same time it appears that the wage increases in high-wage industries were on the average less than that in low-wage industries. This is the convergence pattern among industrial wages alluded to earlier.[28] This indicates that there was a difference in the elasticity of labor supply facing the two sectors. Labor shifted from low- to high-wage sectors, especially after 1939 with the appearance of war-induced employment opportunities. This would increase the likelihood that a greater increase in demand for low-wage products would yield greater price increases than in high-wage products. Nevertheless, the data gave no support to such an expectation. There is no indication that the demand for low-wage products grew more rapidly than that for high-wage products from 1929 to 1948.

What of the other two periods? Here the evidence is mixed. There is clear support for the demand thesis in the 1948–1953 period. In this period there is a strong positive correlation between the initial wage level and the subsequent growth of prices. There is also a strong positive correlation between the initial wage level and the subsequent increase in wages. In this period, the high-wage industries experienced greater wage growth and greater relative price increase than the low-wage industries.[29] Thus, the regional growth patterns appear to be dominated by national demand conditions in the 1948–1953 period.

For the 1919–1929 period there is no evidence that demand conditions had a differential effect on wholesale prices or wages. In view of the divergence of wages among states in this period we should expect to find prices and wages in high-wage sectors growing more rapidly than in low-wage sectors. Actually, we find no pattern at all. There is no relation between the level of wages paid in 1919 and the subsequent growth in prices. Further, there is no relation between the initial level of wages and the subsequent increase in wages. Finally, there is no relation between wage increases and price increases. Despite this lack of confirmation from wage and price data, there are two kinds of evidence that support the demand thesis:

(a) It is clear that the physical output of high-wage sectors grew by a greater proportion than the physical output of low-wage sectors. Output indexes and wage data for 59 manufacturing industry groups

28. The Spearman rank correlation among 34 commodities between the 1929 wage level and the 1929–1948 percentage wage increase is −0.36, which is significant in the probability sense at the 5 per cent level.

29. The rank correlation among 34 industries between the wage level and relative price growth is +0.49. The rank correlation between the wage level and relative wage growth is +0.71. Both are significant at the 5 per cent level.

were examined. A significant positive association was found between the growth of output and the level of wages.[30]

(b) Innovations among the high-wage manufacturing industries appear to have been labor-saving relative to innovations among the low-wage manufacturing industries. This would explain why increases in the demand for high-wage products had not yielded corresponding increases in prices or in wages of this sector.[31]

These two pieces of evidence indicate that demand for high-wage products grew more than demand for low-wage products from 1919 to 1929. While this did not generate a differential pattern of wage or price increases among industries, it apparently affected capital accumulation in the states containing such industries. It also affected wages in the other industries of these states.

3. A third possible explanation is that the marginal efficiency of investment was influenced primarily by wage differentials in the 1929–1948 period, but not in the other two periods. A strong case can be made for the influence of demand in the other two periods, and I have cited the data that support this view.

The one group of products where wage differentials could be expected to have the greatest influence is manufacturing. In this sector one is most likely to find exportable commodities that are neither materials nor market-oriented. In the mining and agricultural sectors, production-function differences are likely to dominate any influence of wage differentials. In the service, transportation, and construction sectors, the growth characteristics of the market are likely to dominate the influence of wage differentials. An examination

30. The following table classifies the 59 industry groups by percentage growth of physical output and wage level. The resulting value of $\chi^2$ is 12.37, which is significant at the 1 per cent level.

| | WAGE LEVEL 1919 | |
| --- | --- | --- |
| GROWTH OF OUTPUT | ABOVE MEDIAN | BELOW MEDIAN |
| Above median | 21 | 8 |
| Below median | 8 | 22 |

Manufacturing output indexes are taken from S. Fabricant [2a].

31. The degree to which an industry has experienced a labor-saving innovation is measured by the change in the ratio of wage payments to value added. The logic underlying this measure can be seen by assuming the production function in an industry to be homogeneous of the first degree in the inputs of labor and capital, and that labor is paid the value of its marginal product. Then, the marginal physical product of labor (MP) and the average product of labor (AP) are both decreasing functions of the ratio of labor to capital (L/C). A decrease in the ratio MP/AP will occur if L/C increases or if there has been an innovation such that at the new equilibrium MP/AP is lower than before. In view of the fact that this was a period of rapid capital accumulation, and that wages in these industries did not fall relative to wages in other industries, it seems unlikely that L/C increased. Therefore, it seems reasonable to attribute declines in MP/AP to the emergence of labor-saving inventions. The ratio MP/AP is measured by the ratio

of the growth of manufacturing employment in the period 1929–48 supports the presumption that low wages were an influence on the marginal efficiency of investment. Table 5 shows the average growth of manufacturing employment in the 48 states, classified in the same fashion as above, *i.e.*, by the growth of total nonagricultural capital, and by the increase in nonagricultural employment. In addition, the states are classified within each box by the average nonagricultural wage. The states with wages below the national average are shown under B, those with wages above the national average are shown under A. X is the average growth of manufacturing employment of the states in the subclassification.

TABLE 5   Average Rate of Increase of Manufacturing Employment in 48 States, Classified by Nonagricultural Wage Level, Growth of Non-agricultural Capital and Increase in Nonagricultural Employment, 1929–1948*

|  |  | HIGH GROWTH OF CAPITAL | |  | LOW GROWTH OF CAPITAL | |
|---|---|---|---|---|---|---|
|  |  | A | B |  | A | B |
| High Increase in Nonagricul-tural Employment | n | 5 | 11 | n | 8 | 0 |
|  | X | 15.98% | 48.29% | X | 47.66% | — |
|  |  | A | B |  | A | B |
| Low Increase in Nonagricul-tural Employment | n | 2 | 6 | n | 10 | 6 |
|  | X | 16.07% | 34.98% | X | 26.14% | 38.27% |

*n: number of states. X: average percentage increase of manufacturing employment. A: nonagricultural wages above the national average. B: nonagricultural wages below the national average.

It can be seen that within the three boxes that permit comparison, the high-wage states showed less increase in manufacturing employment than the low-wage states. This indicates that low wages are an influence on the demand for labor; or more specifically, on the marginal efficiency of investment in manufacturing.

This relation is either much weaker or nonexistent in the other two periods. Thus, there is confirmation that the influence of wage

of the wage bill to value added, which is, essentially, $(MP \cdot P_x)/(AP \cdot P_x)$, where $P_x$ is the price of output. It should be noted that the ratio of wages to value added might fall if there was an increase in the monopoly power of an industry, because the wage would be not $P_x \cdot MP_L$, but $P_x(1 + 1/\eta)MP_L$, where $\eta$ is the elasticity of demand. However, this would have shown up as a price increase in certain industries; and since it fails to show up, I have excluded it as a possible explanation. The relation between the wage level in an industry in 1919, and the change in the ratio of the wage bill to value added from 1919 to 1929 is shown below:

| RATIO OF WAGE BILL TO VALUE ADDED | HIGH WAGES INDUSTRIES | LOW WAGES INDUSTRIES |  |
|---|---|---|---|
| Rose | 1 |  | $\chi^2 = 9.22$, significant at the 1 per cent level. |
| Fell | 21 |  | |

Data are from [18, 20].

differentials on the marginal efficiency of investment was much stronger between 1929 and 1948 than in the other periods. Table 6 shows the same classification of states for the 1919–1929 and 1948–1953 periods. In the 1919–1929 period the influence of wage differentials is much weaker than in 1929–1948 in three cases, and is opposite to what is expected in one case. In the 1948–1953 period, comparison is possible in only three boxes. In two of these the influence of wage differentials is again weaker than in 1929–1948; and in the third, we observe the opposite of what is expected.

TABLE 6   Average Rate of Increase of Manufacturing Employment in 48 States, Classified by Nonagricultural Wage Level, Growth of Nonagricultural Capital, and Increase in Nonagricultural Employment, 1919–1929 and 1948–1953*

|  | | 1919–1929 | | | | |
|---|---|---|---|---|---|---|
|  | | HIGH CAPITAL GROWTH | | | LOW CAPITAL GROWTH | |
|  | | A | B | | A | B |
| High Increase in Nonagricultural Employment | n | 7 | 6 | n | 5 | 6 |
|  | X | 0.80% | 4.56% | X | 8.76% | 16.45% |
|  | | A | B | | A | B |
| Low Increase in Nonagricultural Employment | n | 7 | 4 | n | 4 | 9 |
|  | X | −12.25% | −15.88% | X | −8.10% | −1.91% |
|  | | 1948–1953 | | | | |
|  | | HIGH CAPITAL GROWTH | | | LOW CAPITAL GROWTH | |
|  | | A | B | | A | B |
| High Increase in Nonagricultural Employment | n | 10 | 10 | n | 0 | 4 |
|  | X | 26.69% | 22.41% | X | − | 13.87% |
|  | | A | B | | A | B |
| Low Increase in Nonagricultural Employment | n | 3 | 1 | n | 10 | 10 |
|  | X | 7.66% | 14.22% | X | 5.33% | 6.33% |

*n: number of states. X: average percentage increase of manufacturing employment. A: nonagricultural wages above the national average. B: nonagricultural wages below the national average.

## III.  CONCLUSIONS

1. The role of demand appears to have a strong influence on the relative movements of capital and on the increase in wages in the different states. This appears to be the chief reason why wage convergence failed to appear in two out of three periods; and it indicates strong support for a model of regional growth based on the demand for a region's exports.

2. The influence of wage differentials on the marginal efficiency of investment appears only in the 1929–1948 period. Here we observe a convergence of wages among states. However, this period also witnessed an influence favorable to wage increases which is not likely to

be repeated. This was the increase in the marginal product of labor arising from the relative increase in prices in the labor-intensive sectors of growing states.

3. In all periods examined, interstate migration occurs, as expected, from low- to high-wage areas. Nevertheless, migration does not appear sufficient to produce convergence. It clearly produces less divergence than would occur were migration to halt. The chief influence favorable to the increase in wages appears to be the movement of capital, and this is apparently not explainable by migration patterns.

In view of these conclusions, the prospects for wage convergence appear to depend on three elements: (a) continuation of migration from low- to high-wage areas; (b) elimination of the major driving force behind migration, namely the high population reproduction rate in low-wage areas; (c) the direction of capital formation to low-wage areas. Whether wages will continue to converge in the future depends on the relative strength of these three elements. We have observed two periods in which they interacted to prevent convergence.

## APPENDIX

The influence of accumulation on the marginal physical product of labor may be demonstrated graphically with the aid of the familiar box diagram.[32] In Figure 1 the quantity of labor employed is measured along the vertical axis, capital along the horizontal. Inputs for sector X (labor intensive) are measured from the southwest origin, inputs for sector Y are measured from the northeast origin. The ray from each origin shows the ratio of labor to capital that would be employed at a given set of factor prices in the production of each commodity. At their intersection point $\alpha$, the isoquants (not shown) are tangent to one another; and their slope at this point gives the marginal rate of substitution between $L$ and $C$ employed in both sectors. This slope corresponds to the relative prices of the factors. The dashed line through $\alpha$ is the contract curve showing other maximum values of X that could be produced for other given values of Y. It is assumed that $\alpha$ is the only efficient point in the box with this value of the marginal rate of substitution. Under these assumptions every point on the contract curve will be represented by a corresponding point on a convex production-possibility curve in X and Y. The combination of X and Y at $\alpha$ will be produced only for a unique value of $P_x/P_y$.[33] Therefore, the capital-labor ratios in X and Y will be

32. A complete demonstration is to be found in Rybczynski[13].
33. See Bator[1], Worswick[16], and Green[3].

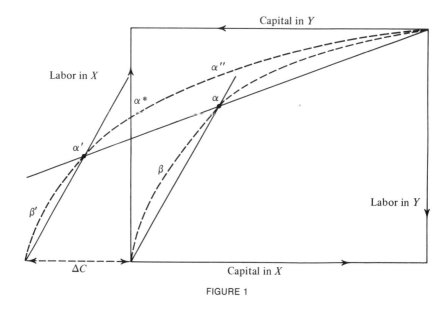

FIGURE 1

used only for that value of $P_x/P_y$. If the value of $P_x/P_y$ changes, then production will shift to some other point on the contract curve,[34] and other values of the capital-labor ratios will be employed.

Now let us increase the amount of capital by $\Delta C$. This shifts the horizontal dimension of the box as shown. At $\alpha'$, where the production of Y has increased and X decreased, the capital-labor ratio is unchanged in each sector, and the marginal rate of substitution between the products X and Y is unchanged. Therefore, the value of $P_x/P_y$ at $\alpha'$ is the same as at $\alpha$. However, if output had shifted to $\alpha*$ (on the new contract curve going through $\alpha'$), the capital-labor ratios in both industries would have risen. This would occur when the price of X had risen relative to the price of Y.

Thus, we have reached the following conclusions:

1. Accumulation will lead to an increase in the marginal physical product of labor when it is accompanied by a rise in the ratio of capital to labor in each industry sector.

2. This will occur when the price of output of the labor-intensive sector rises relative to the price of output of the capital-intensive sector.

3. This means that the output of the capital-intensive sector has failed to expand by enough to leave the ratios of input combinations unchanged.

34. Points on the contract curve are consistent with long-run equilibrium in each industry. Short-run equilibrium positions which are not long-run equilibrium positions represent movements off the contract curve.

4. If accumulation leads to an increase in the marginal physical product of labor, it will also result in a decline in the marginal physical product of capital.

Similar conclusions would be reached if in the initial situation labor was misallocated and wage differentials existed between the X and Y industries. The elimination of the misallocation can, but does not necessarily, provide an impetus to the increase in wages over and above any produced by accumulation. For example, assume that efficient point $\alpha$ is consistent with the long-run equilibrium of demand and supply in industries X and Y. Further, assume that the pre-accumulation allocation was inefficient and was located at $\alpha''$ in Figure 1. This would involve an excessive employment of labor in the labor-intensive sector X.[35] At point $\alpha''$, the price of X relative to Y $(P_x/P_y)$, the marginal physical product of labor in X, and the wage per worker in X all were lower than they would have been at $\alpha$, while the marginal physical product of labor and the wage per worker were higher in Y than they would have been at $\alpha$. If the X sector were large enough, its relatively low wage would overshadow the relatively high wage paid by the Y sector and pull down the total wages paid in the region. In this case the elimination of misallocation and a movement from $\alpha''$ to $\alpha$ would raise the total wage payment.

That this does not necessarily happen, however, can be seen from the following: Suppose that $\alpha''$ were to become an efficient point as a result of the accumulation $\Delta C$; that is, it becomes a point on the new contract curve going through $\alpha'$ and $\alpha^*$. Further suppose that the price ratio in effect of $\alpha''$ remained unchanged due to the nature of changes in demand conditions for the two sectors accompanying the accumulation. The result would be a change in allocation between the two sectors such that the marginal physical product of labor in the two sectors is either lower or unchanged from the situation when labor was misallocated.

This result can be seen in the following way. Initial demand conditions were such that $\alpha$ would be the efficient point with a value of the price ratio equal to $P'_x/P'_y$. At $\alpha''$ the price ratio in effect was lower than $P'_x/P'_y$ because more X and less Y was produced than at $\alpha$. Call the price ratio at $\alpha''$ $P''_x/P''_y$. There is an efficient production point corresponding to $P''_x/P''_y$ which is to the southwest of $\alpha$. Call this point $\beta$. Corresponding to $\beta$ is an efficient point $\beta'$ on the new contract curve with the same price ratio. If when $\alpha''$ becomes efficient, the price ratio remains at $P''_x/P''_y$, allocation will move to $\beta'$. At $\beta'$, the ratio of capital to labor in Y is lower than at $\alpha''$, while the ratio in X is not

35. Such a description appears to be a reasonable explanation of the wide discrepancy in earnings between the services sector and the manufacturing sector to be found in many low-income states prior to the second world war.

perceptibly changed from what it was when $\alpha''$ was inefficient. At $\beta'$, the money wage in X is equal to that in Y. This has been accomplished through a fall of the wage in Y.

We see that the movement from $\alpha''$ to $\beta'$ is a depressant on the marginal physical product of labor outweighing the elimination of the misallocation. Thus, the elimination of misallocation will not necessarily raise wages in a region when accompanied by accumulation. This depends on the final production point.

Note that if $P_x/P_y$ had risen above $P_x''/P_y''$, there could have been an increase in wages. For example, if $P_x/P_y$ had risen sufficiently, allocation could have remained at $\alpha''$ after it became efficient. All the additional capital ($\Delta C$) would then have been used in X to raise the marginal physical product of labor in that sector up to a level where the money wage in X again equaled that in Y.

Thus, the conclusions are the same as before: In order for the marginal physical product of labor to rise as a consequence of accumulation, there must be an increase in the relative price of labor-intensive goods.

## REFERENCES

1. F. M. BATOR, "The Simple Analytics of Warfare Maximization," *American Economic Review* (Mar., 1957), XLVII, 22–59.
2. R. A. EASTERLIN, "Income Differentials Among States, 1880–1950," *Proceedings of the Regional Science Association* (1958), IV, 313–28.
2a. S. FABRICANT, *The Output of Manufacturing Industries, 1899–1939* (New York, National Bureau of Economic Research, 1940).
3. H. A. J. GREEN, "Mr. Worswick on the Production Possibility Function," *Economic Journal*, (Mar., 1959), LXIX, 177–80.
4. F. A. HANNA, "Analysis of Interstate Income Differentials: Theory and Practice," in National Bureau of Economic Research, *Regional Income*, Studies in Income and Wealth, XXI, (Princeton, 1957).
5. C. B. HOOVER and B. U. RATCHFORD, *Economic Resources and Policies of the South* (New York, 1951).
6. E. S. LEE, A. R. MILLER, C. P. BRAINARD, R. A. EASTERLIN, *Population Redistribution and Economic Growth, United States, 1870–1950* (Philadelphia, 1957).
7. M. LEVEN, *Income in the Various States* (New York, National Bureau of Economic Research, 1925).
8. J. R. MEYER and E. KUH, *The Investment Decision* (Cambridge, 1957).
9. R. F. MUTH, "Variations in Levels and Rates of Growth of Per Capita Income," Pt. 4, *Regional Economic Growth in the United States*, Program of Regional Studies, Resources for the Future. (Washington, D.C., mimeo, 1959).
10. D. C. NORTH, "Location Theory and Regional Economic Growth," *Journal of Political Economy* (June, 1955), LXIII, 243–58 [Selection 3 of this volume].

11. D. C. NORTH, "A Reply"; and C. M. TIEBOUT, "Rejoinder," *Journal of Political Economy* (Apr., 1956), LXIV, 165–69.

12. H. S. PERLOFF, "Interrelations of State Income and Industrial Structure," *Review of Economics and Statistics* (May 1957), XXXIX, 162–71.

13. T. M. RYBCZYNSKI, "Factor Endowment and Relative Commodity Prices," *Economica*, N.S. (Nov. 1955), XXII, 336–41.

14. P. A. SAMUELSON, "Prices of Factors and Goods in General Equilibrium," *Review of Economic Studies*, (1953–54), XXI, 1–20.

15. C. M. TIEBOUT, "Exports and Regional Economic Growth," *Journal of Political Economy* (Apr., 1956), LXIV, 160–64.

16. G. D. N. WORSWICK, "The Convexity of the Production Possibility Function," *Economic Journal* (Dec., 1957), LXVII, 748–51.

17. U.S. Dept. of Commerce, Bureau of the Census, *Fourteenth Census of the U.S., 1920*, IV, *Population* (Washington, 1922).

18. ———, *Fourteenth Census of the U.S., 1920*, IX, *Manufacturing, 1919* (Washington, 1923).

19. ———, *Fifteenth Census of the U.S., 1930*, III, *Population* (Washington, 1932).

20. ———, *Fifteenth Census of the U.S., 1930*, III, *Manufacturing, 1929* (Washington, 1933).

21. ———, *Census of Manufactures, 1947*, II, *Statistics by Industry* (Washington, 1949).

22. U.S. Dept. of Commerce, Office of Business Economics, *Personal Income by States Since 1929* (Washington, 1956).

23. U.S. Dept. of Labor, Bureau of Labor Statistics, *State Employment, 1948–1953* (Washington, 1955).

24. ———, *Wholesale Prices, 1913–1927*, Bull. No. 473 (Washington, 1929).

25. ———, *Wholesale Prices, 1929*, Bull. No. 521 (Washington, 1930).

26. ———, *Wholesale Prices, 1947*, Bull. No. 947 (Washington, 1949).

27. ———, *Wholesale Prices, 1948*, Bull. No. 973 (Washington, 1950).

28. ———, *Wholesale Prices and Price Indexes 1954–1956*, Bull. No. 1214 (Washington, 1957).

29. ———, *Monthly Labor Review, 1954* (Washington, 1954).

30. ———, *Employment, Hours, and Earnings*, 1948, 1953 (Washington, D.C. 1948).

PAUL E. SMITH

# 12

## Markov Chains, Exchange Matrices, and Regional Development

In light of the recent attention paid to the appearance and discovery of so-called depressed areas in the United States, and to cold war developments in Latin America and Southeast Asia, it has become understandably fashionable among economists and political decision makers to be concerned with regional economic development. Unfortunately, it is not always clear just what is meant by either "depressed" or "region," although the former term is usually taken to imply that the area in question has a lower per-capita income than other similarly defined areas. We shall adopt this definition for the lack of a better one and avoid the political, geographical, and economic pitfalls of the second problem by merely defining a region as a bordered topological space. Hence, we specify that the inhabitants of some regions enjoy a higher level of living than the residents of others and that it is deemed socially desirable to narrow the income gaps between regions.

Two broad types of solutions, both entailing the geographic reallocation of resources, are often proposed. The first or market solution is in the classical tradition and suggests that, if impediments to labor mobility are absent, human resources will move from the low-income regions to the high-income regions until the income differentials within competing groups are wiped out. In the case of noncompeting groups, public subsidized training programs are sometimes advocated, e.g., West Virginia coal miners are converted into California real estate brokers at government expense. However, recent legislation, possibly due in part to lobbying activities by California real estate brokers, has been aimed in the direction of subsidies to the inhabitants of depressed regions and the raising of the income base in those areas via capital investment.

The purpose of this paper is to explore the possibility of increasing the incomes of some regions relative to those of others. We shall not be concerned so much with the techniques of growth *per se*, but rather with whether such development can be attained within the framework of a model of interregional trade. For this purpose we will find it convenient to employ stochastic or Markov matrices as a useful mathematical tool. The problem will be briefly considered first from the standpoint of comparative statics and then within the

Smith, Paul E., "Markov Chains, Exchange Matrices, and Regional Development," Journal of Regional Science, III, No. 1 (1961), pp. 27–36.

context of a dynamic model. Numerical examples will be used extensively.

## 1.   COMPARATIVE STATICS

Consider $n$ geographic regions $R_1,...., R_n$ which may or may not trade with each other. Each region $R_i$ has income $Y_i$ which it spends either on its own output or the output of other regions, with domestic consumption and imports having linear and homogeneous relationships with its own income.[1] Hence $a_{ij}$ may be said to be the marginal and average propensity of $R_i$ to spend in $R_j$. Therefore, we can write the exchange matrix

$$A = \begin{pmatrix} a_{11}a_{12} \cdots a_{1n} \\ a_{21}a_{22} \cdots a_{2n} \\ \cdots\cdots\cdots\cdots \\ a_{n1}a_{n2} \cdots a_{nn} \end{pmatrix}$$

Clearly $A$ is a square matrix with nonnegative elements and with row sums equal to unity, *i.e.*, $a_{ij} \geq 0$ and $\Sigma_{j=1}^{n} a_{ij} = 1$. This is because no region can make negative expenditures in any region and in equilibrium each region spends all of its income. Therefore $A$ may be called a stochastic or Markov matrix of transition probabilities.

We shall call the subset of regions $R' \subset R$ closed if no region in $R$ imports from any region in $(R - R')$ so that $a_{ij} = 0$ for $i \in R'$ and $j \in (R - R')$. If $a_{ii} = 1$, then $R_i$ spends all of its income on its own output and is said to be an absorbing state or region. Moreover, if $R$ contains more than one closed set, the rows and columns of $A$ can be rearranged into $A^*$. $A^*$ is partitioned with closed sets of coefficients along the main diagonal, *i.e.*,

$$A^* = \begin{Bmatrix} A_1 & 0 & 0 & \cdot & \cdot & \cdot & 0 \\ 0 & A_2 & 0 & \cdot & \cdot & \cdot & 0 \\ 0 & 0 & A_3 & \cdot & \cdot & \cdot & 0 \\ \cdot & \cdot & \cdot & \cdot & \cdot & \cdot & 0 \\ \cdot & \cdot & \cdot & \cdot & \cdot & \cdot & \cdot \\ \cdot & \cdot & \cdot & \cdot & \cdot & \cdot & \cdot \\ 0 & \cdot & \cdot & \cdot & \cdot & \cdot & A_k \end{Bmatrix}$$

where the $A_i(i = 1, \ldots, k)$ are indecomposable or irreducible subsets of coefficients of the decomposable or reducible parent set $A$.

---

1. We assume that prices are held constant so that all variables are expressed in real terms.

The total income of each region $R_i$ is given by summing its sales to itself and all other regions, *i.e.*,

$$y_i = \sum_{j=1}^{n} a_{ji}y_j \tag{1}$$

Hence an equilibrium income vector is a vector $y = (y_1, y_2, \ldots, y_n)$ which satisfies the equation

$$A'y = y$$

or

$$(I - A')y = 0, \tag{2}$$

where $I$ is the identity matrix of order $n$. Equation (2) is seen to be equivalent to the set of $n$ homogeneous linear equations

$$(1 - a_{11})y_1 - a_{21}y_2 - \cdots - a_{n1}y_n = 0$$

$$-a_{12}y_1 + (1 - a_{22})y_2 - \cdots - a_{n2}y_n = 0 \tag{3}$$

$$\cdots\cdots\cdots\cdots\cdots\cdots\cdots\cdots$$

$$-a_{1n}y_1 - a_{2n}y_2 - \cdots + (1 - a_{nn})y_n = 0,$$

whose matrix is $(I - A)$. A basic theorem of linear algebra asserts that a nonzero solution vector $y$ of these equations exists if and only if $(I - A)$ is a singular matrix. We assume this to be the case and concern ourselves only with whether $y$ is non-negative as well. That such an equilibrium vector exists and that all of its elements are positive has already been proven by Gale[3]. For a more general discussion of existence and uniqueness theorems, see Baumol[1].

If $A$ is indecomposable, the equilibrium income vector $y$ is trivially nonunique in that any scalar multiple of a solution vector is also a solution vector. If $A$ is decomposable with indecomposable subsets $A_1, A_2, \ldots, A_k$ and if $y$ is an equilibrium solution vector for $A$, then $y = (y_1^*, y_2^*, \ldots, y_m^*, \ldots, y_k^*)$ where $y_m^*$ is an equilibrium solution vector for the set of regions with the nondecomposable submatrix $A_m$. That is, a solution vector can be found for each submatrix, and these can be suitably ordered so that they are also solution for $A$. Furthermore, a vector, say $cy^*$, found by multiplying any solution subvector by a positive scalar $c$ is also an equilibrium solution vector. Hence for decomposable matrices the general solution vector is nonunique from the standpoint of relative incomes since any non-negative linear combination of the subsolutions is also a solution.

**179**

A simple numerical example may help to illustrate the problem. Consider the three regions represented by the indecomposable matrix

$$A = \begin{pmatrix} 0.5 & 0.2 & 0.3 \\ 0 & 0.6 & 0.4 \\ 0.2 & 0 & 0.8 \end{pmatrix}$$

Inasmuch as each region receives its income from sales either to itself or to other regions, the equilibrium income vector $y$ can be found by simultaneously solving the system of homogeneous linear equations

$$\begin{aligned} 0.5\,y_1 && + 0.2\,y_3 &= y_1 \\ 0.2\,y_1 + 0.6\,y_2 && &= y_2 \\ 0.3\,y_1 + 0.4\,y_2 &+ 0.8\,y_3 &= y_3 \end{aligned}$$

which can be rewritten

$$\begin{aligned} -0.5\,y_1 && + 0.2\,y_3 &= 0 \\ 0.2\,y_1 - 0.4\,y_2 && &= 0 \\ 0.3\,y_1 + 0.4\,y_2 &- 0.2\,y_3 &= 0. \end{aligned}$$

The solution vector is

$$\bar{y} = (y_1, 0.5y_1, 2.5y_1),$$

where $y_1$ may be any arbitrary positive real number. In general, the equilibrium income vector will always take the form

$$\bar{y} = (y_i, b_1 y_i, \ldots b_{n-1} y_i) \tag{4}$$

for any indecomposable model with $n$ regions.

Two tentative conclusions can be derived at this point. In the first place it becomes immediately apparent in the static equilibrium model that if the elements of $A$ are held constant no improvement in a region's relative share of the total available income is possible. Therefore, it follows that any increase in the absolute level of income for a poor region, say Region 2 in the numerical example, must be accompanied by an even greater absolute increase in the incomes of its wealthier trading partners if the exchange model is to remain in equilibrium. The result is a widening of the absolute income gaps between regions.

Secondly, equilibrium growth can take place in the linear exchange model, the limiting requirement being that the growth rate must be the same for each region. As noted above, however, the basic problem is not solved because depressed regions become even more depressed relative to their wealthier neighbors. We remark that this may not be true in terms of utility, depending upon the elasticities of the marginal-utility-of-income schedules of the regions' inhabitants.

The situation is somewhat less hopeless if it is possible to reduce the regional complex into a set of indecomposable subsets of regions. To consider another numerical example, take a five-region model whose exchange matrix, after suitable reorganization, can be written

$$A^* = \begin{cases} \begin{matrix} 0.5 & 0.5 & 0 & 0 & 0 \\ 0.2 & 0.8 & 0 & 0 & 0 \\ 0 & 0 & 0.6 & 0.4 & 0 \\ 0 & 0 & 0.1 & 0.9 & 0 \\ 0 & 0 & 0 & 0 & 1.0 \end{matrix} \end{cases}$$

Note that Region 5 neither exports to nor imports from any other region and that subsets $A_1 = \begin{pmatrix} 0.5 & 0.5 \\ 0.2 & 0.8 \end{pmatrix}$ and $A_2 = \begin{pmatrix} 0.6 & 0.4 \\ 0.1 & 0.9 \end{pmatrix}$ are irreducible submatrices. Proceeding as before, we find that the equilibrium income vector is

$$\bar{y} = (y_1, 2.5y_1, y_3, 4y_3, y_5),$$

where $y_1$, $y_3$, and $y_5$ again are any nonnegative real numbers.

The conclusions are now less rigid than before. Clearly, Region 1's income cannot be increased relative to the income of Region 2, but the combined incomes of Regions 1 and 2 can be raised relative to the incomes of the three remaining regions. The same result is apparent in the case of Regions 3 and 4, and Region 5's income, being independent of the income of any other region, can be increased unilaterally without violating the equilibrium condition. Hence through a suitable process of aggregation, regions can be redefined in a manner such that regional growth is possible in a manner consistent with trade equilibrium. This solution, however, merely amounts to sweeping the income discrepancies under the rug and does not eliminate the original problem.

## 2.  DYNAMIC REGIONAL GROWTH

We now consider the dynamic properties of the model. In particular, we shall begin with a trade equilibrium as defined in the previous section and then examine the consequences of some exogenous shock, e.g., either a one-period injection of income into a depressed region or an increase of autonomous investment which increases that region's income for all subsequent periods. As before, we first investigate the situation for an indecomposable trade matrix.

If we wish to find the interregional distribution of income after $t$ time periods, we know that

$$\sum_{j=1}^{n} v_{ij}(t) = 1 \tag{5}$$

and

$$v_{ij}(t+1) = \sum_{j=i}^{n} v_{ij}(t)a_{ij}, \tag{6}$$

where the number in parentheses dates the associated variable, and the $v_{ij}$ denote the elements of the $i$th row, in $A^t$. Hence the row elements still sum to unity, and Equation (6) introduces a dynamic situation in that a region's income in any time period is given by the total of its sales to all other regions and itself during the previous periods. It follows that the income distribution vector in any period is given by

$$y(1) = y(0)A$$
$$y(2) = y(1)A = y(0)A^2$$
$$y(3) = y(2)A = y(0)A^3$$

and, in general,

$$y(t) = y(t-1)A = y(0)A^t. \tag{7}$$

A few definitions are in order at this point.

1. A state, say $i$, is called *periodic* with period $h$ if a return to $i$ is possible in $gh$ steps, where $g$ is a positive integer and $h > 1$ is the largest integer with this property. Thus $a_{ii}^{(t)} = 0$ where $t$ is not divisible by $h$. A state which is not periodic is called *aperiodic*.

2. A state $i$ is called *recurrent* or *nontransient* if a return to that state is certain. If the probability of a return is less than unity, the state is said to be *transient* or *nonrecurrent*. If the expected recurrence time for $i$ is infinite, the state is said to be *recurrent null*. If the expected recurrence time is less than infinite, the state is called *positive*.

3. A recurrent state $i$ which is neither null nor periodic is called *ergodic*.

4. An income vector $y$ will be called an *equilibrium income vector* if it satisfies the property

$$\bar{y} = \bar{y}A. \tag{8}$$

The corresponding matrix $A$ will be called *stable*.

We find it extremely convenient in the initial period to divide each region's income by the summed income of all the $n$ regions so that

$$\sum_{i=1}^{n} y_i = 1 \qquad (9)$$

for the interregional distribution of income in period 1.

We next state without proofs two basic limit theorems of the theory of discrete Markov chains with a denumerable number of states, and then consider their implications for regional economic development. The proofs are to be found in Bharucha-Reid[2].

*Theorem 1*: If the state $j$ is either transient or recurrent null, then

$$\lim_{t \to \infty} a_{ij}^{(t)} = 0 \qquad (10)$$

for all $i$, where $A^t = (a_{ij}^{(t)})$.

*Theorem 2*: If the exchange matrix $A$ is ergodic, then for every pair of states $i$ and $j$

$$\lim_{t \to \infty} a_{ij}^{(t)} = vj, \qquad (11)$$

independent of $i$, and the $v_j$ satisfy the equation

$$v_j = \sum_{i=1}^{n} v_i a_{ij} \qquad (12)$$

as well as Equation (4). Moreover, the $v_j$ are unique.

The importance of these two limit theorems for Markov chains and their implications for the convergence of regional incomes to an equilibrium is obvious. The theorems assert that if all of the states of $A$ are aperiodic and $A$ is indecomposable then all of the elements of $A^t$ converge toward limiting values as $t$ approaches infinity. Another theorem follows, therefore, that the elements of $y(t) = y(0)A^t$ also converge toward limiting values as $t$ increases without bound.

## 3.   APERIODIC CHAINS

For example, consider a simple model consisting of two regions $R_1$ and $R_2$ with the exchange matrix

$$A = \begin{pmatrix} p & 1-p \\ q & 1-q \end{pmatrix}$$

where $p$ and $q$ lie between zero and one. Using the method of generating functions, we calculate $A^t$ to be

$$A^t = \frac{1^t}{1-p+q}\begin{pmatrix} q & 1-p \\ q & 1-p \end{pmatrix} + \frac{(p-q)^t}{1-p+q}\begin{pmatrix} 1-p & p-1 \\ -q & q \end{pmatrix}.$$

Since $|p\ q| < 1$,

$$\lim_{t\to\infty} A^t = \begin{pmatrix} \dfrac{q}{1-p+q} & \dfrac{1-p}{1-p+q} \\ \dfrac{q}{1-p+q} & \dfrac{1-p}{1-p+q} \end{pmatrix}$$

Clearly, by Equation (7),

$$\bar{y} = y_1, \frac{(1-p)}{q}y_1 \tag{13}$$

A discussion of generating functions and their use is provided in Howard [4] and Saaty [5].

Suppose now that income is increased for one period only in $R_1$ by an amount to $x$. The interregional income distribution converges over time to a new equilibrium given by

$$\bar{y}' = \left((1+x)y_1, \frac{(1-p)(1+x)}{q}y_1\right). \tag{14}$$

An examination of Equation (14) reveals that for the income of Region 1 to increase more than that of Region 2, it is necessary and sufficient that $q > 1-p$, i.e., that Region 1 spends a greater proportion of its income at home than does Region 2. But from Equation (13) this would make Region 2 the initially depressed area, so that the result is the same as for the static model.

A simple numerical example is given by

$$A = \begin{pmatrix} 0.5 & 0.5 \\ 0.4 & 0.6 \end{pmatrix}$$

The equilibrium income vector is

$$\bar{y} = (y_1, 1.25y_1).$$

Since we want income to equal unity,

$$\bar{y} = (\tfrac{4}{9}, \tfrac{5}{9}).$$

In order to illustrate theorem, we assume a transfer from Region 2 to 1 in the initial period so that

$$y(0) = (0.5, 0.5)$$

and examine the behavior of $y(n)$ as $t$ increases indefinitely.

$$\lim_{t \to \infty} A^t = \begin{pmatrix} \frac{4}{9} & \frac{4}{9} \\ \frac{5}{9} & \frac{5}{9} \end{pmatrix},$$

and, therefore,

$$\lim_{t \to \infty} y(t) = \bar{y} = (0.5 \quad 0.5) \begin{pmatrix} \frac{4}{9} & \frac{5}{9} \\ \frac{4}{9} & \frac{5}{9} \end{pmatrix}$$
$$= (\tfrac{4}{9}, \tfrac{5}{9})$$

If income is raised by $x$ in period 0 in Region 1 we get

$$y(0) = (\tfrac{1}{2} + x, \tfrac{1}{2}),$$

and

$$\bar{y} = (\tfrac{4}{9}(1 + x), \tfrac{5}{9}(1 + x)).$$

Hence, $y$ converges to a unique equilibrium with the same relative interregional distribution as formerly.

If $q = 0$, then Region 2 spends all of its income at home, and Region 1 is a transient state such that the equilibrium income vector is

$$\bar{y} = (0, 1),$$

and all of the benefits of any one-shot injections will have accrued to Region 2 once the new equilibrium is attained.[2]

However, if the aid to the depressed region is in the form of capital investment such that the area's output and income are increased during the current and all subsequent periods, the income gap will be partially closed, the amount of the change depending upon the amount of the initial investment and the capital-output ratio. Thus, if the model is in equilibrium in period 0 and income in Region 1 is increased in periods $1, 2, \ldots, n$ by an amount equal to $x$,

$$y(0) = \left( y_1, \frac{(1 - p)}{q} y_1 \right)$$

$$y(1) = \left( (y_1 + x), \frac{(1 - p)}{q} y_1 \right)$$

2. In a typical Markov process Region 1 would clearly be a transient state inasmuch as its limiting state probability is zero. Furthermore, Region 2 is called a *trapping* or *absorbing* state since $a_{22} = 1$, *i.e.*, all income ends up in $R_2$.

$$y(2) = (y_1(1)A + (x, 0)) = \left[ ((1+x)y_1 + x), \left( \frac{(1-p)}{q} (y_1 + x) \right) \right]$$

$$y(3) = (y_1(2)A + (x, 0)) = \left[ ((1+2x)y_1 + x), \left( \frac{(1-p)}{q} (y_1 + 2x) \right) \right]$$

. . . . . . . . . . . . . . . . . . . . . . . . . . . . . . . . . .    . . . . . . . . . .    . .

We conclude that in the case of aperiodic states and indecomposable matrices it is possible to raise the relative incomes of depressed regions through continual and constant injections by an amount equal to the injection.[3]

## 4.  PERIODIC CHAINS

In the case of periodic chains the components of $A^t$ do not converge toward limiting values as $n$ becomes very large but tend to oscillate indefinitely, resulting in an oscillation in the components of the regional income distribution vector. These oscillations, however, are predictable. As defined on paper 12, a periodic chain is a recurrent chain such that for every fixed state the chain will occupy that state with probability equal to one after $h, 2h, 3h, \ldots$ transitions, where $h$ is an integer denoting the periodicity of the chain.

Consider again the simple two-regional model with $p = 0$, and $q = 1$, i.e.,

$$A = \begin{pmatrix} 0 & 1 \\ 1 & 0 \end{pmatrix}.$$

That is, Region 1 spends all of its income in Region 2 and vice versa. We have

$$A^2 = \begin{pmatrix} 1 & 0 \\ 0 & 1 \end{pmatrix}$$

$$A^3 = \begin{pmatrix} 0 & 1 \\ 1 & 0 \end{pmatrix}$$

3. We implicitly assume that no opportunity costs are connected with the initial investment. Hence an increase in the capital stock of depressed regions is not accompanied by a reduction in the income base of other regions.

In general, using an appropriate generating function,

$$A^t = \begin{pmatrix} 0.5 & 0.5 \\ 0.5 & 0.5 \end{pmatrix} + (-1)^n \begin{pmatrix} 0.5 & -0.5 \\ -0.5 & 0.5 \end{pmatrix},$$

where $h = 2$.

Hence the system does not move toward an equilibrium in the sense that the $a_{ij}^{(t)}$ converge to any limiting values. If the initial income vector is $y(0) = (y_1, 1-y_1)$, we have

$$y(1) = y(0)A = ((1-y_1), y_1)$$
$$y(2) = y(0)A^2 = (y_1, (1-y_1))$$
$$y(3) = y(0)A^3 = ((1-y_1), y_1)$$
$$\dots\dots\dots\dots\dots\dots\dots\dots\dots$$

and the interregional distribution of income fluctuates indefinitely for any $y_1 \neq 0.5$.[4]

Suppose next that a one-shot attempt is made to increase income in Region 1. We see that

$$y(0) = ((y_1+x), (1-y_1))$$
$$y(1) = y(0)A = ((1-y_1), (y_1+x))$$
$$y(2) = y(0)A^2 = ((y_1+x), (1-y_1))$$

Once more we note that while Region 1 is better off in an absolute sense it has not gained relatively. Moreover, the amplitude of the oscillation has increased.

If, on the other hand, the injection $x$ is continued indefinitely we have

$$y(0) = ((y_1+x), (1-y_1))$$
$$y(1) = y(0)A + (x, 0) = ((1-y_1+x), (y_1+x))$$
$$y(2) = y(0)A^2 + (x, 0) = ((y_1+2x), (1-y_1+x))$$

We conclude once more, therefore, that the only way a depressed region's income can be increased relative to the income of the other regions of an irreducible exchange matrix, periodic or not, is via either a capital investment program or some other program designed to maintain a continuous flow of new income in the low-income region.

4. If Equations (6) and (7) are used to find an equilibrium income vector, $\bar{y} = (0.5, 0.5)$, in which case both regions would have stable income over time. However, $y(n)$ does not converge to these values as n → ∞.

## 5.  DECOMPOSABLE CHAINS

We now consider the exchange matrix

$$A = \begin{Bmatrix} 0.5 & 0.5 & 0 & 0 & 0 & 0 & 0 \\ 0.4 & 0.6 & 0 & 0 & 0 & 0 & 0 \\ 0 & 0 & 0.5 & 0.5 & 0 & 0 & 0 \\ 0 & 0 & 0 & 1.0 & 0 & 0 & 0 \\ 0 & 0 & 0 & 0 & 0 & 1.0 & 0 \\ 0 & 0 & 0 & 0 & 1.0 & 0 & 0 \\ 0 & 0 & 0 & 0 & 0 & 0 & 1.0 \end{Bmatrix}$$

The indecomposable submatrices $A_1$, $A_2$, $A_3$, and $A_4$ are all familiar to us by this time. The equilibrium income vector is

$$\bar{y} = (y_1, 1.25y_1, 0, y_2, y_3, y_3, y_4).[5]$$

As in the static case a single injection will increase the income of all the regions in any indecomposable submatrix relative to the incomes of other regions. However, in order to raise the income of any single region that is a proper subset of one of the irreducible submatrices, relative to the incomes of all other regions, it is necessary to make the stream of new income in that region continuous. Otherwise the equilibrium requirements would force relative incomes within each submatrix back to their former relationship.

## 6.  CONCLUSIONS

In summary, if the economic development of a region is defined as an increase in that region's income relative to the income of other regions, such growth is consistent with trade equilibrium, and hence possible only under special circumstances. In the first place, the relative incomes of an indecomposable trading bloc of regions can be increased by a once-and-for-all injection. However, the income of a region or regions within such a bloc can be raised relative to the incomes of other regions within the bloc only by continuous injections, hence necessitating either a continuous flow of payments into the depressed region or capital outlays designed to enlarge the region's income base.

We have assumed throughout that the propensities to spend remain constant. Buy-at-home campaigns and import duties, where

5. See footnote 4 with respect to the solution of $A_3$.

possible and in the absence of retaliation, can change the components of a trade matrix in a manner favorable to the depressed region. Moreover, beneficial adjustments in the $a_{ij}$ are apt to take place if the capital projects are designed to produce exported or import-competing commodities, especially if the region enjoys a comparative advantage in those areas. This points out the principal difficulty of such a program; the need for retraining the labor force, whether the solution entails relocating the workers in other regions or the development of new industries in the depressed region.

## REFERENCES

1. W. J. BAUMOL, *Economic Theory and Operations Analysis* (Englewood Cliffs, N.J.: Prentice-Hall, 1961), Ch. 16.
2. A. T. BHARUCHA-REID, *Elements of the Theory of Markov Processes and Their Applications* (New York: McGraw-Hill, 1960), pp. 28–30 and Appendix A.
3. D. GALE, *The Theory of Linear Economic Models* (New York: McGraw-Hill, 1960), Ch. 8.
4. R. A. HOWARD, *Dynamic Programming and Markov Processes* (New York: Wiley & Sons, 1960), pp. 7–12.
5. T. L. SAATY, *Mathematical Methods of Operations Research* (New York: McGraw-Hill, 1959), pp. 77–84.

# 13

LLOYD A. METZLER

# A Multiple-Region Theory of
# Income and Trade[1]

## 1. INTRODUCTION

The theory of employment and income that was developed during the decade of the thirties was concerned primarily with the economic forces governing the level of output in a closed economic system. From the outset, however, it was apparent that the new ideas had important applications to interregional and international problems. In particular, the theory of employment added considerably to our understanding of the mechanism by which an expansion or contraction of income in one region or country is transmitted to other regions or countries. But much of the early discussion of such problems was devoted to a highly simplified model in which the world was divided into two regions or countries; in this model an expansion or contraction of income was assumed to originate in one of the two regions or countries, and the repercussions upon income in the other region or country, and upon the balance of payments between the two, were then examined in some detail.[2] The purpose of the present

1. This paper was written in 1945 but was not submitted for publication because there seemed to be no widespread interest in the subject. In recent months, however, it has become apparent that the general principles of regional income movements are applicable to many other fields besides international trade. Most of the propositions developed in this paper, for example, are applicable to the theory of linear programming and to input-output studies within a single country. See, for instance: David Hawkins and Herbert A. Simon, "Note: Some Conditions of Macroeconomic Stability," Econometrica, XVII (July–October, 1949), pp. 245–248; R. M. Goodwin, "The Multiplier as Matrix," *Economic Journal*, LIX (December, 1949), pp. 537–555; and John S. Chipman, "The Multi-Sector Multiplier," Econometrica, XVIII, pp. 355–374. In addition to these published papers, I have recently read an unpublished manuscript by H. A. John Green dealing with some aspects of the problem discussed in the present paper. In view of the renewed interest in the subject, it seems to me appropriate to present the results of my own investigation.

2. See, for example, my own papers, "Underemployment Equilibrium in International Trade," Econometrica, X (April, 1942), pp. 97–112, and "The Transfer Problem Reconsidered," *Journal of Political Economy*, L (June, 1942), pp. 397–414. See also F. Machlup, *International Trade and the National Income Multiplier* (Philadelphia: The Blakiston Co., 1943). Machlup presents an economic model involving three countries and has also described models involving a larger number. In his more complex models, however, a considerable amount of symmetry is assumed with respect to propensities to spend and to import, and for this reason his results cannot be regarded as completely general.

Metzler, Lloyd A., "A Multiple-Regional Theory of Income and Trade," Econometrica, XVIII, pp. 329–354.

paper is to generalize the earlier discussion by considering a model of an economic system composed of $n$ regions or countries, where $n$ may be either large or small. Although I shall speak hereafter of "$n$ countries," I assume it is clear that the conclusions apply without modification to the regions within a single country or, indeed, to any regional classification of the world economy, such as the economy composed of Eastern Europe, Western Europe, Latin America, and similar regions.

The procedure followed in this paper is essentially the same as that employed in the earlier discussions of the two-country model. The level of output in each of the $n$ countries is assumed, initially, to be in a state of balance in the sense that the country's rate of output of goods and services is equal to the demand for such goods and services. A disturbance of the economic forces governing income is then assumed to take place in one of the countries, and the effects of this disturbance are traced throughout the $n$-country system. Both movements of real income or employment and movements of the international balance of trade are taken into account. In order to isolate the effects of employment and real income, the assumption is made that all prices, costs, and exchange rates remain unaltered. In other words, commodities and services are assumed to be produced and sold at constant supply prices. Exchange rates are assumed to be kept at fixed levels, either by central bank activity or by the normal operations of the gold standard. A free market for foreign exchange is postulated for each of the $n$ countries, and imports are thus supposed to be limited by a country's income or purchasing power, and not by the size of its foreign-exchange reserves.

In the present world of unbalanced trade, dollar shortages, exchange controls, and "hard" or "soft" currencies, this last assumption will doubtless strike the reader as highly unrealistic. I should therefore add that the model of international trade discussed below is not intended as a description of the abnormal conditions prevailing today. Whether the model will or will not be a reasonable description of world trade and employment in the future is a question that can hardly be answered at the present time; the answer obviously depends upon numerous and unpredictable political influences as well as upon more narrow economic considerations, such as the fate of exchange controls, import quotas, and other governmental measures for controlling world trade. But whatever the future development of inter-

---

3. This second example is perhaps slightly misleading, inasmuch as all of the countries concerned have far-reaching import controls which to a considerable extent take the place of exchange controls. It does not seem overly optimistic, however, to conjecture that the import controls within the area, if not those pertaining to imports from countries outside the area, will be gradually relaxed.

national trade may be, there are two reasons, it seems to me, why economic models such as the one given in this paper are useful. In the first place, there are almost certain to be large areas of the world, even in an economic system having extensive trade controls, in which payments between one region and another are made more or less freely. It is unlikely, for example, that any limitations other than the limitation of purchasing power will ever be placed upon transactions between Kansas and Nebraska or upon payments between the North Central States and the New England States in the United States. Likewise, payments between members of the sterling area of the British Commonwealth now occur quite freely despite the limitations upon payments outside the area.[3] Thus whatever happens to inter*national* trade, the model discussed below remains useful as a description of inter*regional* trade. The second and less important reason for regarding the model as useful is the fact that it can be helpful in interpreting economic events of the past. There have been long periods of time — the period under the gold standard before the First World War is an example — when international payments were made without restriction throughout the world. There is no doubt that during these periods limited income was the principal constraint upon imports, and the assumption made above regarding foreign exchange markets is accordingly appropriate for describing such periods.

The international theory of income to be presented below is, in at least two respects, a short-run theory. It is short-run, in the first place, in the same sense that Keynes's *General Theory* is a short-run theory: it takes the rate of current investment in each country either as a given amount or as a given function of income in that country, and makes no allowances either for the effects of continuous investment upon a country's capacity to produce or for the repercussions of a change in such capacity upon the demand for new investment. The theory, in brief, is a *static* theory of income and not a theory of growth; and for this reason it is obviously inapplicable over an extended period of economic development. The theory given below is short-run, in the second place, in its treatment of each country's balance of payments. The procedure followed in this regard is simply to investigate the effects of a given disturbance upon each country's balance of payments on current account, and not to inquire about how a given deficit or surplus in this balance is offset. Nothing is said, in other words, about the role of capital movements in establishing and maintaining equilibrium in the flow of international payments and receipts. Thus, quite apart from the problems of growth, the position of equilibrium described below must be regarded as temporary. For, unless capital movements occur more or less automatically in response to discrepancies in a country's balance of payments on current account, a country with a deficit in its current account will sooner or later have to take measures such as cost deflation or currency depreciation to eliminate the deficit; and these measures, in turn, will affect the equilibrium of income. In other words, the equilibrium of income to be discussed in this paper can exist over a considerable period of time only if international monetary reserves are large or if capital movements are of the equilibrating type.

In demonstrating how an economic disturbance in one country affects income and employment throughout the world, any one of a considerable number of economic events could be selected as the disturbing force. We might, for example, investigate the repercussions of an increase in domestic investment in one of the $n$ countries or of an increase in the consumption of domestic goods; or we might consider the effects of technological changes or changes in tastes which tend to shift the demand for goods and services in some particular country from domestic goods to imports; or we might, following more traditional lines, examine the economic consequences of reparations payments or some other form of income transfer between countries. The international repercussions of all such disturbances, however, have many common features, and it would, accordingly, be needlessly repetitious to consider each of them separately. Indeed, it seems to me that the important elements of an interregional or international theory of employment can, for the most part, be demonstrated by considering only one type of disturbance, namely, a change in domestic investment in one of the $n$ countries. The effects of other, more complex, types of disturbances can then be determined by regarding these complex disturbances as combinations of movements of investment in one or more countries. Thus, for the purpose of income analysis, a reparations payment may be regarded as a combination of investment in the receiving country and disinvestment of the same amount in the paying country. In view of this possibility of transforming other disturbing forces into combinations of movements in investment, the international theory of employment presented below is developed entirely by considering the adjustment of the world economy to a change in investment in one country. The conclusions reached for this particular disturbance may readily be applied to other disturbances as well.

## II.  A SYSTEM OF INCOME EQUATIONS

Neglecting income transfers between countries, the current net income of a particular country is simply the market value of that country's net output of goods and services. The word "net" as used in this connection implies that two deductions are made from the total value of goods and services produced. First, the usual allowance is made for the depreciation of capital. Second, and more important for present purposes, the value of all imported goods and services employed in production is deducted from the market value of such production. This second deduction is necessary because a country's output incorporates not only the services of domestic factors of production, but also many materials and services purchased abroad; and the latter do not constitute income produced within the given country. The concept of income in an open economy is thus a sort of value-added-by-manufacture concept, except that the unit of account is a country or region rather than an industry.

Consider, now, a sum of values consisting of the following items: (1) all expenditures by the residents of a particular country upon consumers' goods and services, including imported as well as domestic goods and services; (2) net investment in plant, equipment, inventories, etc., including investment in equipment produced abroad as well as investment in things domestically produced; (3) exports of goods and services. In what respects does this sum differ from net income as defined in the preceding paragraph? The sum includes, in the first place, the value of imported materials and services employed in domestic production, and these obviously must be deducted in computing the net income produced within the given country. The sum also includes, in the second place, imported finished goods which may have been used either for consumption, for net investment, or for re-export; and since these imported finished goods obviously do not constitute a part of the particular country's current production, their value must likewise be deducted from the total in computing national income. Thus, we find that the total of domestic expenditures for consumption and investment plus receipts from exports exceeds national income by the value of imports, including both imports of finished goods and services and imports of intermediate goods and services. In terms of the final uses of goods and services, national income may accordingly be written as follows:

national income *equals* expenditures on consumers' goods and services
*plus* net investment *plus* exports of goods and services
*less* imports of goods and services.

Three of the items in this summation—consumption, net investment, and imports—are dependent upon the level of income and employment at home, while the remaining item, exports, depends upon income in all of the countries to which the given country is selling goods and services.[4] This immediately suggests that for the world economy it might be convenient to set up a tabular presentation of income similar to the input-output tables developed by Leontief in the study of inter-industry relations.[5] Such a table would show how each country's income is *earned*—in sales at home and sales to other countries—and how income is *spent*—in purchases at home and purchases from other countries. Individual countries or regions, in other words, would replace the individual industries in the Leontief tables; and imports and exports would replace inputs and outputs.

Let $m_i(y_i)$ be the function which shows how *total* imports of the *i*th country from all other countries in the table are related to national income, $y_i$, of the importing country. This total import function will be composed of a number of subfunctions showing how imports from each of the other countries are related to income in the *i*th country. Thus, if $m_{ji}(y_i)$ represents the imports of the *i*th country from the *j*th country, stated as a function of income in the *i*th country, we will have $m_i(y_i) \equiv m_{1i}(y_i) + m_{2i}(y_i) l \ldots$, where the summation is extended over all countries from which the *i*th country imports goods or services. Since one country's imports are another country's exports, the entire pattern of world trade may be described in terms of the import functions, $m_{ji}(y_i)$. The tabular presentation of world income may then be completed by inserting functional relations for each country's expenditures on *all* goods and services. In setting up such total expenditure functions, there is no necessity to distinguish between consumers' goods and net investment, because the one affects income in the same way as the other. Suppose that both consumers' goods expenditures and net investment are dependent to some extent upon income at home, and let $u_i(y_i)$ represent such an expenditure function; $u_i(y_i)$ in other words, shows how expenditure in the *i*th country on *both* consumers' goods and net investment is related to the *i*th country's income. Hereafter, the function $u_i(y_i)$ will be called simply an "expenditure function"; it plays the same role in the present theory of employment that is usually attributed to the consumption function. The quantity $u_i(y_i)$ represents *all* expenditures of the *i*th country on consumers' goods and net investment, irrespec-

4. If the import content of a country's exports differs from the import content of the goods and services produced for home use, total imports will depend not only upon income but also on the composition of income; *i.e.*, upon the way output is divided between exports and goods or services produced for domestic use. Because the demand for the given country's exports is governed in part by income in other countries, and because imports in this instance depend partly upon exports, it follows that imports should really be expressed as a function of income in all countries. But this is a refinement that cannot be incorporated in the present model without complicating it unduly.

5. W. W. Leontief, *The Structure of American Economy, 1919–1929* (Cambridge, Mass.: Harvard University Press, 1941), *passim*.

tive of the source of goods and services purchased. It includes imported finished goods as well as the import content of domestic production. In order to show how expenditure by a given country affects that country's net income, total imports, $m_i(y_i)$, must therefore be subtracted from the expenditure function, $u_i(y_i)$.

The foregoing relations are summarized in Table 1, which presents a hypothetical case of a world economy consisting of three

TABLE 1

| | EXPENDITURES BY COUNTRY 1 (1) | EXPENDITURES BY COUNTRY 2 (2) | EXPENDITURES BY COUNTRY 3 (3) | NATIONAL INCOME (1) + (2) + (3) |
|---|---|---|---|---|
| Receipts from sales by Country 1   (1) | $u_1(y_1) - m_1(y_1)$ | $m_{12}(y_2)$ | $m_{13}(y_3)$ | $y_1$ |
| Receipts from sales by Country 2   (2) | $m_{21}(y_1)$ | $u_2(y_2) - m_2(y_2)$ | $m_{23}(y_3)$ | $y_2$ |
| Receipts from sales by Country 3   (3) | $m_{31}(y_1)$ | $m_{32}(y_2)$ | $u_3(y_3) - m_3(y_3)$ | $y_3$ |
| Total expenditures of each country (1) + (2) + (3) | $u_1(y_1)$ | $u_2(y_2)$ | $u_3(y_3)$ | |

countries. The items in a given *row* of this table provide a classification of the components of a country's national income according to the *sources* from which it was earned, while the items in the corresponding *column* indicate the *uses* of national income. The sum of the items in row 1 thus represents national income of Country 1, while the sum of the items in column 1 shows the total expenditures of Country 1 on all goods and services. In summing column 1, the positive items of imports, $m_{21}(y_1)$ and $m_{32}(y_1)$, will exactly cancel against total imports, which enter negatively in row 1, column 1, leaving only the total expenditure, $u_1(y_1)$.

Consider, now, a more general economic system consisting of $n$ countries. Using the same notation as in the table, we can set up $n$ equations which express the fact that, in equilibrium, each country's output is equal to the demand for this output. Thus we have

$$
\begin{aligned}
y_1 &= [u_1(y_1) - m_1(y_1)] + m_{12}(y_2) &&+ \cdots + m_{1n}(y_n), \\
y_2 &= m_{21}(y_1) &&+ [u_2(y_2) - m_2(y_2)] + \cdots + m_{2n}(y_n), \\
&\cdots\cdots\cdots\cdots\cdots\cdots\cdots\cdots\cdots\cdots\cdots\cdots\cdots && \quad (1) \\
y_n &= m_{n1}(y_1) &&+ m_{n2}(y_2) \quad + \cdots \\
& && + [u_n(y_n) - m_n(y_n)].
\end{aligned}
$$

**197**

Since there are $n$ countries in all, these $n$ equations are sufficient, with given prices and exchange rates, to determine the level of income in each country.

## III.   STABILITY OF THE SYSTEM

Equations (1) are *static* equations; they indicate the levels of income which the system would achieve if consuming and investing habits remained unchanged over a sufficient period of time. They are accordingly useful in solving economic problems such as the ones mentioned earlier. Suppose, for example, that the propensity to consume or to invest in domestic goods were to increase in Country 1; the demand for goods and services would then rise throughout the world economy, and if the system were stable a new equilibrium, corresponding to the higher level of demand in Country 1, would eventually be established in all countries. Equations (1) enable us to show how the new position of equilibrium in each of the $n$ countries compares with the old. This problem is nothing more than a generalization of the familiar investment multiplier.

Before discussing the static theory of income, however, there is a closely related dynamic problem that it will be useful to discuss first. As we shall see, solution of the dynamic problem provides a considerable amount of information about the static theory. If income in one or more of the $n$ countries is not in a state of equilibrium, so that the current level of output differs from the current demand, then the current levels of income, $y_1, y_2, \ldots, y_n$ will not satisfy equations (1). In some instances, the level of output or income, $y_i$, may fall short of demand, while in other instances output will probably be in excess of current demand. Under these circumstances there will be a tendency for the level of output in each country to change, as producers try to bring their production plans in line with current requirements. The changes in output, in turn, will alter the level of income in each country, thereby bringing about shifts of demand and creating further discrepancies between supply and demand. The dynamic problem I wish to discuss is whether such a system has a natural tendency to approach a balanced state or whether discrepancies between demand and supply tend to produce still larger discrepancies. In short, is the system of income equations stable or unstable?

In order to answer this question, some assumptions must be made as to what happens in each country when output differs from current demand. Although no simple model can possibly do justice to such a complex problem, it seems to me reasonable to suppose that producers as a group will react to a discrepancy between output and demand by altering the rate of output. I shall therefore assume that output, and hence income, increases whenever demand exceeds current output and falls when demand is less than current output. Moreover, I shall also assume that the speed with which output plans are altered is directly proportional to the size of the discrepancy between demand and supply; a big discrepancy, in other words, leads to a more rapid response than a small one. Although this second assumption is not absolutely essential, it is an assumption which will simplify our problem somewhat without altering the results in any important respects. Throughout the period of time when income is out of equilibrium, discrepancies between demand and supply are assumed to be met by appropriate adjustments of business inventories.

For any given country, say Country 1, the rate of current net output or national income is $y_1$, while the net demand for this output is $u_1(y_1) - m_1(y_1) + m_{12}(y_2) + \cdots + m_{1n}(y_n)$. The preceding assumptions concerning the behavior of producers may therefore be embodied, as a first approximation, in the following system of dynamic equations:

$$\frac{dy_1}{dt} = k_1[u_1(y_1) - m_1(y_1) + m_{12}(y_2) + \cdots + m_{1n}(y_n) - y_1],$$

$$\frac{dy_2}{dt} = k_2[u_2(y_2) - m_2(y_2) + m_{21}(y_1) + \cdots + m_{2n}(y_n) - y_2], \qquad (2)$$

$$\cdots\cdots\cdots\cdots\cdots\cdots\cdots\cdots\cdots\cdots\cdots\cdots\cdots$$

$$\frac{dy_n}{dt} = k_n[u_n(y_n) - m_n(y_n) + m_{n1}(y_1) + \cdots + m_{n.n-1}(y_{n-1}) - y_n].$$

The constants, $k_i$, in these equations are positive numbers which represent the speeds of adjustment of output in the various countries.

Equations (2) cannot be solved without knowing the explicit form of the expenditure functions and import functions. Since we are primarily interested in the stability of the system and not in its explicit solution, however, we may consider only a linear approximation to (2). Stability of the linear approximation is obviously a necessary condition, although not always a sufficient condition, for stability of equations (2). Expanding the right-hand side of (2) in a Taylor expansion about the equilibrium values $y_1^0, y_2^0, \ldots, y_n^0$, and dropping all except linear terms, we have

$$\frac{dy_1}{dt} = k_1(u_1' - m_1' - 1)(y_1 - y_1^0) + k_1 m_{12}'(y_2 - y_2^0) + \cdots + k_1 m_{1n}'(y_n - y_n^0),$$

$$(3)$$

$$\frac{dy_2}{dt} = k_2 m'_{21} (y_1 - y_1^0) + k_2 (u'_2 - m'_2 - 1) (y_2 - y_2^0) + \cdots + k_2 m'_{2n} (y_n - y_n^0),$$

. . . . . . . . . . . . . . . . . . . . . . . . . . . . . . . . . . . . . . .

$$\frac{dy_n}{dt} = k_n m'_{n1} (y_1 - y_1^0) + k_n m'_{n2} (y_2 - y_2^0) + \cdots + k_n (u'_n - m'_n - 1) (y_n - y_n^0),$$

where $u'_i = (du_i/dy_i)_{v_i}^0$, $m'_{ji} \equiv (dm_{ji}/dy_i)_{v_i}^0$, etc. Equations (3), being linear with constant coefficients, can be solved for any given initial conditions so as to express each of the incomes, $y_i$, as a function of time, as follows.

$$y_i(t) = y_i^0 + A_{i1} e^{\lambda_1 t} + A_{i2} e^{\lambda_2 t} + \cdots + A_{in} e^{\lambda_n t}, \qquad (4)$$

where the $A_{ij}$ are constants dependent upon the initial value of income at time $t = 0$, and where the $\lambda_j$ are roots of the following equation:

$$\begin{vmatrix} k_1(1 + m'_1 - u'_1) + \lambda & -k_1 m'_{12} & -k_1 m'_{1n} \\ -k_2 m' & k_2(1 + m'_2 - u'_2) + \lambda \cdots & -k_2 m'_{2n} \\ \cdots & \cdots & \cdots \\ -k_n m'_{n1} & -k_n m'_{n2} & \cdots k_n(1 + m'_n - u'_n) + \lambda \end{vmatrix} = 0. \qquad (5)$$

In order for $y_1(t)$ to approach its equilibrium value, $y_i^0$, as $t$ increases, it is apparent from (4) that the real parts of $\lambda_1, \lambda_2, \ldots, \lambda_n$ must all be negative. The necessary and sufficient conditions for this to be true may conveniently be expressed in terms of the following $n$th-order determinant:

$$M \equiv \begin{vmatrix} 1 + m'_1 - u'_1 & -m'_{12} & \cdots & -m'_{1n} \\ -m'_{21} & 1 + m'_2 - u'_2 & \cdots & -m'_{2n} \\ \cdots & \cdots & \cdots \\ -m'_{n1} & -m'_{n2} & \cdots & 1 + m'_n - u'_n \end{vmatrix}. \qquad (6)$$

The coefficient $m'_{ij}$ of the determinant (6) represents, of course, the marginal propensity of the $j$th country to import from the $i$th country; i.e., it shows how the demand in Country $j$ for imports from Country $i$ is affected by a small increase in the former country's income. Similarly, the coefficient $m'_j$ represents the marginal propensity of the $j$th country to import from all other countries together, so that $m'_j \equiv m'_{1j} + m'_{2j} + \cdots + m'_{nj}$. Throughout this paper, coefficients such as $m'_{ij}$ are assumed to be positive or zero, which means that all of the off-diagonal elements of $M$ are negative or zero.[6] The coefficient, $u'_j$,

6. If one country's imports from another consisted predominantly of inferior commodities, the former's propensity to import from the latter might conceivably

represents the marginal propensity of the $j$th country to spend, including the marginal propensity to invest, if any, as well as the marginal propensity to consume, and including expenditure on imported finished goods as well as upon domestic goods. Normally $u'_j$ will be less than unity, but if the propensity to invest is large, this need not be true.

I have demonstrated in an earlier paper that, for dynamic systems such as (3) in which all off-diagonal coefficients of the $y_i$ are positive or zero, the necessary and sufficient conditions of stability are identical with the so-called Hicksian conditions of perfect stability.[7] This means that the determinant, $M$, and any set of its principal minors such as

$$1 + m'_i - u'_i, \qquad \begin{vmatrix} 1 + m'_i - u'_i & - m'_{ij} \\ - m'_{ji} & 1 + m'_j - u'_j \end{vmatrix},$$

$$\begin{vmatrix} 1 + m'_i - u'_i & - m'_{ij} & - m'_{ik} \\ - m'_{ji} & 1 + m'_j - u'_j & - m'_{jk} \\ - m'_{ki} & - m'_{kj} & 1 + m'_k - u'_k \end{vmatrix}$$

etc., must be positive. Hereafter, any determinant satisfying these conditions will be called a "Hicksian determinant."[8]

Since the speeds of adaptation, $k_j$, do not appear in the Hicks conditions, it follows that stability of (3) is independent of such speeds. A system which is stable for one set of speeds of adaptation will therefore be stable for all other possible sets. The fact that producers in one country change their production plans more rapidly than producers in another country has no effect upon the stability of the system.

Having established a general set of conditions which must be fulfilled in order that the income equations shall be stable, it is possible to go a step further and show that these Hicksian conditions

be negative. In this event many of the theorems of the present paper would be invalid. The presence of negative propensities to import makes the conditions of stability considerably more complicated. Compare, for example, my conclusions concerning stability with those of John S. Chipman, *op. cit.*

7. L. A. Metzler, "Stability of Multiple Markets: The Hicks Conditions," Econometrica (October, 1945), pp. 277–292.

8. In my earlier paper the conditions of stability were expressed in terms of a determinant whose elements all had signs opposite to the signs of the corresponding elements of $M$. As a result, the formal appearance of the stability conditions was not the same as in the present paper. In the terminology of my earlier paper, stability of the system required that the principal minors, when arranged as above, should be alternately negative and positive, and that the basic determinant itself should have the sign of $(-1)^n$. By changing the sign of each of the elements of $M$, the reader can easily verify that these earlier stability conditions are identical with the ones given in the present paper.

depend, in a unique way, upon the propensities to spend in all countries. In particular, two propositions will be demonstrated. First, if the marginal propensity to spend, including expenditure on investment goods as well as on consumers' goods, is less than unity in every country, the system is necessarily Hicksian and therefore stable. Second, if the marginal propensity to spend is *greater* than unity in every country, the system cannot be Hicksian and must therefore be unstable.

To prove these propositions, it is convenient to use a theorem developed by Mosak.[9] Mosak's theorem, in slightly modified form, is as follows: If an $n$th-order determinant is Hicksian, and if the off-diagonal elements $-m_{ij}'$ are all negative, then the cofactor, $M_{ij}$, of the element $-m_{ij}'$ is positive for all $i$ and $j$. The proof of this theorem is a simple proof by induction. Expanding $M_{ij}$ about the row containing the elements $-m_{j1}', -m_{j2}', \ldots, -m_{jn}'$, we may write

$$M_{ij} \equiv \sum_k - m_{jk}' M_{ij,jk}, \tag{7}$$

where $M_{ij,jk}$ is the cofactor of the element $-m_{jk}'$ in the determinant, $M_{ij}$, and where the summation extends over all values of $k$ from 1 to $n$ except $k = j$. Since $M_{ij,jk} \equiv -M_{jj,ik}$, (7) may be written as follows:

$$M_{ij} = \sum_k m_{jk}' M_{jj,ik}. \tag{8}$$

Now $M_{jj}$ is a Hicksian determinant of order $n-1$. Suppose that Mosak's theorem is true for such an $(n-1)$th-order determinant. Then $M_{jj,ik}$ is positive, and it follows, from (8), that $M_{ij}$ must likewise be positive. Thus, if the theorem is true for the cofactors of an $(n-1)$th-order determinant obtained by deleting the $j$th row and $j$th column of $M$, it is also true for the cofactors of the $n$th-order determinant, $M$. A similar argument applies, of course, to the cofactors of any lower-order Hicksian determinants obtained from $M$ by deleting like rows and columns. To complete the proof we must show that the theorem is true for a low-order principal minor of $M$, such as a second-order minor. A typical second-order minor of $M$ is

$$\begin{vmatrix} 1 + m_i' - u_i' & - m_{ij}' \\ - m_{ji}' & 1 + m_j' - u_j' \end{vmatrix}.$$

The cofactors of the off-diagonal elements of this minor are $m_{ij}'$ and $m_{ji}'$, respectively, and these are both positive. Thus, Mosak's theorem

9. Jacob L. Mosak, *General-Equilibrium Theory in International Trade*, Cowles Commission Monograph No. 7 (Bloomington, Ind.: The Principia Press, 1944), pp. 49–51.

is proved; i.e., we have shown that if the $n$th-order determinant is Hicksian, the cofactors of its off-diagonal elements are all positive.

With the aid of this theorem, the two propositions stated above concerning relations between marginal propensities to spend and the determinant, $M$, may easily be proved. Consider, first, the case in which the marginal propensity to spend is *less* than unity in each country. According to our first proposition, the determinant $M$ is necessarily Hicksian and the dynamic system (3) is therefore stable under these conditions. The proposition will be proved by induction. Since $m_i' \equiv m_{1i}' + m_{2i}' + \cdots + m_{ni}'$, it is clear that the sum of the elements of the $i$th column of $M$ is equal to $1 - u_i'$, where $u_i'$ is the marginal propensity to spend of the $i$th country. Thus, if all $u_i'$ are less than unity, the sum of the elements of each column of $M$ will be positive. Adding all other rows of $M$ to the first row, we may write:

$$M \equiv \begin{vmatrix} 1 - u_1' & 1 - u_2' & 1 - u_3' \cdots 1 - u_n' \\ -m_{21}' & \\ -m_{31}' & \quad\quad M_{11} \\ \cdots \\ -m_{n1}' \end{vmatrix}, \tag{9}$$

where $M_{11}$ denotes the cofactor of $M$ obtained by deleting the first row and first column. Now it is evident that under our assumed conditions $M_{11}$ is an $(n-1)$th-order determinant having the same essential characteristics as $M$ itself; i.e., the sum of the elements of each column of $M_{11}$ is positive. The first column of $M_{11}$, for example, contains all of the elements of the corresponding column of $M$ except the negative quantity, $-m_{12}'$, and similarly for all other columns. It follows that if the sum of the elements of a given column of $M$ is positive, the same will be true a fortiori of the sum of the elements in the corresponding column of $M_{11}$. Any theorems concerning $M$ which are based upon this characteristic will therefore be equally applicable to $M_{11}$. And a similar argument applies to lower-order principal minors of $M$, such as $M_{11.22}$, $M_{11.22.33}$, etc.

Suppose, now, that our theorem is true for the $(n-1)$th-order determinant, $M_{11}$; i.e., suppose that $M_{11}$ is Hicksian. It can then be shown that the $n$th-order determinant, $M$, is also Hicksian. Expanding (9) on the first row and first column, in a Cauchy expansion, we find:[10]

$$M \equiv (1 - u_1') M_{11} + \sum_k \sum_j m_{j1}' (1 - u_k') M_{11,jk}. \tag{10}$$

10. See A. C. Aitken, *Determinants and Matrices* (New York: Interscience Publishers, Inc., 1944), pp. 74–75.

If $M_{11}$ is a Hicksian determinant it must be positive, and $M_{11,jj}$, $M_{11,kk}$, etc., must likewise be positive. Moreover, by Mosak's theorem, $M_{11,jk}$ is positive. Since the $m'_{j1}$ are positive or zero, and since $1 - u'_1$ and $1 - u'_k$ are positive by hypothesis, it follows immediately from (10) that, if $M_{11}$ is a Hicksian determinant, $M$ is positive and is therefore Hicksian.

It has now been demonstrated that if all $u'_k$ are less than unity, and if $M_{11}$ is Hicksian, then $M$ is likewise Hicksian. By a similar argument it can be shown that, if $M_{11,22}$ is Hicksian and if the $u'_k$ are less than unity, $M_{11}$ is necessarily Hicksian. To complete the proof that $M$ is always a Hicksian determinant when the marginal propensity to spend, $u'_k$, is less than unity in every country, it is sufficient to show that the theorem is true for any low-order principal minor of $M$. Consider, for example, the following second-order minor:

$$\begin{vmatrix} 1 + m'_i - u'_i & -m'_{ij} \\ -m'_{ji} & 1 + m'_j - u'_j \end{vmatrix}.$$

Since $m'_i \geq m'_{ji}$ and $m'_j \geq m'_{ij}$, it is easy to show by expanding the above determinant that it is necessarily positive whenever $u'_i$ and $u'_j$ are both less than unity. Moreover, it may be seen by inspection that, under the prescribed conditions, the principal minors are positive. The second-order minor of $M$ is therefore Hicksian, and our proof that $M$ is a Hicksian determinant is complete.

If $M$ is a Hicksian determinant, it follows from the results of my earlier paper that the dynamic system represented by equations (3) is a stable system. This conclusion will perhaps not surprise anyone, since it is simply a generalization of the theory of income stability of a single, closed economic system. It is well known that the multiplier in such a one-country system cannot have a finite value unless the country's marginal propensity to spend is less than unity. I have now established an analogous condition—sufficient but not necessary—for the case of an $n$-country economy.

Consider, now, an extreme case in which the marginal propensity to spend is *greater* than unity in every country. I have suggested above that in this event the determinant $M$ cannot be Hicksian and the dynamic system (3) must therefore be unstable. The proof of this proposition consists of showing that if all $u'_k$ exceed unity the assumption that $M$ is Hicksian involves a contradiction. If $M$ is Hicksian, the principal minor $M_{11}$ is, of course, also Hicksian, which means that $M_{11,jk}$ and $M_{11}$ are both positive. But if the marginal propensity to spend is greater than unity in all countries, $1 - u'_k$ is negative for all values of $k$. From (10) it follows that $M$ must be negative. This contradicts the assumption that $M$ is a Hicksian determinant and proves, in fact, that $M$ cannot be Hicksian. It shows, in other words, that if the determinant is Hicksian so far as its principal minors are concerned, and if all marginal propensities to spend exceed unity, the determinant itself is negative and is therefore non-Hicksian. Employing again the results of my previous paper, it is clear that under such conditions the dynamic system (3) must necessarily be unstable.

I have now examined the stability of income for two different situations. The first, which might be called the normal situation, is the case in which the marginal propensity to spend is less than unity in every country. The second, which goes to the opposite extreme, is the case in which every country has a marginal propensity to spend exceeding unity. In the first situation the system was found to be Hicksian, and therefore stable, while in the second it was found to be non-Hicksian and therefore unstable. Between these two extremes may be found a large number of intermediate situations in which the propensity to spend is less than unity in some countries and greater than unity in others. The basic determinant, $M$, of these intermediate systems may or may not be Hicksian, which means that the systems may or may not be dynamically stable. Broadly speaking, we may say that $M$ will be Hicksian and the system will be stable if the countries with low propensities to spend dominate, while in the converse case $M$ will be non-Hicksian and the system unstable. In any event, the discussion that follows in Sections IV and V below concerning the international repercussions of added investment in one of the $n$ countries is based upon the explicit assumption that the income equations form a dynamically stable system. In other words, the assumption is made that an increase of investment in one of the countries leads ultimately to a new equilibrium of income in all countries, and does not set off a continuous process of expansion culminating in a runaway inflation. This means that, while the propensity to spend may exceed unity in some countries, it cannot do so in all countries; at least one of the countries must have a propensity to spend of less than unity, and the low-propensity countries must be sufficiently important so that the basic determinant, $M$, is a Hicksian determinant.

## IV. INVESTMENT AND INCOME

Having examined the conditions of stability of our income equations, we are now in a position to investigate some problems of comparative statics. Suppose that national income is initially in equilibrium in all countries and that this equilibrium is disturbed by an increase of investment in one of the countries, say in Country 1. If the increase of investment is sustained over a sufficient period of time, and if the income equations are dynamically stable, a new equilibrium corresponding to the higher rate of investment will eventually be established throughout the system. The income of every country will probably be affected to some extent by the expansion of investment in Country 1; and, as national incomes are altered, each country's exports and imports, or its balance of payments on current account, will likewise be changed. The present section is concerned with the changes in income brought about by the higher level of investment in Country 1.

Let $\alpha_1$ represent autonomous or noninduced investment in Country 1. The first equation of the static system (1), including the additional investment, then becomes:

$$y_1 = u_1(y_1) - m_1(y_1) + m_{12}(y_2) + \cdots + m_{1n}(y_n) + \alpha_1. \tag{11}$$

Assuming no change in autonomous investment in the other countries, the remaining $n-1$ equations of (1) are unaltered. Equation (11) and the last $n-1$ equations of (1) thus form a closed system of $n$ equations in which the income of each country may be regarded as a function of $\alpha_1$. In order to see how the increase of investment in Country 1 affects each country, we may differentiate (11) and the last $n-1$ equations of (1) with respect to $\alpha_1$, and solve the resulting linear equations for $dy_1/d\alpha_1$ and $dy_k/d\alpha_1$. It will then be found that

$$\frac{dy_1}{d\alpha_1} = \frac{M_{11}}{M}, \qquad \frac{dy_k}{d\alpha_1} = \frac{M_{1k}}{M}, \tag{12}$$

where, as before, $M$ is the determinant of marginal propensities given by (6). Now, we know from the conditions of stability and from Mosak's theorem that $M_{11}$, $M_{1k}$, and $M$ must all be positive. Both $dy_1/d\alpha_1$ and $dy_k/d\alpha_1$ must therefore be positive, which shows that an increase in investment in one of the $n$ countries increases the level of income in every country in the system. There is, of course, nothing startling or profound about this conclusion; indeed, it is a conclusion which could have been reached intuitively without any mathematics at all.[11] It is therefore important only insofar as it leads to less obvious relations.

11. Any economist who gives the matter any thought will probably feel that to develop the rather complicated theorems of Section III concerning Hicksian determinants and conditions of stability simply in order to prove that an increase in investment in one country causes income to rise in all countries is like using a bulldozer to move an ant hill. His intuitive feeling may be so strong, in fact, that he will prefer to reverse the procedure of the present paper and use what he "knows" about the economic system to prove the theorems concerning determinants in Section III! While the mathematician will doubtless object to this procedure as completely lacking in rigor, I must confess that I have considerable confidence in it, particularly since it was substantially such a trend of thought which first led me to suspect the truth of the mathematical propositions of Section III above.

The expression, $M_{11}/M$, which shows how income in the first country is affected by an increase of investment in that country, is a generalized form of investment multiplier. I wish to show, now, how this generalized multiplier is related to two simpler multipliers that one encounters frequently in the theory of employment. The first of these simple multipliers is the ordinary investment multiplier of a closed economic system, *i.e.*, the multiplier which ignores foreign-trade leakages; the second is the so-called foreign trade multiplier, which makes allowance for foreign-trade leakages but does not take into account the effects of income movements in other countries upon the demand for a given country's exports. If, as before, $u'_1$ denotes the marginal propensity to spend of the first country, and $m'_1$ denotes that country's marginal propensity to import, the ordinary investment multiplier, which assumes that all demand is for home goods, is simply $1/(1-u'_1)$. The foreign trade multiplier, on the other hand is $1/(1-u'_1+m'_1)$. What is the relation of these two simple multipliers to the generalized multiplier given by (12)? Using the stability conditions and Mosak's theorem, it may be shown that, in the normal case in which the marginal propensity to spend is less than unity in every country, the value of the generalized multiplier lies between the ordinary multiplier and the foreign trade multiplier. To prove this proposition, notice first that by adding all other rows to the first row of $M$, expanding on the elements of this new row, and dividing both numerator and denominator by $M_{11}$, we may write:

$$\frac{dy_1}{d\alpha_1} \equiv \frac{M_{11}}{M} \equiv \frac{1}{(1-u'_1)+[(1-u'_2)M_{12}/M_{11}]+\cdots+[(1-u'_n)M_{1n}/M_{11}]} \cdot \quad (13)$$

Since $M_{1k}/M_{11}$ is positive for any value of $k$, and since all of the $u'_k$ are assumed to be less than unity, it is clear that the expression in (13) is less than the ordinary investment multiplier, which in this instance has a value of $1/(1-u'_1)$.

The second limit to $dy_1/d\alpha_1$ may be found by expanding $M$ on its first *column* and again dividing both numerator and denominator of the resulting expression for $dy_1/d\alpha_1$ by $M_{11}$. It will then be found that

$$\frac{dy_1}{d\alpha_1} = \frac{1}{1-u'_1+m'_1-[m'_{21}M_{21}/M_{11}]-\cdots-[m'_{n1}M_{n1}/M_{11}]}. \quad (14)$$

Again, since $M_{k1}/M_{11}$ is positive, the value of $dy_1/d\alpha_1$ given by (14) is clearly *greater* than the foreign trade multiplier, $1/(1-u'_1+m'_1)$. Thus, I have shown that in the normal case in which all marginal propensities to spend are less than unity, the generalized investment multiplier has the following limits:

$$\frac{1}{1 - u_1' + m_1'} < \frac{dy_1}{d\alpha_1} < \frac{1}{1 - u_1'}. \tag{15}$$

These limits derive their importance from the fact that they represent two forms of the multiplier which have played prominent roles in the historical development of the theory of employment.

If one or more of the other countries — i.e., Countries 2, 3, . ., n — has a marginal propensity to spend greater than unity, one of the limits given by (15) *may* not hold. In particular, while the generalized multiplier is always greater than the foreign trade multiplier, as (14) shows, it may in special cases also be greater than the ordinary investment multiplier. Consider, for example, the following system:

$$y_1 = 0.4y_1 + 0.5y_2 + \alpha_1, \qquad y_2 = 0.2y_1 + 0.7y_2. \tag{16}$$

For this system, $dy_1/d\alpha_1 = 3.75$, while $1/(1 - u_1') = 2.5$. Thus, when the marginal propensity to spend of one or more of the "other" countries exceeds unity, the true investment multiplier for a given country may be larger than the ordinary investment multiplier. In most cases, however, it seems probable that the true multiplier will lie between the two simple multipliers, as indicated in (15).

It may be useful at this point to give a brief intuitive explanation of the relations between the three multipliers. The foreign trade multiplier is the smallest of the three because it assumes that a country's exports are given and independent of its imports. In a period of rising domestic income, in other words, the foreign trade multiplier tacitly assumes that increased expenditures on imports represent net leakages from the country's circular flow of income; no allowance is made for the fact that as imports rise the level of income in other countries also rises, and the demand for the particular country's exports therefore rises, to some extent, along with its imports. The generalized multiplier takes account of this secondary rise in the country's exports, and it is therefore larger than the foreign trade multiplier. The ordinary investment multiplier, on the other hand, makes no allowance either for the leakages from the circular flow of income arising from increased imports or for the return of some of these leakages in the form of increased exports; it assumes, instead, that every increase in expenditure represents an equivalent increase in domestic income. Now, since the secondary rise in exports is normally smaller than the increase in imports with which it is associated, it follows that foreign trade usually exerts a retarding effect upon a rise in income originating in domestic investment. In short, the effect of foreign trade is to spread the stimulating effects of investment in one country over the entire economic system, thereby diluting to some extent the stimulus to income in the country originating the expansion. And, because it ignores this diluting effect, the ordinary investment multiplier overstates the rise in income at home to be expected from a given increase in domestic investment.

## V.  INVESTMENT AND THE PATTERN OF TRADE

So much for the effects of investment upon income and employment. I turn now to the related problem of the pattern of trade. As income expands throughout the system, each country's exports and imports will rise, and it is almost inevitable under such conditions that the balance of trade of most if not all of the countries will be affected. In the new position of equilibrium, some countries will have more favorable balances while others will have less favorable balances than in the old. What can be said, in a general way, about the new network of trade compared with the old?

With respect to bilateral balance between individual pairs of countries, there is very little that a general theory such as the one outlined in this paper can predict. The outcome depends entirely upon the particular values of the propensities to spend and to import, and may show wide variation from one economic system to another. With respect to each country's balance of trade as a whole, on the other hand, certain broad generalizations are possible. In particular, we can specify the conditions under which a general expansion originating in Country 1 is likely to lead to an improvement or to a deterioration in a given country's balance of trade with the rest of the world. Since there is no difficulty in forecasting how a given expansion will *initially* affect the balance of international payments, the problem before us is essentially a problem of comparing the initial, or primary, effects with the secondary repercussions. We want to know, in particular, whether the secondary repercussions are likely to reinforce or to offset the primary effects. Consider, for example, the balance of payments of some country other than Country 1, say Country $k$. As investment and income expand in Country 1, the initial effect will probably be an increase in exports from Country $k$ to the expanding country, thereby giving the latter a temporary surplus in its balance of payments. A similar initial effect may be anticipated, of course, in all the other countries dealing with Country 1. But as the other countries' exports to Country 1 rise, their incomes will also rise, and the increase in incomes, in turn, will increase the demand for imports in these countries. The secondary income movements thus tend to offset the initial changes in balances of payments of the other countries.[12] There is no obvious reason, however, why the offsetting movement in each country's balance of payments should always be exactly equal to the initial disturbance. In the new equilibrium some countries will probably have more favorable balances of payments while others will have less favorable ones. What are the circumstances that distinguish the "surplus" countries from the "deficit" countries?

The question may be answered by considering the interrelations between balances of payments and incomes. Although the balance of trade of a given country depends upon the incomes of all countries in the system, there is a convenient way of relating each country's balance of trade to the *income of that country alone.* Thus, from the definition of national income given in (1) above, it follows that the excess of a country's exports over its imports is equal to the excess of its national income over its total expenditure on both consumers' goods and net investment. This is no more than a technical way of stating the common-sense proposition that a country with an export surplus is producing more than it uses itself, while a country with an import surplus is using more than it produces. But it is a technique, as we shall see, which saves a good deal of tedious algebra. Consider, for example, the balance of payments of Country $k$. If $b_k$ denotes this balance, then it is clear from (1) that

$$b_k = y_k - u_k(y_k), \qquad (17)$$

whence

$$\frac{db_k}{d\alpha_1} = (1 - u_k') \frac{dy_k}{d\alpha_1}. \qquad (18)$$

Since $dy_k/d\alpha_1$ is positive, (18) shows that the direction of change of Country $k$'s balance of payments depends upon that country's marginal propensity to spend. If its propensity to spend is less than unity, as will normally be the case, the balance of payments of Country $k$ will be improved by the expansion in Country 1 even after allowing for the secondary rise of imports. But if the country's propensity to spend is *greater* than unity, (18) shows that its balance of payments on current account will be worsened by the expansion in Country 1. In this instance, the secondary rise of Country $k$'s imports will be *more* than sufficient to offset the initial rise of its exports.

12. It was no doubt this offsetting tendency that Nurske had in mind when he said that the theory of employment provides both an explanation of the adjusting process of the balance of payments and a theory of the transmission of business cycles from one country to another. (Ragnar Nurkse, "Domestic and International Equilibrium," in *The New Economics,* S. E. Harris, ed. (New York: Alfred A. Knopf, Inc., 1947)), p. 264.

Now suppose that the marginal propensity to spend of each of the countries 2, 3, . . . , $n$ is less than unity. Under such conditions, the expansion of income in Country 1 improves the trade balances of all other countries in the system; and from this it follows that the trade balance of the country initiating the expansion must be less favorable than before the expansion began. In short, an expansion of income originating in one country normally moves the balance of trade *against* that country and *in favor* of all other countries in the system; as long as marginal propensities to spend are all less than unity, this proposition holds true regardless of the relative sizes of the marginal propensities to import. For this reason we cannot say that, if the other countries' propensities to import from Country 1 are high, the induced expansion of their imports is likely to over-balance the initial rise of their exports, leaving them with less favorable trade balances than before the expansion began. The outcome depends not upon the relative magnitudes of import propensities, but upon the absolute size of each of the propensities to spend. If the marginal propensities to spend are less than unity, the result will be an improvement in the balances of payments of all countries except Country 1, irrespective of the size of import propensities.

If marginal propensities to spend in some of the countries exceed unity, on the other hand, it is possible that some or all of the conclusions of the preceding paragraph will have to be reversed. Consider first an extreme case. Suppose that the propensities to spend exceed unity in *all* of the countries 2, 3, . . . , $n$. Under these circumstances it is clear from (18) that the balance of trade of each of these countries would become less favorable as a result of expansion in Country 1; the secondary rise of imports in each of the countries would over-balance the primary increase in exports. But if Countries 2, 3, . . . , $n$ all have less favorable balances of payments, Country 1 must necessarily have a more favorable balance. After allowing for all repercussions, in other words, expansion of income in Country 1 increases that country's exports more than its imports are increased. Public works, encouragement of private investment, and other measures to expand the employment of resources in Country 1 would not, under the circumstances, create a balance-of-payments problem for the expanding country. Each time Country 1 increased its imports it could count upon an even larger secondary increase in its exports.

It is conceivable that this conclusion would be valid even under less extreme circumstances. Suppose, for example, that some of the countries 2, 3, . . . , $n$ had propensities to spend greater than unity while others had spending propensities less than unity. From (18) it is clear that some of these countries would then suffer a worsening of their balances of payments when Country 1 started an expansion, while others would find their balances of payments improved. And if the sum of all the adverse and favorable changes together were adverse, then Country 1 would obviously have a more favorable balance of payments than in the initial equilibrium. On the other hand, if the sum of changes in the balances of payments of Countries 2, 3, . . . , n were favorable, then the movement of Country 1's balance would necessarily be adverse. Thus, when some of the spending propensities of Countries 2, 3, . . . , n exceed unity, while others are less than unity, it is impossible without additional information to predict the effect of expansion on the balance of payments of the country initiating the expansion. The outcome depends upon a balancing of forces, *i.e.*, upon a balancing of the influence of the stable countries against the influence of the unstable ones.

Thus far we have regarded the balance of payments of Country 1 as a sort of residual; we have described its movement only after seeing what happened to the balances of payments of the other countries in the system. Although this procedure is satisfactory for some purposes, it does not allow us to say much about the *magnitude* of the movement in Country 1's balance of payments. It is therefore useful to examine this balance directly. From (11) and (1) the balance of payments of Country 1 may be written as follows:

$$b_1 = y_1 - u_1(y_1) - \alpha_1. \tag{19}$$

In words, this says that Country 1's balance of payments on current account is the difference between its income and its total expenditure on goods and services, *including in the latter autonomous expenditures*, $\alpha_1$, as well as $u_1(y_1)$. Differentiating $b_1$ with respect to $\alpha_1$, we find:

$$\frac{db_1}{d\alpha_1} = (1 - u_1') \frac{dy_1}{d\alpha_1} - 1. \tag{20}$$

In evaluating (20) we may begin with what I have called the normal case, namely, the case in which all marginal propensities to spend are less than unity. In this case we know from Section IV above that $dy_1/d\alpha_1$ is less than the ordinary investment multiplier; i.e., it is less than $1/(1 - u_1')$. From this fact we can derive the following limits for the movement of the balance of payments on current account of Country 1:

$$-1 < \frac{db_1}{d\alpha_1} < 0. \tag{21}$$

The limits given by (21) show that in the normal case an increase of investment in Country 1 moves the balance of payments on current account *against* the expanding country; and the amount of the unfavorable movement is normally less than the increase of investment. A one billion dollar public works program consisting exclusively of expenditure on domestic goods and services, for example, could not under normal circumstances create a foreign-trade deficit in the expanding country greater than the amount of public works.

If the marginal propensity to spend in the expanding country were *greater* than unity, however, the limits given by (21) would no longer apply. It is apparent from (20) that under such a condition $db_1/d\alpha_1$ would be less, algebraically, than $-1$. The unfavorable movement of Country 1's balance of payment on current account would thus be *greater* than the amount of autonomous investment. An economy characterized by such a high propensity to spend would, of course, be highly unstable, and its instability, in turn, would lead to frequent and severe balance-of-payments problems vis-à-vis the rest of the world.

If the instability is in the rest of the world rather than in Country 1, there may be no balance-of-payments problem at all in the country initiating the expansion. In other words, if a larger number of the "other countries" have marginal propensities to spend greater than unity, while Country 1 has a propensity to spend *less* than unity, (20) shows that the change in the balance of payments of Country 1 may be favorable rather than unfavorable. This would be true whenever $dy_1/d\alpha_1$ were greater than $1/(1 - u_1')$. In such a situation the secondary rise in exports of the expanding country would exceed the rise in imports; the secondary effects, in other words, would more than offset the primary effects. But such an outcome could be expected only under the rather unusual circumstances of high propensities to spend in a considerable number of the other countries.

## VI.  TWO-COUNTRY AND MULTIPLE-COUNTRY MODELS COMPARED

The classical theory of international trade, including the theory of comparative advantage as well as the closely-related theory of the international price mechanism, was developed almost entirely in terms of two countries. Most of the important problems in international economics during the nineteenth century were discussed as though the world economy were divided into two regions, one region being the home country—usually England—and the other region being the "rest of the world." During the interwar period of the present century, this classical procedure came under heavy attack, particularly by the late Professor Graham, who argued with considerable cogency and force that the classical procedure involved a persistent bias.[13] Graham insisted that the traditional, two-country theory greatly exaggerated the role of international demand and neglected the role of shifts in output in determining the terms of international exchange. He argued, specifically, that if one considers a complex world economy in which a large number of countries are trading in a considerable number of commodities, the process of adjustment to a disturbing event in international trade is fundamentally similar to the process of adjustment within a single country. In Graham's view, then, the fact that resources, particularly labor, are more or less immobile between countries does not require, as the classical economists had supposed, a theory of *international* prices, separate and distinct from the theory of prices within a single country.

In concluding the present paper, which has dealt with an international theory of income rather than a theory of prices, there is no need to discuss at length the controversy between Graham and the classical economists. My purpose in raising the issue is not to try to settle it but to raise a similar issue with respect to the international theory of income. If it is true, as Graham argues, that the traditional two-country model of international *price* theory involves a persistent and significant bias, is it also true that an analogous two-country model of international *income* theory involves a similar bias? To put the question another way, is a theory of international income that is founded upon the simplifying assumption that the world economy consists of two regions likely to involve any fundamental errors? The two-country income model, as I indicated earlier, has been discussed by a number of economists, and it should be possible to answer the question raised above by comparing the results of the two-country analysis with those of the generalized theory presented here. Since I am most familiar with my own version of the two-country model, I shall employ it to make the comparison.[14]

On the whole, the comparison does not reveal any basic flaws in the two-country model.[15] There are no processes of income adjustment in the *n*-country model which are not also revealed by the simple two-country model, and in the main the conclusions reached by employing the latter are the same as those reached by employing the former. In my earlier paper, using a terminology slightly different from that used here, I considered altogether three different cases of

13. F. D. Graham, "The Theory of International Values Re-examined," *Quarterly Journal of Economics*, XXXVIII (November, 1923), pp. 54–86, and "The Theory of International Values," *ibid.*, XLVI (August, 1932), pp. 581–616. The ideas contained in these two articles were considerably elaborated in book form. (See F. D. Graham, *The Theory of International Values* (Princeton: Princeton University Press, 1948), 349 pp.)

14. Metzler, "Underemployment Equilibrium in International Trade," *op. cit.*

15. Cf. Machlup, *op. cit.*, p. 197.

the two-country model. The first, or "normal," case was one in which the marginal propensity to spend was less than unity in both countries. The analogue of this case for the $n$-country model is the situation in which the propensity to spend is less than unity in each of the $n$ countries. Under these circumstances both models reveal that an autonomous increase of investment in one country creates a deficit in that country's balance of payments on current account and that the amount of the deficit is less than the autonomous investment. This conclusion of the two-country model, in other words, is in no way vitiated by the complex interactions of trade among a large number of countries. The second case, in the two-country model, was one in which the propensity to spend of the country initiating the expansion, say Country 1, was less than unity, while the propensity to spend of the second country was greater than unity. The analogous situation, in the $n$-country model, is that in which the propensity to spend is less than unity in Country 1 but greater than unity in all other countries. Again, both the two-country and the $n$-country models will lead to the same conclusion: autonomous investment in Country 1 actually *improves* the balance of trade of that country; the induced rise of Country 1's exports exceeds the rise of its imports. The third and final case, in the two-country model, was a situation in which the propensity to spend in Country 1 was greater than unity, while the propensity to spend in Country 2 was less than unity; and the analogue of this situation, in the $n$-country model, is the situation in which Country 1 has a propensity to spend greater than unity, while all other countries have propensities less than unity. In this case also, as in the two preceding ones, the results of the two-country model are consistent with those of the $n$-country model. Either model supports the conclusion that, under the assumed conditions with respect to the propensities to spend, an increase in autonomous investment in Country 1 leads to an unfavorable movement in that country's balance of trade, the amount of the unfavorable movement being greater than the amount of autonomous investment.

Considering the large measure of agreement between the two-country and the $n$-country models, the reader may wonder what purpose is served by studying the generalized theory at all. If the simple theory and the general one both lead to the same results, why bother with the latter? To this question a number of answers may be given. The first and most obvious one is that hindsight is better than foresight. While we might have felt intuitively that the two-country model is satisfactory for most purposes, I doubt whether we could have been sure of this without a careful study of the more general system. A second reason for studying the general theory is that there are certain situations in the $n$-country model for which no analogue exists in the two-country model. This is true, for example, if the marginal propensity to spend is less than unity in Country 1 and in some but not all of the remaining countries. In situations such as this the effects of expansion can be described only by the general, $n$-country model. A third reason for preferring the $n$-country model to the two-country model is that the former provides a good deal more information than the latter about the dynamic stability of our income equations. Although I have used the stability conditions developed above primarily in studying the characteristics of the static equations, these stability conditions are also interesting and useful in other connections as well. It is useful, for example, to know that, if the propensity to spend is less than unity in all regions or subregions of the system, the stability of the income equations does not depend in any way upon how the world economy happens to be divided into national units. As a second example, it could easily be shown from Section III above and from my earlier paper on the stability of multiple markets that any cyclical solutions of the dynamic system are likely to be overshadowed by noncyclical solutions. This means, I believe, that the answer to the riddle of the business cycle is not to be found in horizontal transactions between one region and another, such as those depicted in our $n$-country system.

Perhaps the most important reason of all for studying the $n$-country model is that such a model will probably prove to be the most satisfactory theoretical foundation for an empirical study of the international aspects of income and employment. Although our study of the $n$-country model has not taken us very far, it has, I fear, taken us about as far as we can expect to go without introducing actual numbers in place of our hypothetical propensities to import and to spend. Unfortunately, the limits that we can expect to place upon the movements of our variables from a study of the theory alone are far too broad to be of much practical assistance in the formulation of economic policy. To a country considering the feasibility of a public works program, for example, it is little comfort to know that the unfavorable movement in its balance of trade engendered by such a program will normally be less than the amount of the public works. The country needs to know in addition, what the approximate magnitude of its trade deficit will be and what the repercussions will be on incomes and trade balances in other countries. In order to answer questions such as these, it is obvious that the theory described above must be transformed into an empirical system; and for this purpose the $n$-country system is clearly the appropriate one. Eventually, then, an import-export matrix, similar in many respects to Leontief's input-output matrix for a single country, must be developed for the world economy. Many of the facts needed for such a table are already at hand. Reasonably accurate figures are available, for example, regarding the network of world trade. If these trade figures are to be transformed into propensities to import and to spend, however, they must be supplemented by statistics of national income for each of the countries. Lack of such income statistics has been responsible, more than anything else, for our inability to provide the empirical counterpart of the international theory of income set out above. With the improvement in statistics throughout the world since the end of the war, it is to be hoped that this gap in our knowledge will soon be filled.

# PART V

# REGIONAL ECONOMIC POLICY

# 14

## *Appropriate Goals for Regional Economic Policy*

One of the issues in the current debate on regional economic policy is whether any effort to stimulate growth in particular regions can be compatible with a national growth policy. In this essay, I want to deal with the question in more general terms.

To begin with, I want to put the question: Granted that our primary, if not sole, objective is to accelerate the rate of national growth, which theories of growth and which views of the process of economic progress would make the regional variable interesting and important, and which would make it trivial and irrelevant? In other words, I would like to show how certain frameworks designed for the analysis of national growth problems might very logically and necessarily want to have a significant regional component. It is clear that the regional theorist can work his way back to concern over national growth. Is it also possible that a good national growth theorist might be led logically and necessarily to a concern over the regional deployment of resources? We have many illustrations of good Scotsmen asking, "But what does it all mean for the U.K.?" Can we provide a framework which will impel a good U.K. man to ask, "What's doing in Scotland?"

If economic growth is pursued in the context of a planned economy, the role of regions is fairly clear. You can't very well decide *what* you're going to do without also deciding *where* you're going to do it. And in deciding *where* to do things, you will be making estimates of the impact on growth of alternative locations. What's more, even the *what* will be affected by the "where." You can't decide how much you're going to spend for transport without reference to the regional distribution of population and production, which you also control.

It's not surprising therefore that in the Eastern European countries regional economics and regional planning enjoy much greater relative prestige than they do in the West.

My concern is with advanced market-oriented economies which have a measure of planning and, at a minimum, a deliberate policy to accelerate economic growth in the economy as a whole. I think both the U.S. and the U.K. — despite your recent change in government and our's — fall into this category.

*Chinitz, Benjamin, "Appropriate Goals for Regional Economic Policy," Urban Studies, III, No. 1 (February, 1966), pp. 1–7.*

Now, there is one view of economic growth that has had considerable currency on both sides of the Atlantic, which clearly leaves no room at all for concern over regional dimensions. This is the view that in practice, it is not the rate of growth of capacity but the rate of growth of demand which effectively constrains the rate of growth of per capita output, even in the long run. Whether or not this was explicit in Keynes, it was unequivocally put forth by the most ardent American Keynesian, Alvin Hansen, in his 1938 Presidential address before the American Economic Association. The war and the early postwar years discredited this point of view, but in the late 50's it came back into fashion.

I don't want to make too much of this view because I suspect it borders upon setting up a straw man in order to knock him down. But it's clearly inimical to regionalism. If there is a chronic tendency for the economy to operate at less than capacity because of inadequate effective demand, one would be hard put, on grounds of efficiency alone, to argue that we ought to take measures to enhance the capacity or the fuller utilization of capacity in specific regions. There clearly can't be any gain to the economy as a whole in such policies. But by the same token this view is also inimical to a wider set of concerns such as the pursuit of technological progress — because it dramatises the likelihood of technological unemployment — and the general pursuit of efficiency, because it undermines the connection between factor prices and opportunity costs. You can imagine what happens if the wisdom of specific projects and investments is judged in terms of the alternative of unemployment; a not uncommon perspective in our country.

So we must insist, in order to proceed, that in the long run, abstracting from cyclical fluctuations, the rate of growth of output *per capita* is mainly a function of the rate of growth of capacity. And what concerns us are the factors which determine the rate of growth of capacity.

Capacity depends on the volume of resources and the efficiency of their utilization. Similarly, increments to capacity derive from increments to resources, e.g., through accumulation of capital and/or from increments to efficiency, e.g., through technological innovation. So far, I have defined or illustrated rather than theorized about the growth process. A theory would require me to say something about the conditions under which accumulation and innovation occur. At a minimum, a theory ought to suggest that certain ingredients of growth are more important than others, in the sense of being preconditions of growth or accounting for a larger share of total growth.

There have been theories advanced and there have been attempts to test these theories. I shall not attempt a survey of growth literature;

but what I would like to do is to set up some highly simple categories for the purpose of exploring the possible relevance of regional economics to growth theory.

No one doubts that investment in physical capital contributes significantly to the growth of output *per capita*. How much growth can be attributed to this source is another question to which some investigators have tried to provide an answer. But let us accept for the moment that this is an important level of growth which is certainly implied in policies that are intended to operate directly on investment such as depreciation allowances, investment tax credits and similar inducements. All such measures are intended to raise the expected rate of return on capital investment and thereby encourage a faster rate of capital accumulation.

Is there any reason why such policies should be regionally differentiated if the objective is to get the maximum impact in terms of total national investment? It is important to be clear on one point: if the Board of Trade or whoever administers these inducements wanted to maximize the investment yield from a given amount of public funds and if it had information on the investment demand elasticities of different investors, it could by behaving as a discriminating monopolist induce a larger volume of investment with a given amount of funds than it could by offering a standard set of inducements. The question, then, is whether the aggregate demand for investment can be efficiently disaggregated or sorted out by region, leading to a system of multiple inducements depending upon the responses they are likely to bring forth.

Assume for the moment that we *can* demonstrate that greater inducements are required in one region than in another. Have we established a case for a regionally differentiated inducement policy? This is in fact the kind of policy we have, but I'm sure we'd all be disturbed at the thought that the rationale from a theoretical point of view could come so easily. There is, of course, a fatal flaw in the argument: the separate demand curves are not additive. The same project will be undertaken in one region at one price (inducement) and in a second region at a higher price (inducement). But is there no measure of additivity at all? Are there not investment opportunities which are specific to a region—which are not substitutes for projects in other regions—and which would not be undertaken except with special inducements which may exceed the general level of inducements?

I will return to that question shortly. Let me move to another category: the supply of labor inputs. An ingredient in growth is the labor input *per capita*. Measured in sheer quantitative terms, the input of male labor *per capita* has diminished somewhat, but the input of female labor has trended sharply upward. If we look to greater labour force participation to increase economic growth, do we need to be concerned about regional effects? No matter how mobile we assume or expect male labor to be in the long run we have to recognize that a considerable proportion of the female labor force is captive to the region where the male partner is employed — a pure example of the concept of joint supply — you can't have one without the other. We may argue, if we want to quibble, that in the long run the household will migrate to the point where the joint opportunity of husband and wife is maximized, but this argues for far more mobility than anyone is prepared to assume, since the relevance of opportunities for the wife changes through the family cycle.

It is therefore perfectly consistent with classical free market long-run equilibrium that female labor should be in surplus in certain areas even when there is normally full employment of male labor.

Turning to the quality of the labor inputs, we have a rapidly growing field of research on the growth generating effects of education. Without pretending to settle the thorny issues which surround this question, it is still safe to assert that the rate of growth *per capita* is in part explained by the improvement in the quality of labor through training and education; at least most managers of otherwise free economies are willing to make that assumption and credit investments in education with benefits on the growth account. If a government sets about the business of promoting growth through expenditures on training and education, does it need to pay attention to regional factors?

A program to assist education, rather unlike a program to encourage capital investment, must inevitably cope with all sorts of questions of disaggregation, but not obviously along regional lines. What shall be the mix of assistance as between primary, secondary and higher education? General education and technical education? Shall the awards be made on the basis of potential, or on the basis of need?

Yet, when the institutional setting is taken into account, it is difficult to avoid a recognition of the need to disaggregate by region. In my country, at least, there is a very strong correlation between the quality (and quantity) of education and the economic vitality of the area. Children, like wives, are sufficiently immobile that one cannot assume that they will gravitate to the point of maximum educational opportunity. A region which is economically anemic is likely to underinvest in education, not necessarily in relation to its own resources, but in relation to the social return and the private return to the clientele. Moreover, the institutional fabric is such that one cannot assume that it will upon its own initiative take full advantage of generalized programs of assistance, especially if they require local financial participation.

I come now to a less tangible element in the growth process, one to which we have really become sensitive, mainly because of the challenge of developing the less developed economies of the world, If the term "infrastructure" existed during my graduate student days I must have been leading a very sheltered life indeed; I don't recall hearing the term until much later. The term, I take it, is intended to embrace that kind of capital which has at least two characteristics; it comes in very large lumps, and is (therefore) in most societies — including capitalist — managed in part or in whole by the public sector, transportation and power bring prime examples. What we have come to understand, if not to measure, is that the whole is greater than the sum of the parts, if in counting the parts we neglect the contribution of large blocks of capital which we tend to take for granted — like the streets we drive on, the sidewalks we walk on, the network of communications, the road system, the buildings we live in, etc.

I think it would be unfair to say that we were not aware of the concept of external economies or of its contribution to economic growth; albeit true that classical economics — especially neoclassical economics — is not replete with models which took external economies explicitly into account. The main point is that we assumed that external economies constituted a bonus to straight growth. If you grew and demands increased and you built a lot of capital to *accommodate* the growth, you received as a bonus an additional stimulus to growth. You start with a dirt road; you advance economically; you pave the road to accommodate demand; the next stage of growth comes easier because you have cheaper transportation. What's new in our thinking is that we now believe — or at least some of us do — that we can induce growth by paving the road even though there is only enough traffic at the moment to justify a dirt road.

I said that this change in our thinking was sparked by the challenge of developing the poor countries. But its relevance for the advanced countries rests on other foundations. I am a firm believer in the influence of environment on ideas and theoretical fashions. I think we can attribute the growing emphasis on external economies to the changing structure of economic activity in advanced societies. If the classical economists and their disciples failed to assign what strikes us as proper importance to external economies, we must not forget that they were duly impressed with the overwhelming task of exploiting natural resources and accumulating the "ordinary" kind of physical capital. But the mainsprings of wealth-creation on the margin have shifted proportionately from natural resource exploitation to the clever manipulation of materials at the processing level, and the manipulation of skills and information in the provision of services. We now attach much greater importance to intangibles because the tangibles have receded into the background—economic growth is now much less a function of the natural environment and much more a function of the human and social environment.

If you will forgive the digression, we may now return to the main theme. If social investment is viewed as a tool of economic growth, and not simply as an accommodation *to* economic growth, what about the regional dimension here?

In the United States the relation of social investment to economic growth receives its highest expression at the local level. More and more cities, and even states, emphasize the urgency of renewing and improving their social capital, not just to improve the quality of life in their areas, but also to promote economic development. In former days, the only aspect of public finances which was thought to have a bearing on an area's economic growth was its tax rate. You didn't want to drive industry away by having your local taxes diverge too seriously on the high side from levels prevailing in other localities. Currently, both sides of the ledger, expenditure as well as revenue, are thought to be highly relevant in determining an area's rate of growth. From the locality's point of view, the issue is naturally cast in terms of competition. If we want to draw industry to our locality we need good roads, good housing, good recreational facilities, etc. The natural tendency for the observer is to assume that from a national viewpoint these efforts cancel out. No one doubts the intrinsic value of these investments, but whether they contribute on balance to national growth is quite another matter.

Let me recapitulate. I have said that investments in human resources are bound to have a regional aspect; that inducements to encourage private capital investment might require a regional dimension if there is an element of additivity in the investment demands by region, and just now we have raised the question of social investments.

The latter two issues will fall into place when we consider the role of entrepreneurship in the growth process. All growth studies and growth theories assign an important role to innovation, to changes in production functions which yield higher outputs for given levels of labour and capital inputs. We credit science with invention, but innovation is by definition associated with entrepreneurship.

A number of points about entrepreneurship have impressed me in recent years. First, in a dynamic economy—*i.e.*, rapid change in technology and demand—a major challenge to entrepreneurship is the conversion of old resources to new uses. Secondly, the capacity to adjust is significantly affected by the initial conditions — which in part determine the proclivity for entrepreneurship. Thirdly, the more rapid growth of tertiary or service industries in an advanced economy — certainly in employment, if not in income originating — implies, I think, a relatively greater input of entrepreneurship per unit of output because on the *average* tertiary establishments are smaller than manufacturing establishments. Fourthly, service industries, on the average, are locationally more market-oriented; there is less specialization by region than in manufacturing, hence the entrepreneurial input needs to be more ubiquitous.

The experience of the developing countries and our thinking about them certainly suggests that the quality of entrepreneurship is not a simple function of resources and objective opportunities but depends in a complex way on the heritage of the past: the social and cultural values, the economic experience, traditions, and factors of that nature. In an advanced economy, there is a strong temptation to assume that the capacity for entrepreneurship is secured, and moreover, that its level and quality in the aggregate for the nation as a whole is determined independently of regional factors.

If we argue, however, as I do, that the proclivity for entrepreneurship in time $t$ is a function of the structure of the economic system in time $t-1$, $t-2$, etc., then regionalism becomes significant insofar as the history and heritage of regions differ with respect to those variables which affect what we might call the *entrepreneurial birth rate*. And if, as I have suggested, economic opportunity on the margin assumes more and more the character of tertiary industries oriented to local markets, then there is a compelling need to be concerned about the *fertility* of the local economy in generating entrepreneurship.

What I'm prepared to assert on insufficient evidence is that it is a mistake to assume that all opportunities and all entrepreneurs confront each other, as it were, in the national market, and that the fate of a given region depends on how many of its opportunities are opted for by entrepreneurs. I question the visibility of certain kinds of opportunity; I question the mobility of entrepreneurship; and above all, I assign an important role to history and therefore to regions, in determining the flow of entrepreneurship.

I'm sure there are a lot of loose ends but let me tidy up those which I have explicitly left for now.

1. Regional investment demand schedules can be additive. Thus, a discriminatory inducement policy can be consistent with efficiency.

2. If social investment is relevant to growth, and if certain kinds of impediments to growth are regional in character, then a regionally

stratified program of social investment may contribute to national growth.

If the regional dimension is significant, what does it imply for policy? I come finally to the title of my paper.

1. From the limited perspective of this paper, it is unreasonable to set regional goals in terms of aggregate growth — whether population, labor force, or output. The goal which is suggested by this line of argument is greater progress in productivity and living standards.

2. Although my argument does not lead to a precise definition of regions, it does, I think, suggest a bias in favor of fairly generous boundaries. The net must be large enough to catch all kinds of fish; to embrace a diversified range of opportunities. We certainly cannot hope to generate growth on every corner and in every hamlet. The recent emphasis on growth points within larger regions is certainly consistent with the logic of my argument.

3. Inducement policies should favor indigenous enterprise as against relocations.

4. There should be no bias in favor of manufacturing, or other industries which earn income from the "outside."

5. Relocations should not be evaluated in terms of the number of jobs provided, but rather in terms of the demonstration effect and the generation of external economies.

6. The persistence of high unemployment in development areas should not be taken as evidence that regional policies are not effective. The acid test is relative growth in *per capita* output, which may or may not be accompanied by a reduction in unemployment.

I would like to close by quoting an American colleague. A. O. Hirschman, in a chapter on Interregional and International Transmission of Economic Growth, in his book, *The Strategy of Economic Development*, sums up as follows:

> If only we could in some respects treat a region as though it were a country we would indeed get the best of both worlds and be able to create situations particularly favorable to development.

But in all fairness, let me also quote his footnote:

> We assume that the areas we are talking about have a substantial untapped development potential. There are of course many regions and perhaps even some countries whose natural resources are so poor or depleted that their best hope lies in becoming empty spaces — or at least far emptier than they are now.

NILES M. HANSEN

# 15

# Unbalanced Growth and Regional Development

## INTRODUCTION

In recent years considerable attention has been given to the problem of whether economic development might be best accelerated by "balanced growth" under government direction or by government provocation of imbalances, whereby disequilibria produce positive responses which in turn produce other disequilibria, and so on in the manner of a chain reaction.

The balanced-growth argument for developing lagging national economies has been succinctly stated in the following terms:

> There is a minimum level of resources that must be devoted to . . . a development program if it is to have any chance of success. Launching a country into self-sustaining growth is a little like getting an airplane off the ground . . . . Proceeding "bit by bit" will not add up in its effects to the sum total of the single bits. A minimum quantum of investment is a necessary, though not sufficient, condition of process. This, in a nutshell, is the contention of the theory of the big push.[1]

The "big push" would involve initiating a large number of interdependent projects simultaneously. The principal justification for such action is based on the phenomenon of external economies. Nurske,[2] for example, has pointed out that the marginal product of capital may be greater in underdeveloped areas than in those already relatively industrialized, but not necessarily in terms of private profit, since individual projects in underdeveloped areas are confronted with a high degree of uncertainty concerning whether or not the relevant products will find a market. This disincentive would be overcome if numerous projects were undertaken simultaneously; investments that would not be profitable in isolation become so for the ensemble as a result of mutually favorable external economies.[3]

Hansen, Niles M., "Unbalanced Growth and Regional Development," Western Economic Journal, IV, No. 1 (September, 1965), pp. 3–14.

1. P. N. Rosenstein-Rodan, *Notes on the Theory of the "Big Push"* (M.I.T. Center for International Studies, March 1957), p. 1. The quotation is from *The Objectives of U.S. Economic Assistance Programs* (Washington, D.C.: Center for the Special Senate Committee to Study the Foreign Aid Program, 1957), p. 70.

2. Ragnar Nurkse, "Some International Aspects of the Problem of Economic Development," *American Economic Review* (May, 1952), p. 572; and *Problems of Capital Formation in the Underdeveloped Economies* (Oxford, 1953), Ch. 1.

3. For detailed discussion of various aspects of this approach see also P. N. Rosen-

The applicability of this general approach to problems of under-developed countries has been the target of numerous criticisms,[4] some of which are particularly applicable to problems of lagging regions in mature economies. Specifically, "in practice any implementation of the 'big push' proposals would mean a large public sector. . . . Even if the government were to subsidize private firms, instead of operating public concerns, the extent of regulation would be enormous."[5] In most industrialized economies of the West, institutional patterns would not be compatible with such an approach to developing poorer regions. Moreover, the balanced-growth argument implies a closed economy; but "one way a country can have balanced consumption without balanced production, if it can make or grow or mine anything the world wants, is to import goods it cannot afford to produce."[6] This is especially applicable to regional cases, where free interregional trade makes it relatively (to the international case) easy to avoid many of the difficulties posed by capital "lumpiness."

On the other hand, in some cases balanced growth via the big push thesis might be more relevant to regional than to national cases. One of the principal arguments against its applicability in under-developed countries is that "the resources required for carrying out the policy . . . are of such an order of magnitude that a country disposing of them would in fact not be underdeveloped."[7] But the poverty that characterizes most underdeveloped countries should not be confused with the prevailing situation in lagging regions of industrialized nations. The availability of productive resources in the latter often is not comparable to that in the former. Labor is anxious to find employment and savings frequently are considerable, though they often flow to expanding regions rather than to local projects. In such conditions, as we shall argue, the balanced-growth doctrine is not without value for public policy.

The unbalanced-growth approach has been developed for the most part by A. O. Hirschman and François Perroux. Hirschman has emphasized that investment strategy should concentrate on a few sectors rather than widely dispersed projects; the key sectors would be determined by measuring backward-linkage and forward-linkage

---

stein-Rodan, "Problems of Industrialization of Eastern and South-Eastern Europe," *Economic Journal* (June-September, 1943), pp. 202–11; and Tibor Scitovsky, "Two Concepts of External Economies," *Journal of Political Economy* (April, 1954), pp. 143–52.

4. See, for example, Albert O. Hirschman, *The Strategy of Economic Development* (New Haven, 1958), Ch. 3; H. W. Singer, "Economic Progress in Underdeveloped Countries," *Social Research* (March, 1949), pp. 1–11; Stephen Enke, *Economics for Development* (Englewood Cliffs, 1963), Ch. 16; Marcus Fleming, "External Economies and the Doctrine of Balanced Growth," *Economic Journal* (June, 1958), pp. 241–56.

5. Enke, *op. cit.*, p. 316.

6. *Ibid.*, p. 314.

7. Singer, *op. cit.*, p. 10.

effects in terms of input-output maxima.[8] Development, he argues, has taken place

> ... with growth being communicated from the leading sectors of the economy to the followers, from one firm to another .... The advantage of this kind of ... advance over "balanced growth," where every activity expands perfectly in step with every other, is that it leaves considerable scope to *induced* investment decisions and therefore economizes our principal scarce resource, namely, genuine decision making.[9]

Similarly, Perroux has emphasized that growth does not appear simultaneously and uniformly throughout an economy; rather, it is concentrated, with varying intensity, in certain development poles or propulsive industries.[10]

Even though interregional growth is always unbalanced in geographic terms, it still requires special analytic consideration, for "while the regional setting reveals unbalanced growth at its most obvious, it perhaps does not show it at its best" because successive growth points may all "fall within the same privileged growth space."[11]

The present paper attempts to apply the foregoing theories to intra- and interregional development problems. Primary emphasis is placed on unbalanced growth, since this is the characteristic pattern of development which mature economies have in fact followed and because it generally is still the most feasible approach from an institutional point of view. More important, it is also the most rational approach from a purely economic viewpoint. Before we consider this proposition in detail, it is necessary to define the variables and clarify the terms to be employed in the subsequent analysis.

## TYPES OF INVESTMENT AND REGIONAL PROTOTYPES

Discussions concerning optimal investment allocation frequently distinguish between investment in directly productive activities (DPA) and that in public overhead capital (OC). For present purposes, private investment and investment in DPA are treated as synonymous. OC, however, is divided into two components: social (SOC) and economic (EOC). Projects of the latter type are specifically aimed at supporting DPA, and include roads, bridges, harbors, power projects, and similar undertakings. SOC projects, on the other hand, are more

8. These effects refer, respectively, to induced supply of inputs and induced use of outputs. See Hirschman, *op. cit.*, pp. 100–17.

9. *Ibid.*, pp. 62, 63.

10. François Perroux, "La notion de pole de croissance," *L'économie du XX^e siècle* (Paris, 1961), pp. 142–53 [Selection 7 of this volume].

11. Hirschman, *op. cit.*, p. 184.

concerned with what has been termed "investment in human beings," *i.e.*, education, welfare, and health undertakings. These activities may, of course, contribute to DPA, but the impact of such effects would tend to be less tangible than that associated with EOC activities.[12]

Another refinement concerns the analytic regions to be used. Regional problems are often treated in terms of a twofold distinction between "developed" and "underdeveloped" regions—the familiar North-South problem which characterizes so many mature national economies of the Northern Hemisphere. Here, however, regions are classified into three types: congested, intermediate, and lagging.

Congested regions are characterized by very high concentrations of population, industrial and commercial activities, and public overhead capital. Examples would include the London and Paris agglomerations and much of the megalopolis that extends along the northeastern seaboard of the United States. Such regions have evolved largely through the operation of purely market forces, particularly the wide variety of external economies associated with industrial and commercial concentration. These economies include abundant transportation facilities, proximity to suppliers and markets, skilled labor, and auxiliary business services.[13] However, congested regions have reached the point where marginal external economies accruing to new and existing firms as a result of expanded economic activity are less than the increased external diseconomies resulting from greater congestion, *i.e.*, marginal social benefit is less than marginal social cost. Regarding American experience, Rapkin has found that today "there is little doubt that some cities have developed beyond the optimum point." In large congested cities urban "difficulties are compounded, social and private costs soar, and frictions and waste proliferate."[14] Similarly, two recent French public-opinion surveys indicate that most French citizens, whether residents of Paris or not, would prefer to live in regions other than Paris if opportunities existed for a comparable standard of living. Problems relating to urban congestion were primarily responsible for these negative attitudes. Moreover two-thirds of both Parisian and non-

12. EOC-SOC distinctions are elaborated further in Niles M. Hansen, "The Structure and Determinants of Local Public Investment Expenditures," *Review of Economics and Statistics* (May, 1965), pp. 150–162.

13. These are discussed for example, in Douglass C. North, "Location Theory and Regional Economic Growth," *Journal of Political Economy* (June, 1955), pp. 248, 251–56 [Selection 3 of this volume]; Raymond Vernon, *The Changing Economic Function of the Central City* (New York, 1959), pp. 28–37; Gunnar Myrdal, *Rich Lands and Poor* (New York, 1957), Ch. 3.

14. Chester Rapkin, "Some Effects of Economic Growth on the Character of Cities," *American Economic Review Papers and Proceedings* (May, 1956), p. 297.

232

Parisian respondents favored the use of public policy to limit growth in the Paris region.[15]

Intermediate regions, on the other hand, are those that offer significant advantages — raw materials, qualified labor, cheap power, etc. — to private firms, and where entry of new firms or expansion of existing firms would result in marginal external economies substantially in excess of concomitant social costs. In other words, other things being equal (except degree of concentration), the marginal social product to cost ratio would be greater in these areas than in congested regions.[16]

Finally, lagging regions present few, if any, attributes that would tend to attract new economic activity. They are generally areas characterized by small-scale agriculture or stagnant or declining industries.

## UNBALANCED GROWTH AND CONGESTED REGIONS

Congested regions are the product of unbalanced growth. For the most part, their development begins spontaneously as a result of favorable circumstances, such as privileged location with respect to principal transportation routes or raw materials. Expansion of private investment increases the need for transportation facilities, water, housing, and power. Hirschman provides an apt description of the consequent process:

> Thus, urgent demands for several types of capital-intensive public investment appear and must be given highest priority whether or not they correspond to the government's sense of distributive justice and to its pattern of regional political preference. The public investment in overhead capital in turn makes possible further growth of industry and trade in the favored areas and this growth requires further large allocations of public investment to them.
>
> Determined as it is by the volume of private investment and the general rise in income in the developing areas, public investment clearly plays here an "induced" role, and investment choices are often remarkably and unexpectedly obvious.[17]

However, Hirschman[18] finds that after some time, public investment requirements will decline relative to private investment and that

15. A. Girard and H. Bastide, "Les problèmes démographiques devant l'opinion," *Population* (April–May 1960), pp. 246–87; *Sondages* (1963), No. 4, p. 26.

Extensive documentation concerning numerous types of external diseconomies of overconcentration is provided in K. William Kapp, *The Social Costs of Private Enterprise* (Cambridge, Mass., 1950).

16. This would be the case even if the marginal social benefit to cost ratio in congested regions were not negative.

17. Hirschman, *op. cit.*, pp. 192–93.

18. *Ibid.*, p. 194.

earnings from prior investments can be used to finance a higher share of public investment. This process, he claims, "is implicit in the term 'social *overhead capital.*'" Thus, central government funds are freed for use in other regions and, in the long run, regional differences will tend to disappear.

This argument is questionable on three basic points. First, it ignores the effects of public investment by state (or provincial) and local governments; second, it fails to distinguish between investment in EOC and that in SOC; and, finally, it assumes that reduction in regional income differences should be achieved by emphasis on central government investment (primarily in EOC or DPA) in lagging regions. These propositions require further examination, especially in the context of mature economies.

Concerning the first of these points, the United States data presented in Table 1 show that municipal operating outlays are related directly to population size, implying a direct relationship between

TABLE 1  Average per Capita Expenditures of Municipal Governments, 1962 (by population size class)

|  | CAPITAL OUTLAY | OTHER | TOTAL |
|---|---|---|---|
| Less than 2,500 | 9.43 | 32.48 | 41.91 |
| 2,500–4,999 | 10.05 | 42.24 | 52.28 |
| 5,000–9,999 | 13.63 | 47.09 | 60.72 |
| 10,000–24,999 | 17.26 | 55.17 | 72.43 |
| 25,000–49,999 | 20.66 | 75.41 | 96.08 |
| 50,000–99,999 | 23.79 | 87.66 | 111.46 |
| 100,000–299,999 | 30.36 | 93.76 | 124.12 |
| 300,000–499,999 | 32.48 | 91.56 | 124.04 |
| 500,000–999,999 | 41.27 | 125.23 | 166.51 |
| 1,000,000 or more | 46.80 | 172.31 | 219.12 |

SOURCE: "Finances of Municipalities and Township Governments," *Census of Governments: 1962* (Washington, D.C.: U.S. Bureau of the Census, 1964), Vol. IV, No. 3, p. 34.

per capita capital stock and population. However, there is also a strong direct relationship between capital expenditures (per capita) and population size. Thus, current municipal investment is greatest in areas which have had most investment in the past.[19] Similarly, analysis of census data[20] on direct expenditures of state governments in 1962 shows a strong direct relationship between per capita current operating outlays and per capita capital expenditures. The correlation coefficient relating these variables is 0.731, highly significant at the 99 percent level. These results indicate that, in the absence of central

19. Unfortunately, the data in *Census of Governments* are not sufficiently disaggregated to permit analysis along SOC–EOC lines.

20. The source for the data used in this analysis is *Compendium of State Government Finances in 1962* (Washington, D.C.: U.S. Bureau of the Census, 1963), p. 52.

government regional policy, expansion of public overhead capital would continue to be concentrated in regions already relatively well-equipped in this regard. Still more important in the present context, even where central government investment policy is consciously directed toward favoring lagging regions, it is doubtful whether public investment at all levels of government would, on balance, eliminate regional differences in income or in investment and employment opportunities.

A more precise examination of these issues may be gained by introducing SOC-EOC distinctions, which Hirschman's treatment ignores. The present writer's studies based on standardized Belgian data, covering outlays of national, provincial, and local authorities, show that per capita EOC outlays are directly related to growth factors, while those of SOC are directly related to absolute population size, population density, and degree of commercial and industrial importance. Because of higher SOC outlays, areas of concentrated population and economic activity have significantly higher total public investment outlays (per capita) than other areas.[21] Thus there is no evidence of a tendency for public investment patterns to shift to the benefit of lagging areas.[22]

In general, whatever the merit of Hirschman's argument when applied to EOC, it is highly doubtful when applied to SOC, and thus to public investment as a whole. The evidence indicates that the greatest relative need of lagging regions is for expanded SOC, but there is no evidence that it will be provided as a matter of course by government policy at any level. In this regard, it is relevant to note that the Appalachian Regional Development Act specifies less than 10 per cent of total authorized allocations for SOC activities,[23] whereas, as Caudill has pointed out, the foremost need of the area is for "a comprehensive and effective system of public education," a need which thus far has been "robbed of adequate financing."[24]

The following analysis attempts to deal with these diverse issues in a comprehensive manner. It does not adopt the viewpoint of any

21. Of course, such differences would be even more pronounced to the extent that more economically advanced areas have relatively high growth rates and, therefore, greater EOC expenditures.

22. Hansen, *op. cit.*; see also, Hansen, "Municipal Investment Requirements in a Growing Agglomeration," *Land Economics* (February, 1965), pp. 49–56. The reasons for the high SOC outlays in more advanced areas are complex. For some activities (e.g., police protection) there is undoubtedly a definite need for higher expenditures. Other activities (e.g., education) involve both increased "need" for various skills and increased "wants" resulting from higher incomes and other socioeconomic factors.

23. U.S. Public Law 89–4, Appalachian Regional Development Act of 1965, 89th Cong., March 9, 1965.

24. Harry M. Caudill, *Night Comes to the Cumberlands* (Boston, 1963), p. 136; see also pp. 374–75.

particular type of region; rather, it suggests how a given (politically determined) aggregate of central government funds should be allocated among regions to maximize the concomitant long-run social product from a national point of view.[25]

Finally, it should be emphasized that the relevant net social product function is not linearly homogeneous. Rather, it will have the form (for example)

$$X = [2\theta DP - \lambda(D^2) - \beta(P^2)]^{1/2} + [\rho(\alpha D - D^2) - \gamma],$$

where $X$ = total net social product, $D$ = investment in directly productive activities, $P$ = public overhead capital investment, and $\theta$, $\lambda$, $\beta$, $\rho$, $\alpha$, and $\gamma$ are constants greater than zero.[26] The term in brackets gives the effects of external economies of agglomeration and external diseconomies of congestion. During the initial phases of the region's growth the former produces increasing average returns to scale. Eventually, however, the latter effects become dominant and the bracketed term becomes negative, *i.e.*, $X$ increases less than proportionally with inputs.

The general argument may be summarized by reference to Figure 1. Along any given isoproduct curve, $X_i$,

$$\Delta X = f_s\Delta S + f_e\Delta E + f_d\Delta D = 0.$$

25. Although this implies that per capita real income (including external effects) should be maximized for the nation as a whole, its relevance to income and employment in particular regions will depend on numerous factors, including the magnitude and interregional distribution of backward- and forward-linkage effects associated with various types of investment, and the relative labor intensiveness of various investment projects. Extent of factor mobility also is relevant in this regard. For example, whether public investment in training or retraining workers in lagging region $A$ would increase or decrease employment or per capita income in $A$ or in some more advanced region would depend on such considerations as interregional wage differences and employment opportunities, attachment of workers to $A$ for noneconomic reasons, and the extent to which firms would be attracted to $A$ by trained labor. In any event, there would be a clear net gain in per capita income from a national viewpoint.

26. For the sake of simplicity, all external effects are subsumed under the bracketed term even though $D$-induced $P$ may in turn induce further $D$. A more detailed examination of intersectoral relations would require a system of equations based on input-output data.

For the present equation,

$$f_P = \frac{\theta P - \lambda D}{[2\theta DP - \lambda(D^2) - \beta(P^2)]^{1/2}}$$

and

$$f_D = \frac{\theta D - \beta P}{[2\theta DP - \lambda(D^2 - \beta(P^2)]^{1/2}} + [\rho\alpha - 2\rho P].$$

See H. H. Liebhafsky, *The Nature of Price Theory* (Homewood, Ill., 1963), p. 177.

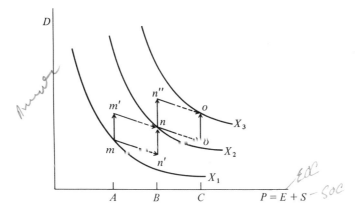

FIGURE 1    Unbalanced growth of public (P) and private (D) investment.

Here $S = SOC$ and $E = EOC$, with $E + S = P$. Thus the cost in terms of $D$ of producing $X_i$ increases if there is less $P$ to help. At the far right, increments to relatively plentiful $P$ do not give any significant decline in $D$. At the far left, $X_i$ eventually becomes vertical since any given $D$ requires a minimum level of $P$. It is assumed that $D$ can be varied continuously but that $P$ is supplied in discrete quanta (e.g., $A$, $B$, and $C$) so that it is not possible to move from $m$ to $n$ (or from $n$ to $o$) via a process of directly and continuously balanced growth of $D$ and $P$. In the initial phase of growth a region which is now congested was at, say, $m$. Factors favorable to private investment result in a gradual movement from $m$ to $m'$. Urgent demands for public investment then induce a delayed, discontinuous "lump" of $P$ and a discrete move to $n$, as implied in Hirschman's analysis above. This forms the basis for a similar movement from $n$ to $o$. As the growth of the region continues there is a relative shift in the composition of $P$; the share accounted for by $E$ (indicated by the dotted portions of segments $m'n$ and $n''o$) declines relative to that accounted for by $S$ (the solid portions).

Furthermore, assuming that $X_0$ is the level of output at which average returns to scale momentarily become constant, there is nothing in the nature of things to halt this process when $X_i > X_0$. Without public-policy measures, growth will continue indefinitely because the external diseconomies in question are generally not internalized costs for private producers.[27]

There are essentially two complementary courses of action available to public-policy makers to prevent further expansion of congested regions far beyond an optimal level. These are direct and

27. Of course, some external diseconomies are internalized in the form of increased transportation costs, higher land prices and higher taxes.

indirect controls on expansion of DPA within such regions, and encouragement of economic growth in alternate regions. In fact, governments have rarely carried out such joint measures in any systematic fashion. France is a significant exception, and even a principal critic of French planning has pointed out that "there has been a virtual absence of dissent to the policy of 'decongestion' which the French government has been pursuing with increasing vigor since 1955,"[28] In its efforts to restrict expansion of the Paris region the French government has relied on numerous devices, such as licensing of new plant construction and expansion, levies on nonresidential building, controls on vacant premises, grants payable to land converted to public uses (parking areas, housing, parks, etc.), decentralization of government agencies, and financial incentives to encourage plant location in other regions. However, this negative approach to decongestion is not satisfactory, for firms have shown a marked disposition to locate as near to the Paris agglomeration as possible and yet be outside the sphere of government restrictions.[29] In the long run, this will merely tend to enlarge the total area of congestion. Thus, positive measures are necessary to induce firms to locate new plants in other regions.

## INVESTMENT IN INTERMEDIATE AND LAGGING REGIONS

The failure of constraints on plant location in the Paris region to benefit more distant regions has led to the suggestion that it would be more practical to initiate "the development of a few major centres, with the state taking a more direct part, even if necessary, under-taking the construction of factory buildings."[30] Similarly, Perroux's[31] concept of development poles has been widely employed in the relevant French literature to support the case for unbalanced growth leading with investment in EOC. But, as Professor Milau has pointed out, "once the theory of growth poles has been accepted, each district of the country is going to demand its own individual pole; unfortunately, no magical means (public or private) is going to cause a pole to

28. Stanislaw Wellisz, "Economic Planning in The Netherlands, France, and Italy," *Journal of Political Economy* (June, 1960), p. 280.
29. See A. Pasquier, "La Normandie: données et problèmes de son expansion économique," *Revue économique* (November, 1956), pp. 939–48.
30. "Political and Economic Planning," *Regional Development in the European Economic Community* (London, 1962), p. 53. This report also recommends equipping industrial estates with "adequate basic services," that is, sufficient EOC.
31. See, for example, the economic planning proposals for various French regions given in *Revue économique* (November, 1956).

spring suddenly out of the ground."[32] But public EOC investment may be rational, given an environment already potentially favorable in one or more aspects to the location of private economic activity. Such conditions might include, among other things, potential sources of cheap power, favorable situation relative to existing transportation routes (given adequate port, canal, or other facilities), abundance of labor with adaptable skills (such as might exist in regions characterized by declining industries), or close proximity to significant raw materials.

In the intermediate regions where these circumstances exist it is reasonable to assume that unbalanced growth will be generated by excess EOC capacity.[33] In terms of Figure 1, the development process begins with a discrete increment of $E(mn')$, followed by a gradual expansion of induced $D$, which moves the regional economy from $n'$ to $n$. In this case the production function assumes the form $X = [2\theta DP - \lambda(D^2) - \beta(P^2)]^{1/2} + [\rho(\alpha P - P^2) - \gamma]$, because now net external effects are induced by $P$.[34] It should also be emphasized that $P$ may continue to induce expansion of $D$ even after $E$ reaches optimum capacity, for, as noted above, regions which have had large amounts of EOC investment tend to spend heavily on SOC even if EOC demand declines.

Finally, whatever the weight of political pressures, it is not economically rational to attempt to induce economic growth in lagging regions via excess EOC capacity, so long as better alternatives exist in intermediate regions. Moreover, it is an empirical fact that out-migration from lagging regions cannot be relied upon to equalize incomes.[35] The situation with respect to SOC, however, is quite different. The SOC needs of lagging regions are relatively great and their SOC equipment is the least well developed; thus, marginal productivity considerations would favor concentrating SOC in lagging regions rather than in areas already relatively well equipped in this regard. Insofar as possible, public outlays should aim at adapting the population for employment in activities with substantial prospects for future expansion. It is possible to develop objective criteria for

32. J. Milau, "La théorie de la croissance et l'expansion régionale," *Economic appliquée* (1956), No. 3, p. 355. The demands in question here are well illustrated by the series of articles cited in the previous note.

33. In France, for example, large investments in port facilities (Dunkirk) and canals (the Moselle River Waterway, linking Lorraine's steel mills to the Ruhr Valley's coal) have stimulated the development of regions favorably located with respect to transportation possibilities. EOC investment in areas characterized by cheap power (the Rhone Valley and the Lacq gas fields in southwestern France) has also initiated significant expansion of DPA.

34. All external effects are subsumed under the bracketed term even if initially induced $D$(or $P$). See note 26.

35. See, for example, E. J. R. Booth, "Interregional Income Differences," *Southern Economic Journal* (July, 1964), pp. 44–51; Girard and Bastide, *op. cit.*, pp. 271, 274.

planning education (and possibly other social investment) for productive purposes in terms of "how much" and "what kind"; such calculations have, in fact, already been made on the basis of United States data.[36]

Of course, availability of SOC will not in itself necessarily induce growth in lagging regions. For example, persons benefited most by SOC investment may migrate to other regions in the absence of supplementary policy measures. Here the balanced-growth doctrine appears more realistic than might be the case within the context of lesser developed nations. Along with investment in the human input it will frequently be necessary to expand EOC facilities and to encourage regional savings, which are often substantial in many lagging regions of mature economies, to find local investment opportunities. Furthermore, the government may promote growth directly by transferring some of the activities of its own agencies from congested to lagging regions. Nevertheless, from a national viewpoint, outmigration from lagging regions should be viewed as a social gain rather than a cause for concern, at least insofar as regional policy aims at increasing welfare rather than maintaining or expanding the number of persons resident in a given area.

## SUMMARY AND CONCLUSIONS

Table 2 contains a somewhat schematic summary of the foregoing discussion. Initially, EOC investment is induced by DPA expansion,

TABLE 2   Regional Growth under Conditions of Induced Public Investment (Phase I) and Excess Capacity of Public Overhead Capital (Phases II and III)

| PHASE | TYPE OF REGION | NATURE OF PUBLIC AND PRIVATE INVESTMENT ACTIVITY |
|-------|----------------|--------------------------------------------------|
| I | Congested | Overexpanded OC and DPA |
| | Intermediate | Deficient EOC |
| | Lagging | Deficient SOC |
| II | Congested | Public controls on expansion of DPA and concomitant OC |
| | Intermediate | Excess EOC capacity |
| | Lagging | Excess SOC capacity |
| III | Congested | Public controls on expansion of DPA and concomitant OC |
| | Intermediate | EOC and DPA approach optimal levels, inducing SOC expansion |
| | Lagging | Balanced growth of SOC, EOC, and DPA |

36. R. S. Eckaus, "Economic Criteria for Education and Training," *Review of Economics and Statistics* (May, 1964), pp. 181–90.

which in turn is a function of those costs and revenues entering into internal calculations of private firms. From the social point of view, public and private investment is overconcentrated in congested areas to the detriment of other regions. In phases II and III, public policy imposes constraints on further expansion in congested regions. The passive role of public investment in phase I is superseded in phase II by projects intended to induce DPA in intermediate and lagging regions. In phase III, EOC and induced DPA have reached a point in intermediate regions where changing tastes and needs induce expansion of SOC; as these regions approach optimal concentration the focus of public policy shifts to the balanced growth of lagging regions, whose populations have been prepared for development opportunities by the SOC investment of phase II.

Interregional equilibrium is attained when the social marginal product (SMP) associated with a given outlay is the same for all types of investment (DPA, SOC, or EOC) and for all regions. For any given investment project $i$ in region $j$, $SMP_i^j = (X - C) \div K$, where $X =$ net social product, including external effects, $C =$ cost of materials, labor and overhead, and $K =$ capital outlay.[37] $X/K$ expresses output per unit investment, and $C/K$ expresses the value of foregone alternative uses of noncapital inputs. It is assumed that prices are rational and that cost and output streams are discounted to the present.

Finally, it may be noted that input-output analysis can facilitate the study of optimal activity location with respect to either the nation as a whole or various regions. For example, J. Boudeville[38] has shown how external economic phenomena and the effects of introducing alternative development poles in various regions may be analyzed in interregional terms by means of a matrix that synthesizes their respective technical input coefficients, propensities to consume, and structures of external trade. Of course, the operational feasibility of such models requires more complex and refined national accounting methods than those now generally employed.

37. This formulation is similar to that given in H. B. Chenery, "The Application of Investment Criteria," *Quarterly Journal of Economics* (February, 1953), pp. 76–96. Strictly speaking, an interest rate should be included in $C$; however, it would not affect relative SMP rankings.

38. J. Boudeville, "La région plan," *Cahiers de l'Institut de Science Économique Appliquée* (January, 1960), Série L, No. 6, pp. 21–43.

STEFAN H. ROBOCK

# Strategies for Regional Economic Development

One of the basic limitations in discussing strategies for regional development is that there are no universal models. National policies and strategies must vary among countries depending upon the country's stage of development, its political system, its social values and goals, its geographical pattern of resources and development potentials, its availability of technical and economic data, and many other factors.

But even though the problem is complex and specific answers have to be related to specific situations, certain basic issues are usually involved and a clarification and improved understanding of these issues can make regional development efforts more realistic and effective.

## AN OPERATIONAL CONTEXT

These issues can be raised in an operational context by visualizing a situation where a distinguished regional scientist has undertaken the task of advising a national minister of planning on regional development. The country might be either developed or underdeveloped.

The planning minister might begin by admitting that his country has given lip service for some time to certain politically popular regional development goals, but that little specific activity has been initiated to implement the goals. These regional development goals are generally threefold: (1) reducing regional income disparities, (2) achieving balanced regional growth, and (3) providing special assistance to distressed areas.

The development official might also feel that it is necessary to emphasize two additional matters to the professional technician:

√ 1. Development policies and priorities are primarily determined by political decisions. The most the technician can do is to illuminate the political process in the hope of improving the quality of political decisions and their implementation.

√ 2. The regional goals already adopted were not supported in terms of maximizing the national economic growth rate. Instead, they were based on considerations of social justice and political

Robock, Stefan H., "Strategies for Regional Economic Development," Papers of the Regional Science Association, XVII (1966), pp. 129–141.

stability. Social justice is to be advanced by an equitable sharing of economic and social gains among people living in all areas. Political stability is to be improved by avoiding growing disparities among political subdivisions that could generate intolerable political tensions.

Whether he approves or not, the regional adviser will have to recognize the political and social emphasis in regional development programs as operational constraints.

## SOME GENERAL PRINCIPLES

After receiving his briefing, the regional scientist might begin his advisory work by identifying a series of general principles involved in developing a program and a strategy. The principles may appear to be simple and noncontroversial to regional scientists. But they are not well known nor thoroughly understood by most development officials and political decision makers.

### The Inevitability of Regional Disparities

Many countries consider the wide economic and social disparities that exist among various regions as a unique and special development problem of the country. A corollary of this conviction, that regional disparities are abnormal and should not be allowed to persist, frequently leads to the doctrine of "equalization" among regions.[1]

It is now becoming better recognized that regional disparities are a universal phenomenon. The economic growth factors of resources, human skills, and access to markets are not evenly distributed among the regions of a nation, and mobility of factors is quite imperfect. Furthermore, "there can be little doubt that an economy, to lift itself to higher income levels, must and will first develop within itself one or several regional centers of economic strength." Consequently, "interregional inequality of growth is an inevitable concomitant and condition of growth itself."[2]

Therefore, "a policy of 'pure equalization' is necessarily a poor policy, although a policy toward *greater* equalization can be, and is likely to be, valid."[3]

1. Walter Isard and Thomas Reiner, "Regional and National Economic Planning and Analytic Techniques for Implementation," *Regional Economic Planning* (Paris: Organization for European Economic Cooperation, 1961), p. 22.

2. Albert O. Hirschman, *The Strategy of Economic Development* (New Haven, Conn.: Yale University Press, 1958), pp. 183–4 [Selection 8 of this volume].

3. Isard and Reiner, *op. cit.*, p. 23.

## Disparity of Regions

The low income regions are frequently considered as homogeneous types. However, for policy and strategy purposes the regions must be differentiated in terms of factors explaining the low incomes and in terms of development potentials. One classification separates the low income regions into (1) depressed areas which are retrogressing, (2) lagging areas which are growing but at slower rates than most other regions and (3) substantially undeveloped "pioneer" or "frontier" regions such as the Amazon River basin in Brazil.

Another operational classification, used by the European Economic Community,[4] is as follows:

(1) Regions including or situated near one or more large industrial centers.

   (a) Zones of "old" industrialization.

   (b) Zones of transformation industries.

   (c) Agricultural zones.

(2) Regions where agriculture is dominant and population is dense.

(3) Regions where agriculture is dominant and population is scattered.

None of these classifications may be most appropriate for a specific country, but the principle of differentiating regions is extremely important.

## People – the Real Issue

The real issue in regional as well as national development is the welfare of people rather than of inanimate political units or geographic areas. Although people may not be highly mobile in some areas of a country and during certain time periods, the mobility of people changes and significant shifts in the location of people can be expected to occur with development.

Political leaders tend to focus on the geographical areas they represent because they are anxious to keep voters in their jurisdiction and to have the population of their areas grow. Nevertheless, the end objective of development – people – is not fixed geographically, and a recognition of this simple but basic fact has profound implications for regional development efforts.

There are exceptions, of course, to the exclusive emphasis on people. A national defense argument has been made in the case of

4. Communauté Economique Européenne, *Objectifs et Méthodes de la Politique Régionale dans la Communauté Européenne* (Bruxelles: 23 Mars 1964), II/720/5/64–F, pp. 11–16.

north Norway that economic activity be decentralized so as to avoid an economic and demographic vacuum in a politically sensitive border area.[5]

## The Crucial Time Horizon

The time horizon is crucial in formulating and implementing regional development programs from several standpoints. One aspect is the usual conflict between short-run and long-range goals.

Political pressures invariably favor short-run objectives and programs, with short-run defined as "before the next election." Yet development efforts which concentrate on short-run objectives are likely to fail in achieving both short-run and long-range goals.[6]

The time horizon is also crucial because the situation of regional inequalities is likely to change over time. Some economists have concluded, based mainly on theoretical analysis, that natural forces tend to create ever greater regional inequalities unless serious governmental intervention occurs.[7]

In my own empirical research, I have previously noted a narrowing of regional disparities in Brazil during recent years,[8] and the similar long-term phenomenon in the United States is well known.

A recent extensive empirical study by Jeffrey G. Williamson, which includes data from twenty-four countries, suggests that regional disparities follow the pattern of "an inverted $U$ over the national growth path," enlarging during early stages of development and narrowing at later stages.[9] However, as Williamson indicates, his research leaves untouched to a large extent the identification of causation.

Assuming that a significant share of the narrowing is from inherent development forces, the possibilities for influencing regional disparities will vary over time and with the stage of development. Furthermore, the costs necessary to reduce regional disparities at an early stage of development may be prohibitive.

During early stages of development, when development resources

5. K. Scott Wood, *The North Norway Plan* (Bergen, Norway: The Christian Mickelsen Institute, July, 1964), p. 23.

6. For a fuller discussion and specific illustrations see Alvin Mayne, "Designing and Administering a Regional Economic Plan with Special Reference to Puerto Rico," *Regional Economic Planning* (Paris: Organization for European Economic Cooperation, 1961), p. 145.

7. Gunnar Myrdal, *Rich Lands and Poor* (New York: Harper & Row, 1958).

8. Stefan H. Robock, *Brazil's Developing Northeast: A Study in Regional Planning and Foreign Aid* (Washington, D.C.: The Brookings Institution, 1963), chap. 3.

9. Jeffrey G. Williamson, "Regional Inequality and the Process of National Development," *Economic Development and Cultural Change, Part II* (July, 1965), p. 10.

are limited, the most rapid progress can often be achieved by concentrating programs in relatively few areas. This is particularly true for industrial development when priority is given to heavy industries which are resource or market oriented and require large production units. The number of projects will be small, and there may be little locational freedom in the selection of plant sites.

In a later stage of industrialization, the possibilities for encouraging a large number of new growing points may increase. Total available investment should be significantly greater, and a change in priorities should give greater emphasis to industries producing intermediate and consumer products. These new circumstances will result in a larger number of projects and greater locational freedom.

## Social and Economic Goals May Conflict

Potential conflicts between social goals and maximizing economic growth are a general problem in development. Such conflicts are particularly acute in regional development because social welfare motivations are so strong in shaping regional development programs from the national level. However, the conflicts may often be overestimated.

The purely economic criterion for allocating development resources and efforts is relatively simple in concept. Priority should be given to alternatives on the basis of greatest marginal contribution to increased output per unit of input.[10] From this principle, the economist often skips to the substantive conclusions that the greatest returns will be achieved by investing in the more advanced and rapidly growing areas.

This factual conclusion is generally based on the assumption that external economies and economies of scale are present to a greater degree in the developed areas than in the backward areas. One implication of this position is that the more developed areas are better equipped with social overhead investment or that increments to social overhead can be added more economically for expansion than in the less developed region.

But this reasoning unless documented should not be accepted as a general guideline. Social overhead facilities in the rapidly developing areas are frequently more overutilized than in the less developed areas and the argument that incremental capacity in the rapidly

10. It should be noted that this criterion frequently is applied in a static way. In terms of immediate results, the return from project A might exceed the return from project B. Over a period of time, however, and taking into account the secondary effects generated by project B, the latter would deserve preference.

developing area will be less costly should also be challenged. In any event, the whole issue must be placed in a time perspective. The argument may be true over the short run in a specific case, but, over a longer period of time, increased overhead investment in the less developed areas may stimulate or support an even faster overall growth rate.

Other circumstances exist where the social goal of stimulating the low-income areas may not conflict with achieving a maximum contribution to economic growth. In many countries, a high priority development goal is to increase foreign exchange earnings. In Brazil, for example, some of the best opportunities in recent years for increasing exports have been in products produced by the less developed areas of the northeast and the north and central interior. Such products as manganese ore, iron ore, and sisal fibers have had better foreign exchange earning possibilities than coffee from the highly developed south. Sugar and cotton, which are produced both in the south and the northeast, have also had good international markets in recent years. The point is that in terms of specific programs and on the basis of economic criteria, the less developed areas may receive high priority in certain national development programs.

The most likely situation, however, may be that the goals of accelerating economic growth and of sharing the economic and social gains among all regions will be in conflict. As will be discussed below, there may be great operational advantages to treating the economic and social issues separately in formulating regional development strategies.

### Some Limitations on Regional Development Efforts

Regional development efforts undertaken either at the national or local level can be greatly reduced in effectiveness because of significant limitations that exist. One of these limitations may be the influence of international markets on significant export production of specific regions.

The case of northeast Brazil illustrates the role of factors outside the control of the region or the nation in reducing regional disparities. The gap between per capita income levels in the northeast and the nation as a whole widened after World War II, but, since 1955, the gap has narrowed significantly. In explaining this phenomenon, the government has emphasized its role in creating a large new regional source of electricity and in investing in the petroleum fields of Bahia.[11]

11. Ministério Do Planejamento E Coordenaçâo, *Programa de Açâo Econômica do Govêrno: 1964–1966*, Documentos Escritório De Pesquisa Ecônomica Aplicada, No. 1 (Novembro de 1964), p. 45.

A former high government official working in the northeast explained the 1955–60 narrowing of regional disparities in terms of the new regional development program of SUDENE, although in fact the new agency did not begin to operate until 1960.[12]

Despite the natural tendency of the government to take credit for this phenomenon, a hard analysis of available data suggests that the dominant force explaining the relative income gains of northeast Brazil was a favorable change previously noted in international markets for several of the key export crops of the region—sugar, cotton, and sisal—and an unfavorable change in the export markets for coffee, which is produced in the higher income areas of the south.[13]

Another limitation on regional development efforts involves the actual geographic impact of investments. The benefits from new investments in a region that can be captured by the region will vary greatly with the nature of the project and the stage of development of the region. Frequently, the actual benefits to a specific region fall far below expectations.

In the United States, many people have attributed the rapid development of the Tennessee Valley region to the large amount of public investment made in the areas. However, most of the first-round stimulus of the investment occurred outside the Valley region. The bulk of the new investment went to the developed areas of the United States to purchase construction equipment, turbines, electric generators, transmission lines material, etc. For many years, Pittsburgh, Pennsylvania, and Schenectady, New York, sites of the major power equipment manufacturers, received more immediate impact than did the Tennessee Valley.[14]

An investment in a low-income area that enlarges the productive capacity of a region can contribute significantly on a continuing basis to regional income and employment. But in a low-income, predominantly agricultural area, a large share of the direct impact of investment expenditures on resource development or industrial projects is likely to be outside the region and even outside the country.

A third limitation on regional development efforts relates to existing deficiencies in data and in tools of analysis. Some scientists and scholars appear to have a professional bias in favor of developing ever more sophisticated tools with increasingly burdensome requirements of data and of technical training. On the basis of personal

12. State income estimates beyond 1960 were not available as of mid-1965 in Brazil.
13. Robock, *op. cit.*, Ch. 3.
14. Stefan H. Robock, "Integrated River-Basin Development and Industrialization: The Tennessee Valley Experience," *United States Papers Prepared for the United Nations Conference on the Application of Science and Technology for the Benefit of the Less Developed Areas, Volume IV, Industrial Development* (United States Government Printing Office, 1963).

attempts to introduce some of the key new tools of regional analysis in operational situations as diverse as those of the southeast of the United States, Bolivia, and India, I have concluded that a great opportunity exists for regional scientists to develop techniques adapted to situations of sparse data and a scarcity of highly trained personnel.

The complexity of many regional analysis tools is not the only operational limitation in the tools and data category. The relevance or appropriateness of certain key tools such as benefit-cost analysis is a related problem. H. C. Bos, in discussing this question, reached the conclusion that "it is necessary to have a method for the appraisal of investment projects which more appropriately takes account of the specific circumstances in underdeveloped countries than benefit-cost analysis as applied in a developed country like the United States does." [15]

The issue of appropriateness of benefit-cost techniques can be broadened beyond the circumstances of underdeveloped countries to development programming in general. In seeking to stimulate development, the principal economic test for a specific project should be its potential for creating and nourishing a major stream of development forces. The orientation of benefit-cost studies is toward making a monetary calculation as an economic justification tool rather than toward providing a guide for economic development.

## Government Policy Decision Versus Investment Decisions

Much of the regional development debate and controversy in specific countries focuses on investment decisions such as priorities and the location of public investment. Nevertheless, decisions on government policies other than public investment may have greater influence on regional patterns.

In the field of tariffs and foreign trade policy, protection for domestic industry, or for specific agricultural products and raw materials, or export subsidies can significantly affect regional development patterns.

In the field of government regulation of business, many policy issues have regional importance. For example, the Tennessee Valley Authority encouraged industrial decentralization through a uniform schedule of electric power rates for all locations in its service area. Obviously, power costs are less at the point of power generation because of savings in transmission costs. But T.V.A. did not want to

15. H. C. Bos, "Discussion Paper," *Regional Economic Planning* (Paris: Organization for European Economic Cooperation, 1961), p. 372.

encourage industrial concentration at a few power-producing locations.

Transportation rate policies can be important, as the southeast of the United States has argued for several decades.[16] Minimum wage regulation which results in narrow regional differentials may inhibit development in labor-surplus poor areas.[17] The distribution of taxing powers between the federal, state, and local governments and other dimensions of tax policy have significant regional implications, as do such programs as national price support and subsidies for the agricultural sector.

Policy discussions may not generate as much regional attention or controversy as investment decisions. The regional implications of the policy decisions are not as clear or visible as the location of a new physical facility. Yet, the policy questions are often the more crucial regional influences.

## Technological Trends as a Major Regional Force

Technology is a dynamic factor that continually operates as a constraint on regional development efforts. Gunnar Myrdal has recently highlighted the matter of capital intensive and large-scale agricultural technology as a barrier to development. He argues that industrialization in most underdeveloped countries cannot generate adequate employment to absorb a large and growing labor force in agriculture, and "agricultural policy must, therefore, be directed toward more intensive utilization of an underutilized labor force..."[18] The solution he proposes, with great implications for rural areas, is the development of labor intensive agricultural technology.

In discussing the problem of urbanization and the desirability of industrial dispersion in India, Professor John P. Lewis notes the role that could be played by smaller scale and less capital intensive technology.[19] An actual project in which small scale technology for cement production was developed to fit the needs of an interior area was the Asimow Project in northeast Brazil.[20]

The technological constraint has many dimensions other than the

16. Calvin B. Hoover and B. U. Ratchford, *Economic Resources and Policies of the South* (New York: The Macmillan Company, 1951), pp. 78–84.

17. Robock, *Brazil's Developing Northeast, op. cit.*, pp. 148–9.

18. Gunnar Myrdal, "Jobs, Food and People," *International Development Review* (June, 1965).

19. John P. Lewis, *Quiet Crisis in India* (Washington D.C.: The Brookings Institution, 1962). pp. 179–82.

20. Morris Asimow, "Project Brazil, A Case Study in Micro-Planning," *International Development Review* (June, 1964).

economic scale of operations. Regional patterns will change with technological changes in transportation and communications, with industrial process developments which alter the pattern of inputs, and with the discovery of new technologies such as water desalinization and nuclear energy.

Without elaborating on the ways in which technology can influence the location of economic activity and regional development patterns, it should be clear that projections of technological trends are necessary in formulating regional development strategies. It should be apparent, also, that programs of technological research which can influence regional patterns might be a component of programs for regional development.

## Need for Special Attention to Urbanization

The urbanization phenomenon in many countries has been a highly emotional issue. The rural fundamentalist view that the only good life is the rural life is widespread throughout the world. It is not surprising, therefore, that much of the official attention given to urbanization treats the phenomenon as an evil force that must be destroyed. And where the matter receives specific attention in development programs, the emphasis is on decentralization and rural improvement programs which implicitly assume that urbanization can be prevented.

Urbanization needs special attention but the issue must be approached realistically and with a minimum of dogma. Urbanization appears to be an inevitable concomitant of economic growth because as Lloyd Rodwin has observed, "Through processes which are not as yet fully understood, growth appears to have a better chance of becoming self-propelled in larger cities...."[21] The real challenge is to understand the role of urbanization in development and to incorporate rational and realistic programs into development planning for guiding and shaping what may be an immutable force or inevitable trend.

## Strategy Guidelines

The hypothetical minister of planning and the regional development adviser, having briefed each other on political aspects and key principles of regional development, can next proceed to formulate strategy guidelines. Much of the strategy, of course, will flow from the general principles previously discussed, and the specific programs

21. Lloyd Rodwin, "Metropolitan Policy for Developing Areas," *Regional Economic Planning* (Paris: Organization for European Economic Cooperation, 1961).

that are undertaken will vary with the circumstances of the specific country.

The strategy guidelines, relating to a wide range of objectives and activities, might be grouped into three categories. The first category involves establishing certain necessary preconditions. The second category includes efforts to inject regional considerations into continuing public and private development activities. The third category comprehends the stimulation of new programs which meet a specific regional development need.

## Establishing Necessary Preconditions

As the Common Market commission has properly stressed, "The choice and putting to work of an economic and social development policy in a region requires a profound knowledge of the present situation and of spontaneous developments that are foreseeable."[22] Because the necessary profound knowledge usually does not exist, because resources will be limited for undertaking technical and planning studies, and because the timing of technical studies must coincide with the timing of political decision making, an explicit strategy should be adopted for increasing the availability of regional data and analyses.

Some features of this strategy should be to establish priorities for specific research and planning activities, to seek out simplified and resource-saving techniques, and to expand the research effort beyond the activities of the national development agencies by stimulating regional, state, and local groups to become actively responsible for planning studies in their areas.

In an operational situation, it is more important to have relatively unsophisticated research results available at the time decisions are being made—providing the planning studies represent an improvement over the prevailing level of knowledge—than to have highly sophisticated and comprehensive studies available after the decisions have been made. In Bolivia, the planning commission, working on its own time schedule and with the most advanced planning techniques, completed its work two years after most of the key decisions had to be made by the government. By the time the studies were available, the planning commission had become almost completely isolated from the center of development decisions and actions.

The decentralization of regional planning and development activities that has been recommended requires that a series of counterpart responsibilities be assumed by national planning agencies. Some

22. Communauté Economique Européenne, *op. cit.*, p. 101.

of these national responsibilities are to support pre-investment studies and research that will better identify and evaluate natural resources, to require that all national planning for specific sectors include an identification and analysis of the regional implications of such plans, to provide national projections that can serve as guidelines for regional studies, and to make technical assistance and technical training available to the regional, state, and local groups that generally cannot compete effectively for the best technical planning talent of a country.

Training programs have a special importance. They can increase the supply of technicians. They can increase the supply of regional data and analyses by including supervised work assignments in the training. And training programs can establish communication channels among the various technicians working in a country.

As more data and knowledge become available, a continuing and multi-dimensional program should be undertaken to upgrade official and popular understanding of regional development issues. In particular, the potentials *and limitations* for influencing regional patterns should be widely publicized.

The regional scientist may regard such educational or "propaganda" activities as beyond the scope of his professional responsibility. Yet, from an operational standpoint, such efforts are absolutely essential for obtaining acceptance of the kinds of programs the technician is likely to prescribe. I have seen excellent results achieved from such efforts in both India and Brazil.

The objective of enlarging public understanding can be approached in many ways. Research studies should be published and public discussions of these studies should be stimulated. The quality of regional development instruction in institutions of higher education should be improved. Training seminars can be sponsored for government officials, academicians, and even politicians as well as for planning technicians.

Another dimension of what I have called establishing the necessary preconditions, in addition to enlarging the technical knowledge and expanding public understanding, is to make a deliberate effort to extend the time horizons for regional development plans and expectations. In part, this objective may be achieved by the program to expand public understanding of regional development issues such as the observed phenomenon that regional disparities are likely to narrow at later stages of development.

An additional and more concrete approach, however, would be to prepare long-range projections or plans in which shifting regional patterns are outlined in some detail. Such national and regional long-range projections were recently completed for Brazil in connection with a planning study for electric power development. The projections suggest, for example, that steel plants are likely to be located in the northeast and in the far south, areas which presently do not have steel production, as national production reaches a certain expected level during the next decade.

Such long-range projections can serve as an implicit future promise to areas presently neglected. And they can reduce current political pressures for short-run measures which result in uneconomic regional dispersion of new economic activity.

## Injecting Regional Considerations into Going Activities

The second stage of regional strategy is to inject regional considerations into activities underway such as decisions on private and public investment as well as on government policy matters. The regional distribution of public investment will be mentioned only briefly because the strategy issues in establishing investment priorities have been widely discussed in professional circles and are better known than most of the other issues included in this paper.

The general problem in public investment decisions is competing priorities for limited resources. Within this framework, the debate continues over the role and the timing of infrastructure investments in depressed or lagging regions and the related issue of regional dispersion of investment versus a concentration of investment in growth points or areas which have high potential for becoming highly dynamic.

My own conviction on these issues is that infrastructure in itself will not generate self-sustaining growth and that infrastructure investment must be related to identified potentials for expanded economic activity in agriculture, mining, manufacturing, or the tertiary sector. On the issue of dispersion versus concentration, the answer will vary over time and depend upon the stage of development.

Increasing the allocation of scarce resources for improving welfare levels at the expense of less expansion in economic output is a difficult decision to make. Nevertheless, a slightly increased share for programs to improve living conditions in the poor areas may be a worthwhile price to pay for greater freedom in selecting more productive locations for the remaining development share.

Furthermore, investment in people through education and health programs, even though widely dispersed throughout the country, may not mean a sacrifice in increased economic growth. Investment in human resources creates a national rather than a locally fixed resource. The people benefited can migrate, if necessary, to areas of more rapid growth to make their contribution.

Influencing private investment may be more important in many situations than public investment. The strategy of using special tax and other financial incentives for encouraging private investment in depressed or lagging areas is well known and effectively applied in many situations. The identification of investment opportunities through technical studies can also be extremely productive in attracting private investment, because a lack of knowledge of area potentials may be an extremely important barrier to regional development.

In addition to private and public investment decisions, regional considerations must be affirmatively injected into decisions on public policies. It should be recognized that the regional impact of certain policies may not be the controlling consideration. Nevertheless, the regional implications of government policies should be analyzed and identified on a continuing basis. Such an investment in technical studies can have a high regional development payoff in a number of situations. In some cases, policy decisions will be modified so that regional development objectives can be better achieved. In other cases, the adoption of policies and programs aside from investment decisions may become an affirmative and effective way of achieving regional development objectives.

## New Programs to Meet Regional Development Needs

In most countries, a strategy of influencing ongoing activities and decisions may not be adequate for achieving regional development goals, and a number of new programs will have to be established to meet the regional development needs. Let me comment briefly on three such programs that may be needed.

Many underdeveloped countries in particular have neglected almost completely the matter of urbanization in their planning and development programs. Therefore, an urgent need may exist for technical studies and for explicit policy formulation on urbanization.

Frequently, a second omission is an affirmative and explicit program to guide and facilitate internal migration. The latter can operate as a powerful factor in narrowing regional income disparities.[23] The

23. The purely statistical results of migration are interesting to note. Regional disparities are generally measured in terms of per capita income. If a number of underemployed or unemployed persons move from a low-income to a high-income area it is likely to reduce regional disparities. In most cases, the out-migration does not affect total output or income in the poor region and per capita income in the poor region will rise. The in-migrants to the high-income region may remain unemployed or work at activities that pay wages that are below regional averages, thus exerting a downward pressure on average per capita income.

European Common Market countries have recognized this and have undertaken affirmative measures to give people throughout the various countries a better opportunity to contribute to and share in overall prosperity by migrating within the E.E.C. area. Migration has been one of the major forces in reducing regional disparities within the United States, Brazil, and many other countries. Yet the common situation is that government programs and policies are neutral or weighted against migration.

A parenthetical comment is that the potential of family planning for reducing regional disparities deserves greater consideration, along with the matter of internal migration.

My final suggestion of possible new programs relates to the matter of technology. Most countries formulate their regional development strategy on the assumption that technological trends are outside of the country's control. At the same time, the goals of achieving geographical dispersion and ameliorating urban congestion may be frustrated by current trends toward larger scales of operation, toward highly capital intensive techniques, and toward processes that make use of inputs most economically available in the few highly industrialized countries responsible for most of the world's technological changes.

Suppose that the social costs of the increased urbanization that are resulting from technological trends were included in the calculations of desirable and feasible technology rather than having such decisions rest solely on private profit criteria. Suppose that the influence of technology on the potentials of achieving regional development goals in an efficient manner were an explicit consideration in technological development. Isn't it likely that the technology options available for countries at all stages of development could be greatly improved?

Suppose the United States, for example, wanted to slow down the urbanization trend and reduce the gigantic demand this is creating on government resources. Is there any doubt that a minute portion of what is being spent on outer space technology could dramatically alter the use of space on earth?

The discussion is growing on possibilities of influencing technological trends as they affect spatial patterns of industrial, agricultural, and urban development in both the developed and the underdeveloped countries. A few successful pilot projects have been completed which have developed highly economic smaller-scale and less capital-intensive manufacturing technologies adapted to the development needs of certain areas. But the discussion has not yet matured to the point that major national or international efforts have focused on a strategy for enlarging the technological options or removing certain technological constraints that limit the potentials for achieving spatial development goals.

These are some of the reflections of an operationally oriented regional scientist on the question of regional development strategies.

INDEX

# Index